Advance praise for
Plan C

A revolution is gaining steam here and elsewhere and it's being led by
communities that are taking responsibility for their energy futures and
food supply while building economies that are fair and sustainable.
It's called *Plan C* and the story is told here by one of the intrepid pioneers
in the movement. Read it, send copies to your city council members,
roll up your sleeves and join in. It's the only decent future we have."

— David Orr, author of *Ecological Literacy* and *Earth in Mind*

This is no sugar-coated vision of how great the world could be if
only magical new technologies appear to replace fossil fuels.
Pat Murphy understands the scale of the challenge facing us and
uses his engineering background to peel away the usual false
solutions. What's left shines with simplicity and common sense:
as the oil age fades to memory, we must use less of Earth's resources
and return to traditional virtues. An indispensable book from
a wise, compassionate, and practical man.

— Richard Heinberg, author of *The Party's Over: Oil, War and the Fate of
Industrial Societies*; Senior Fellow, Post Carbon Institute

Here's a powerful and persuasive glimpse of the future. You may not
agree with every detail and recommendation, but the overriding
message is incredibly important: Cheap fossil fuel has made us
the first humans with no practical need of our neighbors.
That has to change, for reasons ecological but also psychological.
The world on the other side of cheap oil may be a little less comfortable
·than the one we grew up in, but it may also be much sweeter

— Bill McKibben, author of *Deep Economy*; co-founder 350.org

The rich are getting richer and the poor are getting poorer much faster now than at any time in the past. The world is at peak injustice, and that one point, and its ramifications, make *Plan C* essential reading.

— Albert Bates, author of
The Post Petroleum Survival Guide and Cookbook

There are many people who tell us that the skies are about to open up and unleash a deluge of environmental crises upon us. But Pat Murphy does more than forecast disaster — he's right there with you, handing out umbrellas, bringing around the boats and showing us how to get to safe, dry ground. *Plan C* is a powerful tool for creating a viable future.

— Sharon Astyk, author of *Depletion & Abundance:*
Life on the New Home Front and *A Nation of Farmers;*
and publisher/blogger, www.sharonastyk.com

Plan C is a tour de force encyclopedia of sustainability.
A highly readable cornucopia of no nonsense facts, insights,
and suggestions for action, it is an essential desk reference
for every citizen, public official, and business leader concerned
with addressing the challenge of peak oil and climate change.

— David C. Korten, author of *The Great Turning:*
From Empire to Earth Community and
When Corporations Rule; and board chair *YES!* magazine.

In *Plan C*, Pat Murphy has not only shown us the life we *should* lead —
he has shown us the life we ***must*** lead — if we are to survive on this planet.

— Adam Corson-Finnerty, author of *World Citizen: Action for Global Justice*

PLAN C

Community Survival Strategies for Peak Oil and Climate Change

PLAN C

Community Survival Strategies for Peak Oil and Climate Change

Pat Murphy

NEW SOCIETY PUBLISHERS

Cataloging in Publication Data:
A catalog record for this publication is available from the National Library of Canada.

Cover design by Diane McIntosh. Images: iStock/Bob Randall.

Printed in Canada. First printing May 2008

Paperback ISBN: 978-0-86571-607-0

Inquiries regarding requests to reprint all or part of *Plan C* should be addressed to New Society Publishers at the address below.

To order directly from the publishers, please call toll-free (North America) 1-800-567-6772, or order online at www.newsociety.com

Any other inquiries can be directed by mail to:

New Society Publishers
P.O. Box 189, Gabriola Island, BC V0R 1X0, Canada
(250) 247-9737

New Society Publishers' mission is to publish books that contribute in fundamental ways to building an ecologically sustainable and just society, and to do so with the least possible impact on the environment, in a manner that models this vision. We are committed to doing this not just through education, but through action. This book is one step toward ending global deforestation and climate change. It is printed on Forest Stewardship Council-certified acid-free paper that is **100% post-consumer recycled** (100% old growth forest-free), processed chlorine free, and printed with vegetable-based, low-VOC inks, with covers produced using FSC-certified stock. Additionally, New Society purchases carbon offsets based on an annual audit, operating with a carbon-neutral footprint. For further information, or to browse our full list of books and purchase securely, visit our website at: www.newsociety.com

NEW SOCIETY PUBLISHERS
www.newsociety.com

Recycled
Supporting responsible use
of forest resources
www.fsc.org Cert no. SW-COC-1271
© 1996 Forest Stewardship Council

This book is dedicated to Wendell Berry,
who provided me with the vision for a sustainable, more agrarian world,
and to Noam Chomsky, who gave me the courage to speak out
against the injustice of many of our national policies.

Contents

Acknowledgments

T HE BEST SYNONYM for community is cooperation. Cooperation always
implies sharing, and this book was written within that context. While I
wrote this book I was part of many different communities of interest as well as
my own community of place — Yellow Springs, Ohio. I want to acknowledge
many of the people who helped me, particularly those who have spoken at
Community Solutions (CS)'s annual conferences on peak oil and solutions
held in Yellow Springs since 2003.

I first acknowledge the many members of the peak oil community with
whom I have spent the last several years on a truly astounding journey. Foremost
of these are Richard Heinberg, Colin Campbell and Matt Simmons. Richard
Heinberg first introduced me to peak oil at lunch in 2001 in Santa Rosa,
California. I met Colin and Matt at ASPO Paris in 2003 and have avidly followed the work of all three ever since.

Economics drives our world today, but the neoclassical economic view has
led us to disaster. I was fortunate in finding the leaders of a new form of economics including John Ikerd and Michael Shuman who have spoken at CS
conferences. Their writings, as well as those of Michael Perelman, Herman
Daly and Michael Albert have formed my economic views.

Advocates of simple living who have influenced me include Vicki Robin,
Jim Merkel, John de Graaf, David Wann and Marilyn Welker. Vicki spoke at a
CS conference, and I have spoken at Simplicity events put on by Marilyn
Welker in Columbus, Ohio. Jan Lundberg has been arguing for simplicity for
years, and my talks with him have been an inspiration. Julian Darley and
Celine Rich of Post Carbon Institute are key contributors to the views

reflected in this book. Jan and Julian have both been speakers at CS conferences.

My organization's long term relationship with the Fellowship for Intentional Community has affected this book. Key contributors in that vein have been Laird Schaub and Harvey Baker. Harvey spoke at our first CS conference on peak oil.

I have been heavily influenced by the co-housing and eco-village movements. Diana Leafe Christian, Patricia Allison, Liz Walker, Peter Bane and Richard Olson have spoken on these topics at CS conferences. Peter has further helped me to understand permaculture, and Richard and Cheyenne Olson have supported me with advice and help in other ways. My visits to Earthaven in North Carolina and Berea Ecovillage (developed by Richard Olson) in Kentucky have been instructive.

When it comes to understanding food, Robert Waldrop and Sharon Astyk (as well as Peter Bane, Editor, *Permaculture Activist*) have been great teachers. All three have spoken at CS conferences. Robert's *Running on Empty* Internet discussion group has contributed greatly to my understanding of a new world coming. Andrew Manieri, founder of a community supported agriculture farm in Yellow Springs, has also contributed to my understanding of food and permaculture.

Yellows Springs has provided me with a wonderful place in which to work, live and experiment. I am grateful to my village council, particularly president Judy Hempfling and vice president Karen Wintrow who chair the community's Electrical System Task Force (ESTF) of which I am a member. Community Solutions' board has been most supportive, and I thank trustees Lynn Sontag, Heidi Eastman, Deb Kociszewski, Carol Gasho, Bob Brecha and Saul Greenberg. I particularly thank Bob Brecha for his technical support and the enjoyment of serving with him (and Carol) on the Yellow Springs ESTF. Bob has been a speaker at our conferences on the topic of straw bale houses.

I very much appreciate the work of Affordable Comfort Incorporated, one the nation's most important organizations in dealing with energy and housing for the poor. I give special thanks to Linda Wigington who is the point person for ACI in developing strategies for deep retrofitting of existing homes. Jeff Christian of the Building Technology Center at Oak Ridge National Laboratory in Tennessee introduced me to high performance building. Both Linda and Jeff have spoken on house energy reductions at our conferences.

Thanks to our staff including Jeanna Breza who manages the office and shipping of our film *The Power of Community: How Cuba Survived Peak Oil*. Bob Bingenheimer has served us for years in our marketing activities and developed many of the graphics in this book. Eric Johnson deserves recognition for his work as editor of our film. John Morgan helped also as an editor of my writings, as a photographer at our conferences and for the film, and most important, as an impressive model for low-energy living.

Special thanks to Roy Eastman, who reminds me that we do have to manage things, balance budgets and get along with people. Roy is also part of the ESTF, an advisor to me on building retrofit technologies and an ex-trustee of Community Solutions.

Larry and Gail Halpern have been working to curtail their energy use since they attended our first Peak Oil Conference. Larry spoke at a recent conference on the steps they took to cut their energy use 50%. They are powerful examples of curtailment practices.

Thanks to Bob Steinbach, one of our conference speakers, who told me that the Smart Jitney idea was not crazy and encouraged me to continue.

Many thanks to my editor Betsy Nuse who did a masterful job in reducing my bulky manuscript to its current form. Her patience and encouragement were important.

Our three trips to Cuba and the making of our film were vital to the concepts in this book. Thanks to Global Exchange and Rachel Bruhnke, my tour guide on our filming trip, as well as to the wonderful Cubans who showed me what is possible. Cuba is a place where community is strong, allowing people to curtail at a rate yet unachieved anywhere else in the world.

The writings of Australian Ted Trainer heavily influenced this book, and he deserves special recognition. David Orr, who spoke at one of our conferences, has influenced me for years.

Special thanks to Megan Quinn Bachman, Outreach Director at Community Solutions, who read every word of this book more than once, made lots of comments and — most importantly — helped keep the organization focused and kept getting out our message while I concentrated on writing.

There is often a person of whom one can say "this book would not have been written without his or her help." This honor goes to Faith Morgan, my wife and the president of the board of Community Solutions, who read every word of the book many times and edited many versions. Together with Megan and Jeanna, she kept the organization running efficiently while at the same time growing much of our food. She also planned and directed the first *deep gut rehab* energy retrofit of one of our buildings, using the German Passive house as the model. Faith was the director of our film on peak oil and Cuba.

There are dozens of other people who could be mentioned — these are the ones I remember most. It is working and living with people like these that make me confident in the power of community to overcome a mere reduction in our material standard of living.

Preface

WE ARE FACING MULTIPLE GRAVE WORLD CRISES — peak oil, climate change, inequity and species extinction to name just a few. When I began this book our situation was very serious — now it is life threatening. The survival of industrial society as we know it today is in doubt. Twenty years of so-called *sustainability* conversations have led nowhere, and green has degenerated into a marketing term. The time for scientific and technological solutions to problems caused by science and engineering is long past. Survival requires that we begin to see that energy technology is the root cause of many serious world problems. As William Jevons pointed out decades ago, ever more efficient machines designed by scientists and engineers means ever-increasing consumption of fossil fuels and more generation of CO_2.

Our problem is cultural, not technical. It is a character issue, not a scientific one. We have never bothered to ask or answer the question "What is energy for?" We have allowed cheap fossil fuels to change us from citizens into mere consumers. We in the modern world have become addicted to consuming energy. In the past, our spiritual traditions warned us against materialism — an older name for our current addictive consumerism. But contemporary religions seem to concede that humanity's main purpose is to consume the products of a fossil fuel-based, perpetual-growth economy. As Wendell Berry says:

> The churches generally sit and watch and even approve while
> our society hurries brainlessly on with the industrialization of
> child-raising, education, medicine, all the pleasures and all the

practical arts. And perhaps this is because religion itself is increasingly industrialized: concerned with quantity, "growth," fashionable thought and an inane sort of expert piety. From where I'm looking, it seems necessary for Christians to recognize that the industrial economy is not just a part of a quasi-rational system of specializations, granting the needs of the body to the corporations and the needs of the spirit to the churches, but is in fact an opposing religion, assigning to technological progress and "the market" the same omnipotence, omniscience, unquestionability, even the same beneficence, that the Christian teachings assign to God.[1]

Plan C offers an alternative perspective to the ever more frantic technical proposals for continuing our soul destroying and life endangering way of living. This book opens with a few chapters intended to "make a searching and fearless moral inventory of ourselves," a starting point for many 12 step programs. In Part I, I take that moral inventory, describing the morally central core issues of fossil fuel depletion, human-caused climate change and global inequity. I relate peak oil to our *economy* — a word which, together with *free market*, defines us principally as self-centered consumers rather than as caring citizens. The growth economy has been based on the principle "greed is good," and the results are disastrous. I review the history of imperialism, especially in the West, and the greed and violence it displays towards the planet's human and non-human inhabitants. I show that US imperialism has its own history of greed, aggression and cruelty, extending within as well as beyond the national borders. The automobile — possibly the most destructive machine ever built, both of the physical world and of human communities — is addressed along with the electricity generating power plant, the fixed counterpoint to the automobile. The automobile and power plant are the key technologies that produce the CO_2 that is so dangerously altering the planet's climate. Finally I summarize the two institutions, the corporation and the media, that deliberately foster the delusion that the pursuit of personal satisfaction will advance the social good, which keeps us in a trance that *all will be well*.

Part II is solution focused and covers strategies and action plans. Curtailment and community define the underlying philosophy of this book, with curtailment being the action and community the context. Curtailment accepts the facts that we have squandered our children's birthright, and so must now radically reduce our consumption of fossil fuels. Community is the core aspect of a new set of values and a new consciousness that must replace the consumer driven mentality. Next I define some of the expertise and abilities we need to develop to live in a low energy world. This brings abstract national problems down to the personal level so we can recognize our own culpability for our personal day-to-day choices and habits. It also describes the major areas for individual energy reduction in the household sector — our cars, our homes and our food.

I devote four chapters to the household economy — that part of the GNP under personal direct control. The problems and solutions for buildings, for cars and for our food are described in detail. All of us must in fact regain a set of skills and knowledge which atrophied while we put our trust in corporate producers. These are not *tips* chapters but rather explanations of what we must know in order to make good decisions and to determine which skills we will need for the new world economy.

In Part III, I discuss the new cultural context that we must create to survive. I emphasize the personal steps we must take, in particular breaking our addiction to machines that use fossil fuels. I discuss the media and emphasize our need to break free from this second addiction, one that allows society to be controlled by powerful corporations. I also cover the current focus on localization — an effort to counter the destructive trend toward globalization. This analysis emphasizes the need to avoid concentrating on government and corporate action, since that might keep us from making far more significant personal changes. Finally I close the book with thoughts on community revival and renewal, as these represent the heart and soul of the post fossil fuel society. I envision a society based on cooperation and care of the planet rather than competition and exploitation of planetary resources. I describe a new world view, with community as the new context for living, and I identify some key elements of community. The most important element, relationships, is the essence of community and, as such, offers a challenge to our current societal celebration of individual material pursuits. The difference between the current culture and this new one are covered in detail, and the core values of the two options are compared.

This is definitely a numbers book. It is focused on analysis and shows by such analysis the tremendous risks we are taking as we attempt to perpetuate, by dubious technological means, the fossil fuel-based society and growth oriented economy. It is also historical. It challenges the authority of our scientific and technological communities and exposes our poor collective record when it comes to managing fossil fuels and CO_2 responsibly. And it also challenges Americans' view of themselves by taking a close look at our violent history. It is my belief that if we cannot penetrate the distortions that obscure our true political and social history and the hype that offers us *techno-fixes*, then life in the future will be very difficult indeed.

My thesis is that the best of American culture has been seriously degraded since becoming addicted to oil. We used to have fewer material goods but better relationships. The country was less violent. Our citizens sought to avoid entanglement in foreign affairs. The United States had cleaner water, healthier ecosystems, and more caring human relationships. It had neighborhood schools and unlocked doors. It had community in the best sense of that word. Much of this has been lost. We have gained wealth but we are losing our souls. The national soul desperately needs rework. Our best examples of community-focused living, and the sustaining relationships it fosters, show us exactly what to strive for. But the time remaining is limited, and the urgency of engaging ourselves in this work can not be overstated.

PART I

One

Fossil Fuel Depletion and Climate Change

"**Y**OU CAN'T FIGHT PROGRESS," "you can't go home again" or "there is no turning back" are statements representing a view that the industrial way of life is inevitable and good. Serious problems are appearing everywhere. People are more and more concerned about peak oil and climate change. The film *An Inconvenient Truth*[1] together with the latest reports of the Intergovernmental Panel on Climate Change (IPCC)[2] have suddenly raised the question of the survival of the species. Nor is this simply a theory — almost everyone is aware of the changes of climate in their own neighborhood with different rainfall patterns and warmer temperatures. All governments have recognized the harsh realities and are frantically trying to determine strategies. The 2007 United Nations Framework Convention on Climate Change verified the seriousness of the global situation.[3]

We at Community Solutions have long been opposed to the world paradigm of continuous economic growth rolling over all resistance.[4] Rather we are committed to small community in its various forms — small towns, villages, neighborhoods of cities — and work to preserve them as best we can regardless of how many farmers in the developing world are moved into ghettos or how many small farmers in the US are forced to leave their farms and move to factory jobs in industrial cities. We believe small, local communities can be more energy efficient and are preferable to the megalopolises of the globalized free market.

Is dependence on fossil fuel and the resulting industrialization a mistake? Will the effects of fossil fuel depletion and climate change cause us to move to smaller communities with local economies again? Will global warming force true sustainability on the world? It is important for every person to become more than just familiar with these issues. We must begin to make them the highest priorities in our lives. It is necessary that we stop living by burning fossil fuels and generating greenhouse gases.

Peak Oil

Peak oil is the term used to describe the point in time at which oil production reaches its maximum and then begins to decline. After 140 years the world has consumed about half the oil available. In the next 40-50 years all the oil in the earth will have been burned. But long before then the amount of oil available each year will begin to decline.

The concept of peak oil was formulated in the late 1950s by M. King Hubbert, an oil geologist who worked for Shell Oil Company. Hubbert wrote a ground breaking report which measured oil reserves as well as their pattern of depletion. He noted that the world had been searching for, finding and developing oil for more than 75 years and that, based on the data available from these decades of exploration, it was possible to determine how much oil had existed in a given area (such as the lower 48 US states) and to predict when it would be half gone. He further pointed out that at the time an oil reservoir deep in the earth was drawn down to half full, oil production would begin to decline and continue to decline until the reservoir was empty.

At an oil conference in 1956 Hubbert predicted that oil production would peak in the US lower 48 states around 1970.[5] Oil professionals ridiculed the prediction. However, to everyone's surprise, oil production in the US lower 48 states did peak in 1970 as Hubbert predicted, and the rate of production has been

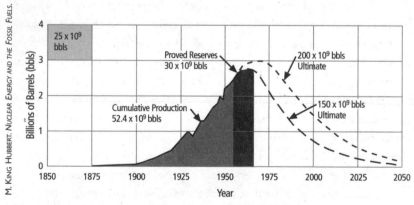

1.1: *King Hubbert's Original US Peak Oil Curve (Lower 48 States)*

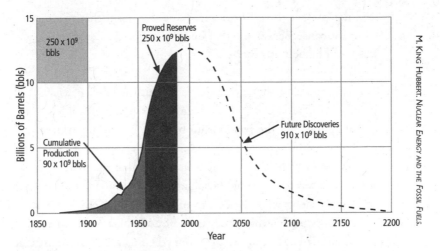

1.2: *King Hubbert's Original World Peak Oil Curve*

declining steadily ever since (Fig. 1.1). In the same presentation Hubbert gave a preliminary estimate for world peak production to be the year 2000 — off by only five years if one accepts the increasingly popular view that *regular* oil production peaked in 2005 (Fig. 1.2). In spite of Hubbert's accuracy, it was hard for people who believe in a world without limits to take him seriously. Hubbert commented "The consumption of energy from fossil fuels is thus seen to be but a 'pip' rising sharply from zero to a maximum, and almost as sharply declining, and thus representing but a moment in human history."[6]

The oil shocks of the 1970s increased interest in determining a date for world peak oil, and in 1980 *The Global 2000 Report to the President of the United States* — begun during the Carter administration — was published.[7] This report included coverage of peak oil. At that time, there were significant differences between official government positions and Hubbert. The US Geological Survey (USGS) argued that Hubbert's estimate of 175 billion barrels of oil reserves in the US was too low. Vincent McKelvey, the Assistant Chief Geologist of the Department of Interior, supported the USGS estimate of 590 billion barrels. In the discussion on the differing viewpoints, the report summarized a fateful decision.

> As a result of this disagreement, the committee's summary report
> did not base its recommendation on Hubbert's projections and

did not present the oil depletion issue in a form that made clear the consequences and the course of action that should be taken if Hubbert was correct.[8]

In 1986 six years after the government's report, the book *Beyond Oil: The Threat to Food and Fuel in the Coming Decades* described in detail the work of King Hubbert and pointed out the relationship between oil consumption and the economy.[9] This superbly written book became a key resource for publications on peak oil in the early 2000s. Popular belief has it that the marketing campaign for the book was upstaged by the Challenger explosion in the same year. If true, this event along with the efforts of Vincent McKelvey to discredit Hubbert will be key points when the history of peak oil denial is written.

Peak oil resurfaced in Europe in 1997, the year English oil geologist Colin Campbell published *The Coming Oil Crisis*.[10] Campbell had been a well known oil-hunting geologist for over 30 years. He founded the Association for the Study of Peak Oil (ASPO) in 2001. In June 2003 ASPO changed its title from Association for the Study of Peak Oil to the Association for the Study of Peak Oil and Gas, adding natural gas resources to its areas of analysis. ASPO provides depletion information that is as accurate as possible rather than focusing on politics or activism. Each monthly newsletter contains an analysis of one of the major oil producing countries in the world. ASPO's oil and gas depletion chart is now known around the energy world.

ASPO has been critical in educating people about the coming peaks in oil and natural gas production. ASPO's date for the peak of regular oil was 2005. For regular oil plus deep water, heavy oils and natural gas liquids the estimate for peak is 2010 (Fig. 1.3).[11] Without the activities of this organization and its subsidiaries in other countries there would be much less general knowledge available to the public. Oil companies such as ExxonMobil and Shell argue that there is much more oil to be discovered, discounting historical trends by suggesting new technology will find new supplies. The United States Geological Service (USGS) supports this contention and claims that there is much more oil remaining than ASPO estimates. However, oil companies and the USGS have done a poor job of predicting resources in the past and in some cases have deliberately misled the public.

In his book *The Hype About Hydrogen*, Joseph Romm praised Shell Oil's technical skills saying "The Royal Dutch/ Shell Group [is] probably the most

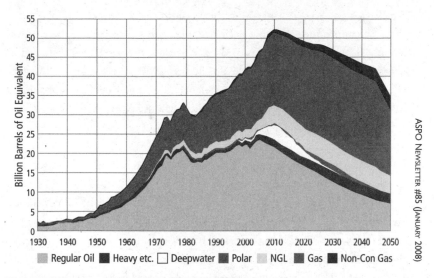

ASPO NEWSLETTER #85 (JANUARY 2008)

1.3: *ASPO Peak Oil and Natural Gas Chart (2006 Base Case)*

successful predictor in the global oil business".[12] Yet in January 2004, the energy industry was rocked by scandal when Shell, one of the four major public oil companies in the world, lowered their proved reserves. This so called successful predictor not only reduced its proved reserves by 20% but admitted that both its chairman and chief exploration officer had deliberately misrepresented the size of their reserves. Shell paid almost $700 million in fines for this action.[13] Other oil companies are equally uncaring about the public. In late 2007, British Petroleum paid out $373 million dollars in fines and restitution for oil spills from pipeline breaks, violation of the Clean Air Act in conjunction with a refinery explosion and driving up the price of propane. [14] In March 2006 the largest independent oil operator, ExxonMobil, ran ads in the *Wall Street Journal*, the *Washington Post* and the *New York Times* which claimed that peak oil is decades away, attempting to discredit what it called the theory of peak oil.[15] Chevron advertisements extol the growth of the world's population not as a problem but as a solution to the energy problem, implying that the increasing population will provide more ingenious people to look for fossil fuel alternatives.[16] Chevron's costs for such campaigns are in the tens of millions of dollars.[17]

Obviously proved reserves are not proved at all. This term simply misleads the public, disguising the fact that the oil experts guess at what is available. The term proved reserves also has a political context. The amount of oil OPEC countries can produce and ship is tied to a certain percentage of their proved reserves. If they increase their proved reserves, they are then allowed to increase their production as well. So, in the 1980s the country of Kuwait increased its proved reserves. Within a short time the other OPEC countries increased their proved reserves accordingly, regaining parity with Kuwait. This marketing move was never rescinded; most OPEC reserves are consequently highly suspect.[18]

A legitimate estimate must be based on the amount of oil being discovered and the amount of oil being produced and used. In 2006 the ratio was 1 to 6 — one barrel of new oil was discovered for each six barrels of oil consumed. This is obviously unsustainable (Fig. 1.4).

In February 2007 the US Government Accountability Office (GAO) published a major report stating that peak oil will occur between now and the next few decades.[19] The report noted that the wide spread in their estimated dates was due to lack of data, data which is in the files of domestic oil companies (who hold them confidential) and major oil producing countries around the world (who also keep this data secret). Unfortunately, the world is held hostage to commercial interests who, by combining their confidential data, could accurately predict the date of peak oil. No one country or company controls more

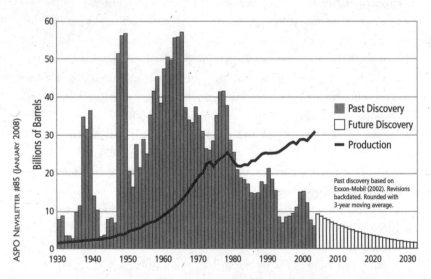

1.4: The Growing Discovery Production Gap (Regular Conventional Oil)

than a fraction of the oil resources; in the case of the four major corporations, no more than a few percent each. How, when obviously they have an incomplete view of the whole resource, can oil producers continue to insist that peak oil is fiction and that the US need not reduce its oil consumption?

Peak Natural Gas

In the US, oil provides 40% of total energy consumed, natural gas 22% and coal 22%.[20] Oil has been the main concern of those involved with fossil fuel depletion, with a primary focus on transportation. Most people in the US perceive *the energy crisis* as an increase in gasoline prices; however, all fossil fuel prices have been increasing in recent years and peaks in supply of all three fuels will occur. Natural gas production peaked in the lower 48 US states in 1973, only three years after the peak in US oil production in the same states. Fortunately for the US, under the rules of the North American Free Trade Agreement (NAFTA) Canada must supply as much natural gas to the US as it requires. Canada cannot husband gas for its own needs or for its future generations. The US currently consumes about 50% of Canada's natural gas production. The peak in North American gas (US and Canada combined) occurred in 2002.[21]

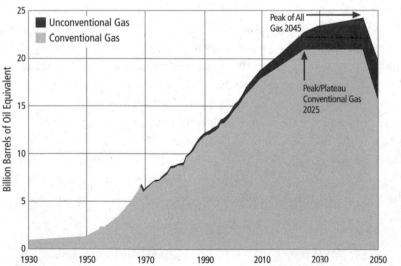

1.5: *World Peak Natural Gas*

Natural gas has a different depletion pattern than oil. The halfway point of peak oil occurs when about half the oil is gone. But in the case of natural gas, production does not necessarily decline at the halfway point. Rather production remains at a relatively constant rate until there is a sudden falloff that can be very steep.

It is therefore more difficult to predict the amount of natural gas in an area based on a peak occurrence. The ASPO chart for natural gas worldwide shows a more gradual buildup of production, a plateau and then a steep decline. Colin Campbell projects that world natural gas production will peak in about 2045 (Fig. 1.5).[22] Most of the natural gas remaining is in Russia and the Middle East — not easily accessible to the US.

Peak Coal

The United States has more coal reserves than any other nation. Many people in the US feel that coal will replace oil and natural gas. The media religiously state that the nation has a 250 year supply, a number that has been bandied about for decades. But like oil and natural gas, this optimistic projection is looking more and more inflated. Roscoe Bartlett, a Republican member of the US Congress from Maryland, has given numerous talks to Congress on peak oil and coal. He points out that the popular notion of a 250 year supply assumes current use rates. But at a compounded annual increase in consumption of 2%, the supply time drops from 250 years to 85 years. He also points out that if coal, which is a solid, is converted into a gas or a liquid in order to replace gasoline or natural gas, then the supply drops further to 50 years since extra energy is needed for the conversion.[23] Other more recent information also calls into question the popular number of 250 years. The Energy Watch Group, an advisory organization to the German government, in its 2007 coal report challenged this number.[24] Another study by the European Commission's Institute for Energy aimed to estimate the coal supply prospects for 2030 and beyond. Their analysis concentrated on coal used to generate steam for electricity, since the power generation sector is by far the largest user of coal worldwide. The report includes the following points.

1. The supply base of coal is being continuously depleted. World proven reserves (i.e. the reserves that are economically recoverable at current economic and operating conditions) of coal are decreasing fast.

2. Coal production costs are steadily rising all over the world, due to the need to develop new fields, increasingly difficult geological conditions and additional infrastructure costs associated with the exploitation of new fields.

3. The lion's share of world proven coal reserves is concentrated in six countries (USA, China, India, Russia, South Africa and Australia) who hold 84% of world hard coal reserves.

4. The immense growth in coal consumption since 2000 has not been matched by a corresponding development of proven coal reserves, despite the increase in world coal prices. In fact, from 2000 to 2005, the world proven reserves estimate dropped by almost a third, from 277 to 155 years.

5. If the 2000-2005 evolution in the proven reserves-to-production ratios for coal, gas and oil continues, the coal ratio could relatively quickly decrease to those of natural gas and oil. The world could run out of economically recoverable (at current economic and operating conditions) reserves of coal much earlier than widely anticipated.

6. While in the past coal has been traditionally perceived as an abundant, widely available, cheap, affordable and reliable energy source, the coal of the future may look quite different.[25]

In his analysis of the coal situation, Richard Heinburg reveals the startling fact that the energy provided by coal in the US peaked in 1998! Unlike oil or natural gas, coal has several different grades. The grades vary greatly in their heat content.

Anthracite: 30 MJ/kg
Bituminous: 18.8-29.3 MJ/kg
Sub-bitiminous: 8.3-25 MJ/kg
Lignite: 5.5-14.3 MJ/kg

The US may have passed its peak of high quality (anthracite and bituminous) coal production in the Appalachian and Illinois areas. Production of sub-bituminous coal from Wyoming has been growing to make up for this

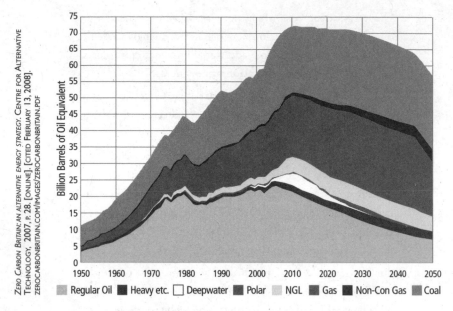

ZERO CARBON BRITAIN: AN ALTERNATIVE ENERGY STRATEGY. CENTRE FOR ALTERNATIVE TECHNOLOGY, 2007, P. 28. [ONLINE]. [CITED FEBRUARY 13, 2008]. ZEROCARBONBRITAIN.COM/IMAGES/ZEROCARBONBRITAIN.PDF

Regular Oil ■ Heavy etc. □ Deepwater ■ Polar ■ NGL ■ Gas ■ Non-Con Gas ■ Coal

1.6: *Oil, Gas and Coal Production Projections*

depletion. The energy content of coal burned peaked in 1998 at 598 million tons of oil equivalent (Mtoe). In 2005 energy content had fallen to 576 Mtoe.[26]

Figure 1.6 shows the combination of oil and its variants, natural gas and coal. It suggests a plateau of hydrocarbon usage and a steady decline beginning sometime in the next decade.

Peak Uranium

In 2007 the price of uranium recorded its biggest percentage increase since its use began almost 40·years before (Fig. 1.7).[27] The demand for uranium is growing due to a resurgence of interest in nuclear power. According to the International Atomic Energy Agency, 34 new nuclear reactors are presently under construction, adding to the current 439 reactors worldwide.[28] The nuclear power industry was adversely affected by the accidents at Three Mile Island in the US and Chernobyl in Russia. Large amounts of enriched uranium from Russian nuclear bombs were used for reactor fuel, providing a brief increase in supplies. The estimates for uranium resources are as vague and uncertain as those for coal. In a 2006 report the Energy Watch Group suggested a peak uranium date around 2050.[29]

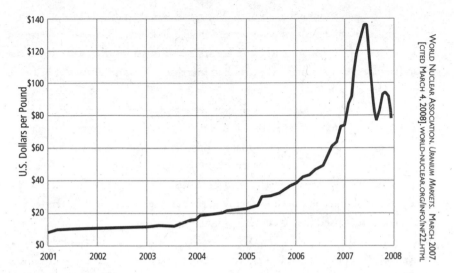

World Nuclear Association, *Uranium Markets*, March 2007. [cited March 4, 2008]. world-nuclear.org/info/inf22.html

1.7: *World Uranium Price*

Climate Change and Global Warming

The Intergovernmental Panel on Climate Change (IPCC) was established in 1988 by two United Nations organizations, the World Meteorological Organization (WMO) and the United Nations Environment Programme (UNEP). The role of the IPCC is to assess, comprehensively and objectively, the scientific information relevant to understanding the risk of human-induced climate change. One of its main goals is to publish special reports to support the UN Framework Convention on Climate Change (UNFCCC), the document behind the Kyoto Protocol. The IPCC does not carry out research, nor does it monitor climate or related phenomena. It bases its assessments on peer reviewed and published scientific literature.[30] IPCC reports are widely cited in almost any debate related to climate change; national and international responses to climate change generally regard the UN climate panel as authoritative.

The executive summary of the 1990 IPCC report noted that emissions resulting from human activities are increasing the atmospheric concentrations of such greenhouse gases as CO_2, methane, CFCs and nitrous oxide. The second report published five years later (1995) concluded that greenhouse gas concentrations had continued to increase and noted that the climate has changed over the past century (air temperature has increased by between 0.3 and 0.6 °C since the late 19th century). The balance of evidence suggested a discernible human influence on global climate. The third report, published in 2001, said that an increasing body of observations gave a collective picture of a warming world and other changes in the climate system. Emissions of greenhouse gases and aerosols from human activities had increased. New evidence showed that most of the warming observed over the last 50 years has been attributable to people. The Fourth Assessment Report was completed in early 2007. The key conclusion of the report was that warming of the climate system is unequivocal. Most of the increase in global average temperatures since the mid 20th century was due to human activity. Hotter temperatures and rises in sea level will continue for centuries even if greenhouse gas levels are stabilized. The report noted that the amount of temperature and sea level rise is dependent on the fossil fuels used in this century (Fig. 1.8).[31]

Shortly after the IPCC's 2007 report was issued, newer studies became available that provided a more up-to-date analysis. In an article entitled "Global warming 'is three times faster than worst predictions,'" Geoffrey Lean reported on two studies released after the latest IPCC report. These studies found that emissions of carbon dioxide have been rising at three times the rate of the 1990s. The Arctic ice cap is melting three times as fast — and the seas are rising twice as rapidly — as had been predicted. One study, published by the US National Academy of Sciences, showed that carbon dioxide emissions have

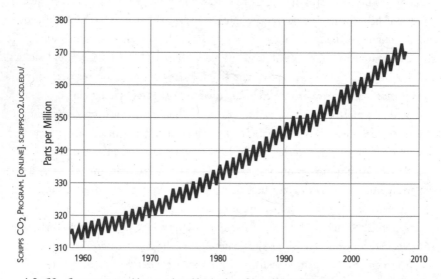

1.8: CO₂ Concentration Measured at Mauna Loa Observatory, Hawaii

been increasing by about 3% a year during this decade, compared with 1.1% a year in the 1990s, suggesting that IPCC's dire forecasts likely understate the threat facing the world. A second study by the University of California's National Snow and Ice Data Center showed that Arctic ice has declined by 7.8% a decade over the past 50 years, compared with an average estimate by IPCC computer models of 2.5%.[32]

CO_2 levels reached a 650,000 year high in 2006 — 381.2 parts per million. Spring now arrives 13 days earlier in many parts of North America than it did 30 years ago. The planet's ability to absorb CO_2 through soil and sea chemistry has steadily declined.[33] Climate change is real. Twenty years after the first warning, early prognoses have not only turned out to be accurate but are probably conservative.

Issues and Choices for the Future

In recent years, the news has not been good. Peak oil, although clearly understood in the 1970s and 1980s, was not taken seriously — only in the last few years has it been a topic of discussion. Common sense, the intuition of all people that there are limits to everything, did not prevail and the US accepted a neoclassical economic view that growth could be limitless. The theory of peak oil is now being verified as country after country reaches peak. Natural gas has already peaked in North America. Other fossil fuels will also peak — or may be completely depleted — in this century. But suddenly the prospect of peaking, with its dire consequences, becomes insignificant when related to climate change. Climate change theory now tells us that we should not burn what fossil fuels remain. Life on the surface of the planet can only continue if most of the remaining fossil fuels are left in the ground.

How rapidly must we respond? And how can we measure the change needed? Recent information from the IPCC gives a sense of how much we must reduce our generation of CO_2 and in what time frame. George Monbiot summarized the most recent IPCC estimates for CO_2 reductions. He calculated that the current generation of CO_2 in the world is about four tonnes per person. He determined from the IPCC forecast that this must be reduced to less than one tonne by 2050, a reduction of about 4.5% per year.[34] Figure 1.9 shows the CO_2 generated by the 33 most populous countries that make up 80% of the world's population. The more industrialized countries are far from the goal of being sustainable.

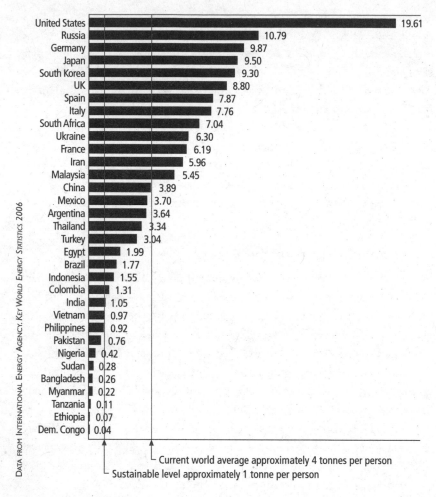

DATA FROM INTERNATIONAL ENERGY AGENCY. KEY WORLD ENERGY STATISTICS 2006

Current world average approximately 4 tonnes per person

Sustainable level approximately 1 tonne per person

1.9: *Actual CO$_2$ emissions per capita (in tonnes) — 33 most populous nations containing 80% of world population*

The burning of fossil fuel has created a chasm toward which humanity is rushing. The more fossil fuels we burn, the deeper the chasm. Many hope that acquiring great wealth will keep them from the chasm, ignoring the fate of billions of less well-off people. Some try to build partial bridges in anticipation, hoping to somehow jump over the chasm. Most people simply deny its existence. Will society be more affected by climate change or fossil fuel depletion? Will humanity be able to reduce emissions enough to mitigate the damage already done? The questions are difficult. The US must step on the brakes and pull over to the side of the road for a few decades while it designs a new low energy way of living, as it is by far the largest consumer of fossil fuels and generator of CO_2. But before we can begin designing we need to explore the nature of our current fossil fuel based economy and find a new economic system that serves community and nature rather than destroying them.

Two

Peak Oil — Peak Economy

I N TODAY'S MEDIA much of the discourse about the economy lacks substance but uses an extensive vocabulary of metaphors. The economy has a wide repertoire of actions — it can *tank, implode, derail, grow, shrink, stagnate, flatten, boom, explode, soar, collapse, run down* and *strengthen*. The economy is apparently temporal since bad policies can *kill* it. Those who like speed metaphors can say the economy *slows, accelerates* or *speeds up*.

These metaphors give the impression that the economy is some physical creature. A child, overhearing a conversation using such terms, might ask for a picture of economy or maybe even a video with examples of it imploding or exploding. A parent might tell the child that economy is just an adult's way of talking about money or that economy is the word we use to describe our income and savings. We might go on to explain that all these words simply mean we are either getting more money and can buy more things, or we are getting less money and can buy fewer things.

The main indices that measure the economy are the Gross National Product (GNP) or the Gross Domestic Product (GDP). In the case of the US these indices are measured in dollars, not feet, miles, temperature, weight, volume or rate of acceleration. They are simply dollar numbers which are composed of the sum of many other dollar values representing particular sources of revenues and expenditures. The GNP or GDP cannot explode or tank but they can increase and decrease by a quantitative dollar amount.

Growth is the measure of a positive change in the economy or, in our words, a measure of how much more money is available. *Economic growth* sounds nicer than *making more money*, perhaps because Christian tradition states "the love of money [economic growth, goods and services] is the root of all evil." But most Americans love money and have created a culture where money is the primary measure of success or progress. Economic growth or a growing economy is a euphemism for getting richer.

Fossil Fuels and the Economy

How is it that our economy grew so much in the last century, particularly after World War II? And why has the US economy apparently been so successful? Was it the American character? Was it Yankee ingenuity and innovation? Was it some breakthrough in thinking? Or was it simply the fact that the nation sat on a huge reservoir of fossil fuels — oil, coal and natural gas? This is the most likely factor. Fossil fuel use began with coal and moved to oil. But it was not until after World War II that oil's use became widespread worldwide, that oil consumption began growing exponentially and North America began its romance with driving and the suburbs. Throughout the world people began to radically alter their lives by using long stored energy created 100s of millions of years ago.

Energy was linked to modern capitalism at its birth in the late 18th century at the beginning of the coal fueled Industrial Revolution. Adam Smith, author of *The Wealth of Nations* (1776), created the intellectual framework that defined the free market of today's dominant economic theory. He coined the expression *the invisible hand of the market* to argue that personal self-interest would result in the most efficient use of resources, with public welfare following as a byproduct. Smith concluded that state and personal efforts to promote social good are less effective than unbridled competition in a free market environment. Within a few years of the publication of Smith's *Wealth of Nations*, James Watt obtained his early patents on an advanced steam engine and began manufacturing these machines, marking the beginning of the Industrial Revolution. Thus, modern economics and modern technology began at the same point in history — in fact, Watt and Smith knew each other. Statements such as "our economy is fueled by cheap energy" might be more correctly stated as "our economic theory is based on the concept of an infinite supply of fossil fuels and an infinite 'sink' (air, oceans, land) for its waste byproducts." The direct connection between economic growth and fossil fuels was aptly described by oil geologist and ASPO founder Colin Campbell.

The *Industrial Revolution* opened in the mid 18th Century with the exploitation of coal, initially in Britain, providing a new fuel for industry, transport and trade, which grew rapidly. The Oil Age dawned 100 years later, initially to provide lamp-oil for illumination, but later to fuel transport, following the development of the internal-combustion engine. Electricity generation expanded widely, fuelled first by coal, but later mainly from oil, gas and nuclear energy. This epoch has been widely seen as one of amazing technological progress, which has conditioned many people to think that there must always be a technological solution.

The *Industrial Revolution* was accompanied by an equally important, but less visible, *Financial Revolution.* In short, commercial banks lent money in excess of what they had on deposit, effectively creating money out of thin air, but the system worked because tomorrow's expansion provided collateral for today's debt. It was effectively a system of confidence, an intrinsic element of all debt. So, it might be better termed the *Financial-Industrial Revolution.*

The World's population expanded six-fold exactly in parallel with oil, which provided much of the fuel with which to plough the field, and bring food and manufactured goods to market, thus indirectly supporting the Financial System. The international[ization] of transport of food reduced the risk of local famines when harvests failed for climatic and other reasons.

The Second Half of the Oil Age now dawns and will be characterized by the decline of oil, followed by gas, and all that depends upon these prime energy sources. The actual decline of oil will be gradual at less than 3% a year: such that the production of all liquid hydrocarbons in 2020 may well have fallen to approximately what it was in 1990. In those terms, it does not appear to be a particularly serious situation. But in reality, it is a devastating development because it implies that the oil-based economy is in permanent terminal decline, removing the confidence in perpetual growth on which the Financial System depends. Without the assumption of ever-onward growth, borrowing and lending dry up: there being little viable left to invest in. It follows that there will be a need to remove vast amounts of so-called Capital, which in fact was not Capital in the sense of being the saved proceeds of labor, but merely an expression of speculative confidence in ever onward economic growth. This in turn leads to the conclusion that the World faces another Great Depression, triggered more by the perception of long-term decline of the general economy rather than the actual decline of oil supply itself which is gradual not cataclysmic. The World is definitely not about to run out of oil, but it does face the onset of decline having consumed about half of what is readily available on the Planet.[1]

Growth Economics and Inequity

Ivan Illich, theologian, philosopher and historian, pointed out the destructive power of modern capitalistic institutions, which, to survive, must have an unending supply of consumers. They must create needs faster than they create satisfaction. As people try to meet these unnecessary needs they consume more and more fossil fuels and other nonrenewable minerals. As they consume the finite resources of the earth, massive amounts of toxins are created. In his seminal essay *Energy and Equity* Illich discusses the contradiction that comes with the joint pursuit of equity and industrial growth. He says equity and energy consumption can grow concurrently only to a certain level. Below that level, technology improves the conditions for social progress and above it energy consumption leads to greater inequity. A high energy consuming society leads to social relationships dictated by fossil fuel based machines.[2] The economist Jeffrey Sachs, who helped design the blueprint for the economic disaster that overtook Russia after the USSR was dismantled, compares the world at the beginning of the industrial revolution and the result almost two centuries later.[3]

Figure 2.1 shows the change in the distribution of the world's income in different regions over a period of almost two centuries of so called free market activity and increasing consumption of fossil fuels. The huge imbalances are obvious. The roughly 2 to 1 ratio between the richer areas and the poorer areas of 1820 rose to a roughly 12 to 1 ratio by 1998 — and that ratio has increased each year since! Sachs suggests that the poorer nations will eventually reach the same level as the richer ones, but he does not see the connection between wealth and energy consumption nor does he measure the environmental devastation that would arise if by some miracle such parity were achieved. Like most other economists, Sachs has rationalized the constant increase of inequity with some hoped for technology that will eventually *level the playing field*.

Economic growth is the first goal of most nations and one might hope that all people would be better off financially. Most people in the world — even in the United States — don't feel better off. The increasing level of inequity in the

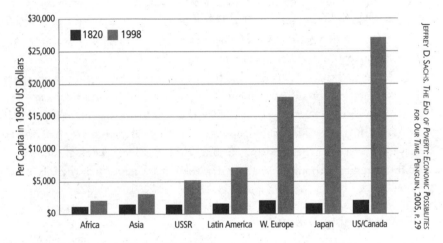

2.1: *Wealth Distribution by Region 1820/1998*

Jeffrey D. Sachs. *The End of Poverty: Economic Possibilities for Our Time.* Penguin, 2005, p. 29

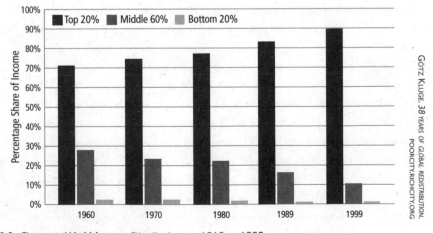

2.2: *Change in World Income Distribution — 1960 to 1999*

Götz Kluge. *38 years of global redistribution.* poorcity.richcity.org

US leads many to be in danger of untimely death simply because they cannot afford a doctor. The inequity trend that began in 1820 continues today — and is accelerating.

The fossil fuel-based free market has brought greater and greater inequity. Figure 2.2 shows the increasingly unequal distribution of income worldwide, the result of economic policies and competitive values of the last four decades of the 20th century, a period in which the growth economists have been most influential. In the last 40 years, the income share of the poorest 20% of the people in the world has decreased almost 50%, while the income share of the richest 20% has increased by 40%. This difference is worsening, a predictable outcome in a dog-eat-dog world where competition for money is the fundamental premise of modern economics.

The same situation exists within the US, although the inequity is not quite as extreme.[4] In the US, we lament the shrinking of the middle class and the disappearance of safety nets. Just since the year 2004, the income share of those in the upper 20% of the population has increased to more than 50%, a level not seen since the period just prior to the Great Depression of the 1930s.[5] More significant though is the fact that the rate of inequity in the US is still increasing.

Rationalizing Inequity

Growth economists deal with increasing inequity by using three metaphors. The first is a *rising tide lifts all boats*. This statement implies that economic growth (recall that this means nothing more than an increase in the average income of all workers) will provide more wealth to each person. The metaphor is deliberately misleading since income increases are not distributed equally — more goes to the rich than the poor. It is more accurate to state that some boats rise, and some sink.

The second metaphor is the *trickle down theory*, which argues that if the rich get richer some percentage of their riches will trickle down to the less rich, making them better off than they were before. As we have seen, on a worldwide basis such trickling is minimal if it exists at all. But economists argue that life is still better for those with low pay because society has advanced to such an extent that even those in poverty are better off than they were in the past, even though in the past they earned a higher percentage of available income. The poor have generally not subscribed to this argument.

The third, the *growing pie* metaphor, is a modified version of trickle down. It suggests that even if one's slice of the economic pie is decreasing relative to others, the size of the pie itself is increasing so each person increases their income by some amount even though inequity is also increasing.

All three of these metaphors are used to justify the existence of elite people or groups with incredible wealth and power who take a greater percentage of the available income and wealth each year. Economists argue that such elite are superior humans who create more wealth for the rest of us, no matter how unequal the distribution. Technical entrepreneurs are particularly lauded for their superiority.

Economics, Energy and Income

When the economy is discussed along with energy, an additional set of metaphors is used.

> Energy is the *glue* that makes our economy work.
> Energy is the *engine* that drives our economy.
> Our economy *runs* on oil (or cheap energy).
> We can't *grow* our economy without cheap oil.
> Cheap oil *fuels* our economy.

Energy use and economic growth are closely linked. The relationship is consistent in all regions and countries of the world. Developing countries like

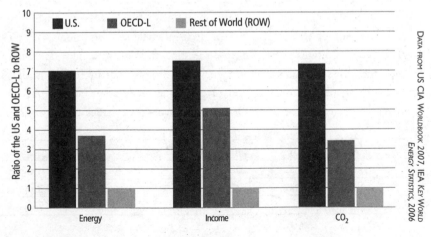

Data from US CIA Worldbook 2007, IEA Key World Energy Statistics, 2006

2.3: *Correlation between Energy, Income and CO$_2$ Emissions*

China are using more and more energy as they attempt to build societies like the US. And, just like the US, inequity is increasing in those countries. As noted earlier, the measure of a growth economy is the measure of its GNP or GDP, which is a measure of personal income change. What we have yet to understand is that this is simply the measure of fossil fuel consumption. All wealth and prosperity is the measure of a person's or a country's access to fossil fuels.

Few contemporary economists appear to understand or care about the relationship between fossil fuel distribution, climate change and poverty (or inequity). Figure 2.3 depicts a simple relationship: personal income (or national GDP) is proportional to fossil fuel consumption which is proportional to CO_2 pollution. This figure divides world population into three groups: the United States (US), a subset of the members of the Organization for Economic Cooperation and Development (OECD)[6] and the Rest of the World (ROW).

The population of the US is about 300 million people, 4.5% of world population. The OECD-L grouping (OECD members except US, Turkey and Mexico) contains roughly 10.5% of the world population, about 700 million people. It includes Western Europe along with Canada and the industrial counties of Asia — Japan, South Korea, Australia and New Zealand. The third group, ROW, has about 5,700 million people — 85% of the world's population. The PPP (national yearly GDP divided by population), annual fossil fuel consumption (barrels of oil equivalent or boe) per capita and annual CO_2 generation (tonnes of CO_2) per capita are included in Figure 2.4.

This simple analysis shows the correlation between energy consumption and income, supporting the argument that oil consumption (along with CO_2 generation) and one's personal income are linked. Within each group of countries, the ratios are roughly equivalent. This implies that increased income is based on increased consumption of oil (as well as other fossil fuels) and increased generation of CO_2. Or, in simple words, wealthier people consume

Region	Pop.	% Pop	PPP	BOE/c	CO_2/c
US	300 million	4.5%	$43,800	57.8 boe	19.6 tonne
OECD-L	700 million	10.5%	$29,915	30.9 boe	9.3 tonne
ROW	5,700 million	85.0%	$5,832	8.3 boe	2.7 tonne

2.4: *Income, energy and CO_2 per capita values* — US, OECD-L, ROW
DATA FROM US CIA WORLDBOOK 2007, IEA KEY WORLD ENERGY STATISTICS, 2006

more oil and pollute more; poor people consume less oil and pollute less. Thus the standard of living of every person on the planet is based on how much energy he or she uses and how much pollution he or she generates.

So called economic miracles of the past, including the Green Revolution, were based on the increased consumption of oil and other fossil fuels. When these resources begin to decline, our income will decline with them and we will become poorer. Soon the party of the century will be over, and in the cold light of dawn we will begin the long process of cleaning up the mess. Oil geologist M. King Hubbert concluded his 1976 paper "Exponential Growth as a Transient Phenomenon in Human History" with these observations.

It appears therefore that one of the foremost problems confronting humanity today is how to make the transition from the precarious state that we are now in to this optimum future state by a least catastrophic progression. Our principal impediments at present are neither lack of energy or material resources nor of essential physical and biological knowledge. Our principal constraints are cultural. During the last two centuries we have known nothing but exponential growth and in parallel we have evolved what amounts to an exponential-growth culture, a culture so heavily dependent upon the continuance of exponential growth for its stability that it is incapable of reckoning with problems of non-growth.

Since the problems confronting us are not intrinsically insoluble, it behooves us, while there is yet time, to begin a serious examination of the nature of our cultural constraints and of the cultural adjustments necessary to permit us to deal effectively with the problems rapidly arising.[7]

Twelve years later, Dr. Hubbert said in an interview, "Our window of opportunity is slowly closing... at the same time, it probably requires a spiral of adversity. In other words, things have to get worse before they can get better. The most important thing is to get a clear picture of the situation we're in, and the outlook for the future — exhaustion of oil and gas, that kind of thing — and an appraisal of where we are and what the time scale is. And the time scale is not centuries, it is decades."[8]

What's in Store for the USA?

The language we use to describe the economy keeps people from looking at physical reality. *Economic growth* means more money and pollution while *economic stagnation* or *shrinking* means less money and a cleaner environment. Peak oil implies the end of economic growth which will likely result in pay cuts, lay-offs, foreclosures and repossessions. The question is, "can we manage what is inevitable in such a way as to lessen the ill effects?" One country — Cuba — did, after its sudden economic collapse when their oil supplies were unexpectedly cut off by Russia in 1990. Cuba's experience was very traumatic and difficult as the country transitioned from an industrial society to a more agrarian one, with a major reduction in standard of living. Yet it maintained free medical coverage and education, and a life span equal to the US.[9]

One might hope that advanced industrial nations will do as well as Cuba, applying their technical and social innovations to minimize the effects of peak oil. More likely we could suffer as much as poorer nations. Possibly a people with more wisdom might have already devised a way of living not dependent on increasing fossil fuel consumption. However, since the 1970 US oil production peak, Americans have consistently bought larger homes, larger cars, driven more, flown more, eaten more energy-expensive meat and, in general, consumed with no limits. The US has no low-energy infrastructure and no plan to develop one. Thus when world peak oil occurs, the falling tide will lower all boats (sinking many of them), the trickle down will dry up and the metaphorical pie will shrink. The *safety net* (some type of minimal government support for the poor) may be completely shredded, leading to great suffering. After the first oil crisis, the US could have made the decision to choose a qualitative way of life rather than a quantitative one. Massive amounts of investment could have been made in wind and solar energies. Much smaller and more efficient cars could have been made. Houses could have been built both smaller and with better insulation. Government funding might have gone to supporting family farms instead of industrial agribusiness.

Recall Colin Campbell's prediction that declining oil supplies will remove the confidence in perpetual growth on which the world's financial system depends. Capital which in theory has been saved from the profits of productive growth, will shrink because much of it — such as inflated stock market and home prices — is more speculative than real. High mortgage payments, natural gas bills and gasoline costs will make all commodities less and less affordable. When people understand that their incomes are in decline, borrowing and lending will decline as well. The result will not simply be a decline of 3-5% per year (the estimated rate of oil production decline). The decline of oil, the principal driver of current economic growth, will undermine the very foundations of our current economic system, setting the scene for a Second Great Depression if a new economics is not developed.

Community Economics

Earlier in this chapter we noted that Adam Smith believed that personal self-interest would result in the most efficient use of resources, with public welfare resulting as a byproduct. Smith implied that the accumulation of material goods is the highest aim of humanity, ahead of any moral, ethical or spiritual considerations and also ahead of concern for others or the environment. Modern economic doctrine also includes the concepts of specialization (assembly lines to increase efficiency), standards (eliminating uniqueness and craftsmanship), routinization (eliminating creativity), control (a wage earner instead of business person) and disposability (goods made to be nonreparable). Advertising became a tool to turn optional wants into seductively addictive needs. Finally, current economic doctrine espouses private ownership instead of public ownership of land and enterprises.

To support this doctrine of material consumption, economists must assume that the natural world offers a limitless source of the raw materials necessary to create the finished goods we will consume. Their view is that if a natural resource (such as oil) declines, then capital, technology and the incentive for personal gain will stimulate human ingenuity to find a replacement. This idea is being severely tested as governments and technologists appear powerless to deal with peak oil and climate change. Economists also use a concept they call *externalization*, invented to deal with the contradictions of basic economic doctrine. Whenever an economist cannot rationally explain a problem, he or she deems it to be an *externality*. This means the *problem* is not taken into account when calculating economic costs. For example, the area of dead ocean at the end of the Mississippi river is deemed an externality. Ignoring it allows one to justify ongoing pollution as economical. But the greatest externality now is the atmosphere and increasing CO_2 levels, which dramatizes the dangerous nature of such ideas.

Fortunately, there is a new breed of economist whose focus is on contemporary, community-based, steady-state economics. Examples are Herman Daly,

Richard Douthwaite, Michael Perelman, John Ikerd, Michael Schuman and Michael Albert.[10] Their community-centered versions of economics are complex and rich. They do not agree with the principle that self-centered individual pursuits will always benefit the community nor that resources are infinite. Rather, the community is held as more important. Cooperation is preferred to competition. And these economists know that economic activity takes place on a finite planet. Figure 2.5, by Herman Daly, illustrates a more realistic world view. It shows that the economy (designated as a square with inputs and outputs of material and energy) is contained within a finite ecosystem, represented by the oval. The economy can *grow* (use more and more energy and material) — but only until it reaches the limits of the ecosystem (where the square hits the edge of the oval). It cannot grow outside of that boundary, thus putting a finite limit on resources used. In this community based economy, the natural world is not seen as an externality, but considered as an integral part of the economy.

Burying old economic theories, abandoning products that require excessive burning of fossil fuels, drastically curtailing dependence on oil-burning machines and beginning to rebuild local infrastructures for food and services are good first steps. In the last sentence of Perelman's book, *The Perverse Economy*, he states "We should move as quickly as possible to a more democratic, more egalitarian, more sustainable society before it is too late."[11] Locality is a vital part of this new sustainable economics; this implies local design, local manufacturing, local savings, local investment and local food production. It means the decline of transnational corporations and the rebirth of locally owned and operated businesses. And a new economy must also be one based on a different concept

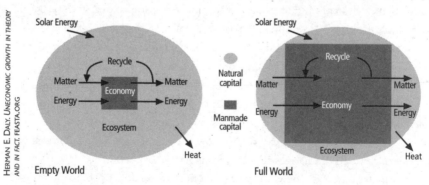

HERMAN E. DALY, *UNECONOMIC GROWTH IN THEORY AND IN FACT.* FEASTA.ORG

2.5: *A Macro View of the Macroeconomy*

of the consumer, as someone who is a neighbor, a fellow citizen and a member of the community. It is only recently that Americans have begun to refer to themselves as consumers. Possibly we can begin to view ourselves as citizens again — that is people who know they are not rugged individualists but members of a community.

As we assessed the role of the growth economy as a cause of peak oil and climate change, we must also reassess our role in the world for the same reason. The fossil fuel era is also the era of the inequitable, violent and over-consumptive American Empire — which was made possible by energy. We must understand the resulting suffering so that we can more easily give up our non-sustainable way of living.

Three

Peak Oil — Peak Empire

As peak oil approaches, tensions are rapidly building in the world. China's growing consumption of oil is said to be a threat to US national security. Japan speaks of taking more of a leadership role in Asia even if it means rearming. Russia is accused of backing off from the free market economy. US officials have said that American soldiers will be in Iraq another 12 — even as much as 50 — years. Inequity is increasing as globalization spreads. Unless the tremendous inequity in fossil fuel use and the equally unfair imbalance in CO_2 generation are addressed, conflict is inevitable. Wars of national energy liberation are highly likely unless remaining fuels are allocated based more fairly than under the current free trade axiom.

Fuelling America's Prosperous Way of Life

When the US was attacked on 9/11, President Bush announced that people hate Americans because of our freedom.[1] Others say that the rest of the world hates Americans for the way the US and all other colonial powers have plundered and murdered them for their resources — thereby depriving them of their freedom and wealth. The US's disproportionate consumption of oil is just one of the manifestations of this imperialism.

I do not intend to criticize or moralize about the country's past or blame current leaders or institutions. Rather I want to examine the ways we Americans relate to each other, to other people and to the natural world. This is necessary to fully understand the implications — both to US citizens and others — of a high energy way of living which is protected by high energy weaponry. This way of life will be short lived as limits to mineral resources and pollutant sinks are reached.

A person with newly diagnosed heart disease learns that the path to health is based on changing pleasurable, but harmful, habits and patterns of eating. Only after making changes does he or she become aware that poor eating habits and a bad lifestyle had actually obscured the pleasures of good health. We Americans find ourselves in this situation today. We are addicted to pleasures derived from cheap and abundant resources and blind to the consequences. It is important that people in the US acknowledge that many people in the world have good reason to hate and fear our country. This awareness may help direct this nation to overcome its harmful habits and energy addictions.

Peak Empire

President Bush claims Americans are good while Osama bin Laden says they are evil. Bin Laden argues that his Arab world has been exploited for decades by western powers. History shows a consistent pattern of stronger nations controlling weaker ones. The Roman Empire was content to control an area around the Mediterranean in close proximity to Rome. The empire of the Netherlands extended to Indonesia. The Spanish Empire focused its conquests in South America, beginning with an assault on the Maya and Aztec civilizations, and including the distant Philippines. But it was the British Empire that first established control on a global basis.

The extent of England's colonialism was celebrated by the slogan "The sun never sets on the British Empire." It represented what was possible with a conquering attitude, advanced weaponry and a lack of scruples. In 1900, Britain had the largest empire in world history, dwarfing preceding empires in size and numbers of people exploited. With a population at that time of 37 million people, Britain controlled and exploited one-fourth of the population of the world (440 million people) and 12 million square miles of the earth's land surface. Fifteen years later, at the end of World War I, Britain took more territory from the Ottoman Empire, particularly parts of what are today many members of the Organization of Petroleum Exporting Countries (OPEC). To understand the numbers of people colonized, the extent of the control and the duration of this empire we must consider the countries occupied and the years spent under British control. Figure 3.1 is a list of British-controlled countries with their independence dates. Most were occupied in the 18th and 19th centuries.

Many British today view their period of empire with nostalgia and pride. However, for the countries occupied, the period of British rule was extremely

Africa		
Egypt - 1950	Uganda - 1962	Botswana -1966
Sudan - 1956	Kenya - 1963	Swaziland - 1968
Ghana - 1957	Malawi - 1964	Zimbabwe - 1980
Nigeria - 1960	Tanzania - 1964	Namibia - 1990
Sierra Leona - 1961	Zambia - 1964	
South Africa - 1961	Gambia - 1965	
Asia		
Australia - 1901	Burma - 1948	Maldives - 1965
New Zealand - 1907	Sri Lanka - 1948	
Nepal - 1923	Bhutan - 1949	
India - 1947	Malaysia -1963	
Middle East		
Cypress - 1961	Kuwait - 1961	Oman - 1967
TransJordan - 1961	Bahrain - 1967	Aden - 1967
Palestine - 1961	Qatar - 1967	Yemen - 1967
Worldwide		
Canada - 1867	Tonga - 1970	Nassau - 1984
N. Borneo - 1963	W. Samoa - 1978	Pitcairn Isl. - 1984
Guyana - 1966	Solomon Isl. - 1978	Brunei - 1984
Fiji - 1970	Filbert Isl. - 1984	

3.1: *Former British Colonies & Their Independence Dates*

INSTITUTE OF COMMONWEALTH STUDIES LIBRARY, FORMER BRITISH-ADMINISTERED TERRITORIES AND COMMONWEALTH COUNTRIES. COMMONWEALTH.SAS.AC.UK/RG_COLONIES.HTM

painful. Although Britain was far and away the most formidable colonizer, other European nations were equally voracious if not as effective. France was a close second, conquering and controlling much of North Africa as well as what was called French Indochina (Vietnam, Laos, Cambodia). The French Empire in Northern Africa included the countries of Algeria, Morocco, Tunisia, Mauritania, Libya, Niger, Mali, Chad, Central African Republic, Gabon and the Republic of the Congo. King Leopold of Belgium, writes historian Adam Hochschild in his book *King Leopold's Ghost*, established a rule of terror that would culminate in the deaths of 8 million indigenous people in the Congo from 1885 to 1909.[2] Spain and Portugal decimated and enslaved the whole continent of South America and much of Central America, killing tens of millions of people. The Netherlands (current population of 16 million) controlled and exploited Indonesia (current population of 238 million) from the early 1600s to 1949.

Just Rule — Saving Souls and Free Trade

It is the nature of aggressive empires to see themselves as benefactors and saviors of the people whom they conquer. How did the British justify their subjugation, killing and exploitation of other peoples? Even before Darwin wrote about survival of the fittest, the Industrial Revolution was used by European countries to prove their intellectual superiority. But in addition to this, there was a growing idea of moral superiority, including the conceit that if the conquerors were not superior, God would not have given them their colonies. Thus, Britain saw its destiny in becoming an imperial power as the raising of the level of civilization in backward nations, a destiny pre-ordained by God. From this spiritual base came the concept of what the British called *just rule*, expressed in many writings of the time. For example, Brigadier General John Jacob in a communication from the early 1800s, asserted, "We hold India, then, by being in reality, as in reputation, a superior race to the Asiatic; and if this natural superiority did not exist, we should not, and could not, retain the country for one week. If, then, we are really a morally superior race, governed by higher motives and possessing higher attributes than the Asiatics, the more the natives of India are able to understand us, and the more we improve their capacity for so understanding, the firmer will become our power. Away then with the assumption of equality; and let us accept our true position of a dominant race."[3]

"One Brit is worth two Frenchies or a hundred Wogs" is an old expression from British colonial days. The statement equates the life of one Englishman with the lives of two Frenchmen (Britain's historical competitor) and 100 Wogs, a derisive term for the darker-skinned people of Africa and Asia. Another expression — "Life is cheap in the Orient" — means Asian (or African) lives are less valuable than those of Europeans. These expressions show the deep racial prejudice that separated colonizing nations from those they conquered in Africa, Asia, the Middle East, as well as North and South America. At the 1919 Paris Conference after World War I, Japan proposed a clause on racial equality which read "The equality of nations being a basic principle of the League of Nations, the High Contracting Parties agree to accord, as soon as possible, to all alien nationals of States members of the League equal and just treatment in every respect, making no distinction, either in law or in fact, on account of their race or nationality." This proposal was defeated. The British Foreign Secretary, Lord Balfour, had said about the clause that the notion that all men were created equal was an interesting one, but that he did not believe it. "You could scarcely say that a man in Central Africa was equal to a European."[4]

Free trade is a second justification for controlling weaker nations. History is replete with descriptions of Britain's military expeditions to "keep trade routes open," including campaigns throughout Africa and Asia. Today, *free trade* is the favored rationale for exploitation, as most people simply do not believe in racial and cultural superiority any longer. Military intervention has to some extent been replaced by trade embargoes and other financial mechanisms to maintain control over weaker nations, the 10-year-long embargo on Iraq being a recent example. And the World Trade Organization, dominated by the US, sets policies that favor developed nations.

Superior Character or Superior Weaponry?

Britain fought the Battle of Omdurman in 1898 against a Muslim army in Sudan. Using the technology of the machine gun, the British killed 20,000 Muslims in the battle. Forty-eight British soldiers were killed. Winston Churchill reported, "Thus ended the Battle of Omdurman — the most signal triumph ever gained by the arms of science over barbarians."[5] It was not simply superior weaponry that defeated native peoples in their own land. Rather, it was the willingness to use this weaponry to slaughter large numbers of people. Some scholars have noted that such killings were based on the fact that the other races were viewed as inferior. But more astute observers have suggested that it is first necessary to define other people as inferior before one can justify killing them, taking their land and resources and enslaving them for profit. The British were the founders of the slave trade between Africa and the Americas. This horrible and shameful time in history could only be justified by assuming Africans were not people — thus they could be treated as commodities which could be bought and sold for profit. Today Anglo American and European countries have even greater superiority in weapons, but offer only slightly more subtle justifications for military action — bringing supposed freedom and democracy rather than civilization. However, we can hope that peak oil and a careful study of history will soon expose this charade.

During the Vietnam War, it was common to hear the number of Vietnamese killed that day on the US evening news. Eventually the brutality displayed caused a reaction against the war. Today in Iraq the press only reports US casualties as significant — avoiding any mention of Iraqi casualties. US weapons are now *smart* and its soldiers use *surgical strikes*, giving the impression that weapons can now distinguish between the other country's army or terrorists and non-involved citizens. But murdering many of *them* — including civilians — while keeping our own casualties to a minimum is still the primary military strategy of modern warfare, especially effective against the poorly armed people of the majority world.

The American Empire

After the American revolution of 1776, colonists continued British policies of genocide, slavery and conquest. Over the next two centuries the US killed 8-10 million Native Americans[6] and took their lands, leaving a small number today either dispossessed or living in poverty on government controlled reservations. The US in the Southern states and the British in their Central American colonies enslaved or killed more than 28 million Africans, moving them to the Americas to be worked to death in horrible conditions using torture and murder to maintain obedience. This period of slavery lasted from 1450 to 1850.[7]

In the mid-19th century (1846-1848), the US attacked Mexico and seized half of its territory. The US expanded further into the countries of the Pacific, including the euphemistically called *opening up* of Japan by Admiral Perry in 1853. In 1896, the US declared war on Spain, subsequently conquering Cuba, the Philippines, Puerto Rico, Guam and Midway, with the result that the US became a major colonial power in the Pacific. In the same year the US seized Hawaii. During the Philippines Insurgency (1899-1902), an independence effort by the native people, 220,000 Filipinos were killed while 4,234 Americans died.[8]

The US also participated in and signed the Treaty of Berlin in 1896, which divided the continent of Africa among the major European powers; this treaty was probably one of the most destructive acts in human history.[9] Toward the end of the 19th century, the US supported Britain in the forceful *opening up* of China. In 1900, the United States played a significant role in continuing this policy by suppressing the Boxer Rebellion in China using military resources still deployed in the Philippines. By the beginning of the 20th century most of the populations of China, India, Indonesia and Africa as well as smaller nations, were under the control of European powers and the US. Japan and Thailand were the only unoccupied nations in Asia, and in Africa only Ethiopia and Liberia were unoccupied. This is a testament to the power and aggression of the US and Europe.

The conquered world was stable for a few decades, and imperial powers seemed content to maximize their tribute under the guise of so called *free trade*. The British sale of opium to the Chinese is one example of such free trade. When the Chinese objected and tried to stop the practice, Britain attacked and occupied parts of China until the ban was lifted. What was once called *opening up* is now called *globalization* and is frequently achieved by financial pressure and control.

Two World Wars

Competition to control the world led to continuous shifting of the European power structure, with frequent renegotiation and reformation of allegiances. World War I began in August 1914 with the assassination of the leader of an occupying country (Austria-Hungary) by a citizen of a subjugated one (Serbia). By 1917 the European powers were at a military stalemate, with a huge number of battle casualties from trench warfare. This stalemate ended in early 1917 when the US decided to support Britain and France against Germany and entered the war. This ultimately led to cessation of hostilities in November 1918. As the Ottoman Empire had sided with Germany, the conquering nations divided it into a number of smaller nations. Until this time, what Europe calls the Middle East was the one major area of the globe that had to a degree escaped European control. With the post-war division the oil resources of the Arab world passed into European hands, and a long era of conflict in the Middle East began.

Within two decades the US was at war again, this time with Germany and Japan. Tensions between Japan, Europe and the US had been building since World War I when Britain and the US insisted that Japan build fewer warships than they were building. Japan had studied US and British imperialism and was emulating it successfully, invading China in 1937 with oil and steel supplied by the US and Britain. It is estimated that 6-10,000,000 Chinese were killed during the period Japan occupied the Asian continent.[10] Some historians suggest that 260,000 to 350,000 noncombatants were killed in a single incident — the Rape of Nanking.[11] Eventually the US decided to limit Japan's expansion since that country began to encroach on territories controlled by Britain and the US. In July 1941 the US and Britain placed an embargo on scrap steel and oil. This was a dire threat to Japan's imperial interests. Japan responded by attacking the US military base of Pearl Harbor in Hawaii six months later.

Most of the allied casualties of World War II were in Europe. Although many Europeans and Americans think the US and Western Europe dominated the fighting against Germany, most of the battles took place between Germany and Russia. More than ²/₃ of German troops killed in the war were on the Russian front. Russia suffered 20 million dead while the US, Britain and France's combined deaths totaled about 1 million.[12] It is rare to see due credit given to Russia for its participation in winning this war. In spite of the tens of millions of casualties suffered by China and Russia at the hands of Japan and Germany, the US and its European allies began a Cold War based on ideological differences with Russia and China immediately after the end of World War II. Germany and Japan were transformed from enemies to friends, and top priority was given to restoring these countries to their previous positions in the economic power structure.

Kill Ratios

After World War I a leading British statesman, Lloyd George, when arguing against some military limitations wrote in secret that, "We have to reserve the right to bomb the niggers."[13] Today Britain and the US continue to reserve the right to bomb Islamic people in oil-producing nations. One of the derisive names used to describe Arabs is "sand nigger." The Battle of Omdurman, mentioned earlier, resulted in the deaths of 20,000 Muslims and 48 British soldiers. The ratio of killings on each side, called the *kill ratio*, in this battle was about 400 to 1. This was not exceptional in colonial days. The British used artillery and machine guns against spears and arrows. The kill ratio at Omdurman shows both the technical superiority and the brutality that made it possible for the British to rule so much of the world.

The European colonial powers were weakened by World War II, and many of the colonized nations, including Indonesia and India, were eventually able to gain independence. Other colonized nations, such as Kenya and Algeria, had to fight longer to obtain freedom from Britain and France. In much of colonized Africa and Asia, wars of national liberation led to independence but with horrible casualties on the part of the colonized compared with minor losses on the part of the colonizers.

It has been argued that war is less brutal today or even that war is more humane. A more contemporary example is Britain's role in Kenya, one of the last major colonies of their empire. Kenya gained its independence in 1963 after a decade-long revolution. Books such as Caroline Elkins's *Imperial Reckoning: The Untold Story of Britain's Gulag in Kenya* and David Anderson's *Histories of the Hanged: The Dirty War in Kenya and the End of Empire* tell what happened during this particularly bloody anti-colonial war. These books reveal the astonishing depths to which the British sank to forestall the inevitable demise of their imperial enterprise. In Kenya deaths during the independence struggle were 63 British soldiers and 32 British settlers versus 50,000 natives (with 1,000 hanged) resulting in close to a 500-to-1 kill ratio.[14]

According to Vietnamese government figures, 5 million Vietnamese died during their war with the US. American deaths of 57,000 yield a kill ratio of 88 to 1.[15] Small, so-called US police actions, show even higher ratios. In 1989, the US invaded Panama to overturn the dictator Noriega, who was a long time

Time Period	Countries	Colonizer Casualties	Colony Casualties
1885-1909	Belgium vs. Congo	Negligible	8,000,000
1898	Great Britain vs. Sudan	48	20,000
WWII	Japan vs. China	83,000	25,000,000
WWII	Germany vs. Russia	5,000,000	20,000,000
1950-63	Great Britain vs. Kenya	95	50,000
1954-62	France vs. Algeria	20,000	600,000- 1 million
1960s-70s	US vs. Vietnam	57,000	5,000,000
1965	Indonesia vs. Indonesia (US backed)	Negligible	500,000
1989	US vs. Panama (extraction of Noriega)	23	3,000
1991	US vs. Iraq (First Gulf War)	343	146-206,000
1991-2001	US vs. Iraq (blockade)	Negligible	500,000 to 1 million
2003-07	US vs. Iraq (Second Gulf War)	About 4,000	About 1.2 million

CALCULATED BY THE AUTHOR FROM MULTIPLE SOURCES

3.2: *Historical Casualties (Deaths) Comparisons*

CIA asset. A US-based independent Commission of Inquiry headed by former US Attorney General Ramsey Clark estimated the number of Panamanian civilian casualties at more than 3,000. There were 23 Americans killed, a kill ratio of 130 to 1 (Fig. 3.2).[16]

For those who think these statistics for the killing of colonized people are long past, one need only analyze Iraq. At the beginning of hostilities in 1991 the combined populations of the US and nations supporting its military actions in Iraq exceeded 500,000,000 people. Iraq, a country deeply in debt and with a decimated military exhausted by the ten-year Iran/Iraq war of the 1980s, had an approximate population of 24,000,000. Reports of the first US attack on Iraq in 1991 referred to the air war against retreating Iraqi troops as a "turkey shoot." A Greenpeace report by Peter Bahouth and William Arkin estimated Iraqi deaths to be between 146,000-206,000, compared with 343 Allied troops, for a kill ratio ranging from 425 to 1 to 600 to 1.[17] A state of aggression continued for the next decade as the US and Britain patrolled and bombed northern and southern no-fly zones in Iraq. An economic blockade was applied.

These economic sanctions imposed by the US following the first Iraq war led, according to the UN, to 500,000-1,000,000 additional Iraqi deaths. In May of 1996, 60 Minutes aired an interview with Madeleine Albright, who at the time was President Clinton's Ambassador to the UN. Correspondent Leslie Stahl said to Albright, "We have heard that a half million children have died. I mean, that's more children than died in Hiroshima. And — and you know, is the price worth it?" Madeleine Albright replied "I think this is a very hard choice, but the price — we think the price is worth it." No American or British citizen died from this blockade.[18] ·

In late 2006 a team of researchers at the Johns Hopkins Bloomberg School of Public Health published in Lancet, Britain's leading medical journal, a study of deaths since the beginning of the second invasion of Iraq. This study showed that the Iraqi death rate due to violence exceeded 650,000. American deaths for the same period were about 3,500, giving a kill ratio of about 170 to 1. By comparison Human Rights Watch estimated Saddham Hussein's regime killed 250,000 to 290,000 Iraqis over 20 years.[19]

In September 2007, the British polling firm Opinion Research Business published the results of a new study that estimated 1,220,580 violent deaths since the US invasion of Iraq.[20] This is consistent with the Johns Hopkins study, which if updated, would also be more than a million. These estimates include civilians killed in the war, but not those who have died because of public health problems created by the war, including breakdowns in sewerage systems and electricity, shortages of medicines and food.[21] As of November 2007, US total troops killed since the beginning of the war were approximately 3,875 giving a kill ratio of about 315 to 1.[22]

Combining the approximate 200,000 Iraqi deaths in the first war, the approximate 750,000 deaths from economic sanctions and the approximately 1,200,000 deaths from the second Iraqi war gives a total number of deaths exceeding 2 million as compared to the US approximate military deaths of 4,000 — a 500 to 1 ratio. This is severe punishment for a nation that was not involved in the 9/11 attack and which did not have nuclear weapons. And the killing continues.

It is informative to look at how many Americans were killed by terrorists in the 22 years from 1983 through September 11, 2001. In 1983, 63 people were killed in a suicide bombing attack at the US embassy in Lebanon. In the same year, also in Lebanon, another suicide bombing attack killed 241 US Marines. In late 1983 a third suicide bombing attack killed 5 people at the American embassy in Kuwait. In 1984, also in Lebanon, a truck bomb attack killed 24 people at a US embassy annex. Two Americans were killed in late 1984 during the hijacking of a Kuwait Airlines flight. Another American was killed the next year during the hijacking of a TWA flight from Athens to Rome. Also in 1985, an American was killed during the hijacking of a cruise ship, the *Achille Lauro*. Later that year airports in Rome and Vienna were bombed, killing 20 people. In 1986, two Americans were killed when a bomb was detonated at La Belle, a discotheque in West Berlin known to be popular with off-duty US servicemen. A Turkish woman was also killed, and nearly 200 others were wounded. In 1988, a PanAm flight from London to New York was destroyed in flight from a bomb explosion, killing 270 people. The 1993 bombing of New York's World Trade Center killed six people. In 2000, the USS Cole was attacked by suicide bombers, killing 17 people. And in 2001, the September 11 attack killed approximately 3,000 people. So, about 3,700 US citizens, not counting military casualties (about 4,000), were killed by terrorists in this 22-year period.[23] This is a tiny number compared to the millions of Iraqi dead, not to mention unknown number of Afghanis killed during the same period.

Kill ratio numbers show the superiority of the weapons of colonizing nations, both in the East (Japan) and in the West (Europe and US). They attest to the fact that the US is now the most powerful nation on earth and probably the most powerful nation in history, if by powerful we mean the ability to deploy extremely destructive weaponry efficiently anywhere in the world. It certainly does not show that the US is the kindest or the fairest nation in history. History shows that the more powerful the nation, the more brutally it has behaved. And the US has shown that, like the older colonizing powers such as Britain and France, it is not above using torture. Naomi Klein in an article about torture describes a conversation from the 1966 Gillo Pontecorvo film *The Battle of Algiers*. A French officer, Col. Mathieu, finds himself in a situation familiar to top officials in the Bush administration relative to torture in Iraq. Mathieu is being grilled by journalists about allegations that French paratroopers are torturing Algerian prisoners. He neither denies the abuse nor claims that those responsible will be punished. Instead, he tells the reporters, who work for newspapers that support France's continued occupation of Algeria, that torture "isn't the problem. The problem is the FLN (National Liberation Front) wants to throw us out of Algeria and we want to stay.... It's my turn to ask a question. Should France stay in Algeria? If your answer is still yes, then you must accept all the consequences."[24] His point, as relevant in Iraq today as it was in Algeria in 1957, is that brutality and torture are required to occupy a nation against the will of its people. Those who benefit from such an occupation, and in the case of Iraq this benefit is oil, cannot morally separate themselves from the torture and killing that is required. His words may well have been said in many different ways by many American officers serving in Iraq.

Who benefits from fossil fuel driven Globalization?

Rich powerful countries (15% of the world's population) say they are attempting to help the poorer countries (85% of the world's population) to become developed (e.g. wealthy like the rich) by innovation, free trade and loans. Yet every year through the actions of corporate globalization, the IMF and the World Bank, the poor get poorer. In reality, richer countries pay lip service to aiding developing countries. Far more money is spent on the military than on aid. In an article entitled "The Polarized World of Globalization," Vandana Shiva takes exception to Thomas Friedman's rosy depiction of globalization in his book *The World is Flat*. Friedman argues that globalization is a leveler of inequity and notes three periods of improvement, beginning in 1492 with the voyages of Christopher Columbus. Shiva, however, sees it another way.

For us in India the first wave of globalization was driven by the first global corporation, the East India Company, working closely with the British government, and did not end until 1947 when we got Independence. We view the current phase as a recoloniza- tion, with a similar partnership between multinational corporations and powerful governments. It is corporate-led, not people-led. And the current phase did not begin in 2000 as Friedman would have us believe. It began in the 1980s with the structural adjustment programs of World Bank and International Monetary Fund (IMF) imposing trade liberal- ization and privatization, and was accelerated since 1995 with the establishment of the World Trade Organization (WTO) at the end of the Uruguay Round of the General Agreement of Trade and Tariffs.[25]

Noam Chomsky, in his book *Year 501 — The Conquest Continues*, like Friedman picks the year 1492 as the beginning of a major change in the world. But whereas Friedman argues that this year began significant improvements, for Chomsky, this is when the exploitation of most of the people on the planet began. Chomsky particularly shows how the economic policies of the US dec- imated many countries in Latin America.[26] He also exposes the strategies of the World Bank, WTO and IMF in attaining the classic aims of colonialism subtly under the rubric of globalization. And he calls attention to the creation of persistent poverty in the United States, as free markets run amuck, destroying jobs, lives and savings and increasing inequity via the process of vicious com- petition. In *Hegemony or Survival*, Chomsky enumerates the tremendous dangers that are coming ever closer to the US itself as the economic conquest continues.[27]

Another extremely important book, *Confessions of an Economic Hit Man* by John Perkins, a former economist for an international consulting firm, exposes the way US intelligence agencies and multinationals cajole and blackmail for- eign leaders into serving US foreign policy and awarding lucrative contracts to American business. Perkins explains how he created bogus economic projec- tions in order to convince foreign governments to accept loans from the World Bank and other institutions to build dams, airports, electric grids and other infrastructure which they could not afford. The loans were given on condition that construction and engineering contracts went to US companies. The deals were supported by bribes to foreign officials. But it was the taxpayers in the foreign countries who had to pay back the loans. When governments could not repay, the World Bank or International Monetary Fund would take charge of the country's economic system, dictating everything from its spending budget to security agreements and even its United Nations votes. Perkins notes that this was a clever way for the US to expand its empire at the expense of citizens in the developing world. By thus explaining the huge debt burdens that many poor countries cannot handle and pointing out the corruption and manipulation involved, Perkins destroys the fiction that poorer countries are responsible for getting themselves into debt.[28] Thus the promoters of globalization have conquered the rest of the world, not just through military might, but also through control of the world economic structure, destroying the once relatively equitable distribution of income as well as more sustainable local lifestyles. When peak oil arrives, the poorer countries of the world will be hard-pressed simply to survive, much less pay back debts incurred by trickery.

Peak Conflict

The huge inequities in world energy consumption are also fueling international tension. Matthew Simmons, author of *Twilight in the Desert*, says the two main drivers for future energy demand are Prosperity and Poverty. Prosperity is *us*, the 1 billion people who use 85% of modern energy and who don't want to give up our way of life, a lifestyle that depends on using more each year. Poverty is *them* — the 3 billion people who use the other 15% and 2 billion people who use almost none and who would like to have a better life by using some of what is left.[29] This tension cannot but lead to unrest, and as oil shortages become severe, resource wars between wealthier countries and poor ones are likely. The present position of the privileged and powerful industrial nations — us — could become increasingly unsupportable, and a vicious competition for fossil fuel resources will begin. As resources decline the poor will experience the results first. At some point the rich world will have to make the choice of sharing shrinking resources or taking an ever increasing share of the smaller amount in order to maintain their *standard of living*. Currently the second option seems to be preferred. But this may not be possible. It is one thing to watch Americans on TV driving SUVs while the viewer in the developing world walks or rides a bicycle. It will be another when the same viewer may no longer be able to afford cooking fuel or fuel to run irrigation pumps or have money to buy food.

In 1976, as oil prices began to soar in the world's first energy crisis, Paul Erdman wrote a book called *The Crash of '79*, a fictional account of war in the Middle East. At the book's climax atomic weapons were used to make the oil fields in Saudi Arabia inaccessible, leading to the collapse of the world's economy and financial system.[30] Although Erdman's book was fantasy, a real life possibility is described in Gerald Posner's *Secrets of the Kingdom: The Inside Story of the Saudi-U.S. Connection*. Posner suggests that the Saudi oil fields and facilities are already mined with explosives and devices which emit low radioactivity that can contaminate the sites for decades.[31] To the US, the supposedly beneficent leader of the free world, this may seem to be a strategy of madmen, but to countries who have been occupied by colonial powers over many decades it may seem like a sensible strategy. Similar protective measures might be taken by Iran. Certainly Iraq, with millions dead from attacks and embargoes, has little loyalty to colonial powers and might wish that it had mined its oil fields when it had the chance.

Americans' attitudes of righteousness and arrogance blinds them to the dangers of our situation. We assume that we will prevail in any conflict that may arise because of the nation's overwhelming military power and its willingness to use it. When US *bunker buster* nuclear weapons are available people may believe that they can easily destroy the most hardened sites of the nation's enemies while remaining out of their reach. But the next war may well be different. Consider the casualties in Europe or the US which would result from a nuclear attack by terrorists in the Middle East on the Saudi oilfields, refining facilities and shipping facilities. Such casualties would not be the direct result from the weapons used, but would occur as a result of the disruption of basic life support systems that need fuel to operate. Could Europeans survive a winter without fossil fuels from Russia or Saudi Arabia to heat their homes? Would the industrial food system continue to function? Would there be mass starvation in the US and other affected countries? Would the resulting economic chaos lead to another Great Depression?

Such a prospect seems horrifying and mad. But in war all actions are those of mad people. Is it not madness to have nuclear weapons that can destroy all life, ready to fire at a few minutes' notice? This is the strategy of the nations who now dominate the world. Would the poor people of the world consider destruction of the Saudi oil infrastructure to be evil or simply good tactics against what they perceive as a powerful and merciless foe? Would people who are concerned about the future of the planet's ecosystems possibly view such an act of violence as a way to end the destruction of the planet by those of us living lifestyles which are destroying our planet's carrying capacity?

Armageddon is a mythical battle predicted to occur in the Middle East which will be followed by a thousand years of peace. A battle in that part of the world that destroys its fossil fuel resources would certainly eliminate the prospect of world-wide wars, since such wars could not be fought without fossil fuels.

A Different Path

What should Americans do? Although the obvious question, it is perhaps the wrong one. The more significant question is "Who shall Americans become?" Many US citizens believe that the US is the leading light of freedom, the best country in the world (or maybe even in history), and that any resistance to its goals comes from evil people — typically dark-skinned people in faraway places. However, this attitude could destroy the entire planet.

America must give up the beliefs that its world is the best of all possible worlds, that inequity is the natural state of mankind, that wealth is the nation's birthright, that war is an extension of diplomacy, that the environment will always provide limitless sources of materials and that pollution will not negatively affect our lives or the planet. If the country's efforts continue to be focused on keeping the economy (a.k.a. personal pursuit of money) booming, then the situation is hopeless.

The United States of America has had its day in the sun, and its record is not a good one. However, if we consider the facts presented here then Americans have the chance of becoming something other than a nation of mere consumers. There is still time to become a nation with new values, and the world needs a different kind of US citizen — one no longer addicted to the consumption patterns made possible by cheap oil. Peak oil and climate change provide an opportunity for all Americans to face the truth of what they have been doing, whether they like to admit it or not. People might regret the inevitable reduction in their standard of living (how much money they make), but they could rejoice that the suffering of billions caused by Western imperialism will now decrease, that US culture, currently based too much on greed and hatred, can evolve to something higher and more laudable. America must fundamentally change its national character. The first step is to understand more about our current culture.

Four

Peak America — Is Our Time Up?

IN THE PREVIOUS CHAPTER I analyzed the United States' imperial role in the world — both historically and at the present time. This chapter looks at US culture — an increasingly materialistic one — in which consuming has become the nation's psychological reason for existence. Just as the US threatens the stability of the world with its imperialistic tendencies, it also poses a threat to its own people as the standards of care and community decline and it becomes more difficult for average Americans to attain or sustain well-being.

How does this bode for America's place in the world? Is the so called American Century over? When the impact of peak oil really hits, how will the nation deal with it? Will Americans cooperate with the rest of the world in sharing scarce resources, or will they rely on the country's position as the only Superpower to try to bully the world?

Measuring US Inequity

There are several ways to measure the quality and health of a society. One way is to look at the distribution of income and wealth over time. Another is to ask how generous a nation is at home and abroad. A third is to compare the level of violence in one society with other similar cultures. And finally, spending for social good can be compared with military expenditures.

As I have previously noted, inequity is increasing worldwide. Inequity is also increasing in the US. Figure 4.1 shows the change in the distribution of income in the US in the 20th century. Inequity was highest during the roaring 1920s. In the 1930s and '40s, Franklin D. Roosevelt passed laws to make incomes more equal. But since the Reagan era of the 1980s, the trend has reversed. A further

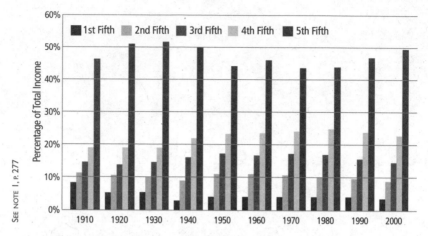

4:1: *Income Distribution in the US 1910-2000*

breakdown of the data shows that the share of income that goes to the top 5% increased from 16.6% in 1970 to 22.3% in 2006. In 2004, the amount of income going to the top 20% actually passed the 50% mark for the first time since the 1930s. The percent going to the top 20% increased even more in 2005 and 2006.[1]

In blunt terms, the poor are getting poorer and the rich are getting richer. In fact, except for the top 20% of the population, people in the US are getting poorer as more income shifts to the very top. The American Dream has become less and less attainable for more than 80% of our population. The difference between the top fifth (the richest) and the bottom fifth (the poorest) of US citizens is greater than what it was at the beginning of the Great Depression of 1929 — with no Roosevelt New Deal in sight.

Figure 4.2 shows the continued move toward higher levels of inequity in more recent times. In 2006 persons in the top 20% earned about 15 times that of the lower 20% — a historical record for the US. In that year the Gini index for the US, which is used to measure inequity, reached an all time high. This index is calculated so that 0 corresponds to everyone having the same income and 1 corresponds to one person having all the income. A Gini coefficient of 0.3 or less indicates substantial equality. A coefficient of 0.3 to 0.4 is generally considered acceptable and 0.4 or higher is considered too large. A value of 0.6 or higher is predictive of social unrest.[2] Surprisingly, US inequity is greater than in most other nations in the world. The 2007 *CIA World Fact Book* includes the Gini coefficient for 120 out of about 220 nations. The total population of

Year	Number (thous.)	Lowest fifth	Second fifth	Third fifth	Fourth fifth	Highest fifth	Top 5 percent	Gini Index
2006	116,011	3.4%	8.6%	14.5%	22.9%	50.5%	22.3%	0.470
2000	108,209	3.6%	8.9%	14.8%	23.0%	49.8%	22.1%	0.462
1990	94,312	3.8%	9.6%	15.9%	24.0%	46.6%	18.5%	0.428
1980	82,368	4.2%	10.2%	16.8%	24.7%	44.1%	16.5%	0.403
1970	64,778	4.1%	10.8%	17.4%	24.5%	43.3%	16.6%	0.394

4.2: *Change in Income Distribution in the US 1970-2006*

DATA FROM US CENSUS BUREAU. CENSUS.GOV/

those 120 countries (including the US) is 6.2 billion, about 94% of world population. The average Gini coefficient for these nations was 0.412 compared to 0.470 for the US. The European Union Gini index was 0.312.[3] This data shows that incomes in the US are more unequal than in most countries in the world and are significantly more unequal than incomes in Europe.

Figures 4.1 and 4.2 are based on income distribution (what each person earns in a year). Figure 4.3 illustrates wealth (assets accumulated over years or generations). Inequality in wealth is also increasing,

	Top 20 percent	Bottom 80 percent
1983	81.3%	18.7%
1989	83.6%	16.4%
1992	83.7%	16.3%
1995	83.9%	16.1%
1998	83.4%	16.6%
2001	84.5%	15.5%

4.3: *Distribution of net worth and financial wealth in the United States, 1983-2001*

G. WILLIAM DOMHOFF. *Power in America: Wealth, Income, and Power.* SOCIOLOGY.UCSC.EDU/WHO-RULESAMERICA/POWER/WEALTH.HTML

with the top 20% claiming an additional 3.2% of the total in the period from 1983 to 2001. Not only is more total income being allocated to the wealthy, but the inequity in accumulated wealth is also increasing.

Measuring US Generosity

Another measure of the health of a society is how generous the affluent are to the poor. Figure 4.4 shows the Official Development Assistance (ODA) measured as a percentage of Gross National Income (GNI) by the Development Assistance Committee (DAC), consisting of 22 nations of the OECD. This figure shows that the US falls well behind the rest of the developed world. Relative to the other affluent OECD nations the US is quite stingy. The UN set a target for the richer nations to contribute .7% of their Gross National Index (an index similar to GDP and GNP) to the poorer nations. The average

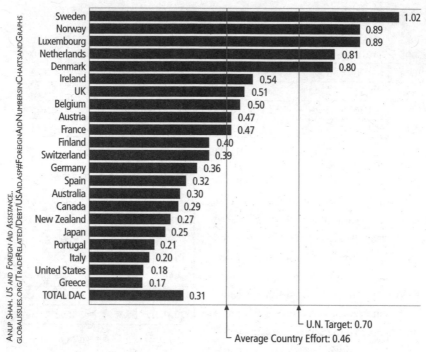

Net Official Overseas Development Assistance (ODA) in 2006 as percent of Gross National Index (GNI) for 22 Nations.

4.4: *Net Official Overseas Development Assistance (ODA) in 2006 as percent of Gross National Index (GNI) for 22 Nations.*

contribution for these wealthier nations is .46% while that of the US is .18%, only marginally above that of Greece. The US allocation per year comes to $76 per person, hardly generous considering that the average per capita income in the US is much greater than the other nations. Compare this to the approximately $2,090 per US citizen spent yearly on the military.[4] The US is responsible for over 50% of the arms expenditures in the world.[5] These two numbers give a sense of the values of the nation.

Violence in the US

Some historians have suggested that the wealth of the US resulted not only from the plenitude of natural resources but also from the genocide of about 10 million Native Americans and the enslaving of tens of millions of African-Americans. Although its past history was violent, could the US now have evolved to a more peaceful state? Figure 4.5 shows how US compares to its partners in the G7.

Country	Population	Murders per100k	Rapes per100k	Assaults per100k	Prisoners per100k	Gini Index
US	301,139,947	4.3	30	757	715	.460
Germany	82,400,996	1.2	9	142	96	.283
France	63,713,926	1.7	14	176	95	.267
UK	60,776,238	1.4	14	746	120	.368
Italy	58,147,733	1.3	4	50	100	.360
Japan	127,433,494	0.5	2	34	54	.381
Canada	33,390,141	1.5	73	712	116	.331
US to G6 Ratio		3.8/1	2.5/1	3.3/1	8.1/1	1.5/1

Crime Statistics: Murders, Rapes, Assaults and Prisoners per capita (most recent) by country nationmaster.com/.

4.5: *Comparison of Violence in the US and other G7 Nations*

This figure shows various crime levels in the richer group of nations known as the G7. In per capita terms, the US has the worst record in murders, assaults, prisoners and inequity. Only Canada is worse than the US in rapes. The bottom line of the table compares the US to a weighted average of the other six nations (the G6). America has 3.8 times as many murders per capita. The ratio for rapes is 2.5 to 1, assaults 3.3 to 1, and inequity 1.5 to 1. In terms of prisoners, the US has an incredibly high ratio of 8.1 to 1.

To round out the picture, the US is the only G7 nation that does not provide health care as a right to its citizenry. Higher education is increasingly becoming too expensive for average US families. Efforts to protect the environment are under continuous attack. And, while tax cuts make the rich even richer, the US Congress seeks cuts in domestic programs to pay for an oil war in the Middle East. If these are the nation's priorities at home, there is little wonder that the US's shining light of freedom and democracy has dimmed in the eyes of the world.

Selling our souls for gasoline

As pointed out in Chapter 2, the dominant economic theory in the US for the past 60 years holds that the pursuit of self-interest is the engine of economic growth which will ultimately benefit all of society. There are clear benefits from the creative dynamism that is released in free markets. But the *greed is good* economic theory, maintained with nearly religious fervor, has tended to create extremes of wealth and poverty along with unsustainable environmental destruction. It is questionable if the nation can or will evolve into a sustainable and fair system. Under this doctrine have the great quantities of goods and services brought notable happiness? Statistics suggest otherwise.

Figure 4.6 shows that the percent of people who are very happy has not increased as average US income increased.

Figure 4.7 compares the US GDP (Gross Domestic Product) and GPI (General Progress Indicator). The GPI measures a wide variety of societal and ecological characteristics to determine rates of progress in areas other than financial. In the US, GPI has been flat or declining since the 1970s.

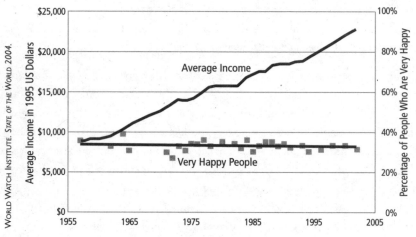

4.6: *Average Income and Happiness in the US 1957-2005*

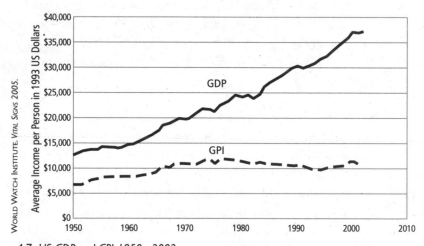

4.7: *US GDP and GPI 1950 - 2002*

For centuries, many spiritual traditions have taught that one should avoid focusing on the accumulation of material goods. Jesus' familiar *Sermon on the Mount*, based on the theme "For what is a man profited, if he shall gain the whole world, and lose his own soul"? [6] is rarely heard today. In the last half of the 20th century, particularly the last 25 years, the US and affluent nations of Europe have rejected these traditions and adopted the religion of growth economics, the fundamental principle being that if everyone pursues his or her own self interest, then society will benefit materially — and that material benefit is all that matters.

In 1985, one of the leading financial crooks in the US, Ivan Boeský, told an audience of Stanford business students "I think greed is healthy. You can be greedy and still feel good about yourself."[7] None of the executives at Enron, Arthur Anderson, Tyco or WorldCom reported feeling bad about themselves — but they did feel bad about getting caught. In 2005, top executives of WorldCom responsible for an $11 billion fraud (which destroyed the life savings of thousands) were sentenced to an average jail term of about seven years.[8]

This new culture of greed is tragic. But the greatest tragedy will be this culture's legacy to our children and grandchildren. Over the last 60 years, American materialism, based on cheap, abundant oil, has blossomed. On April 18, 1977 President Jimmy Carter addressed the nation on the energy problem saying, "Our decision about energy will test the character of the American people and the ability of the President and the Congress to govern this Nation. This difficult effort will be the 'moral equivalent of war,' except that the country will be uniting its efforts to build and not to destroy."[9] In the ensuing three decades, the nation has failed to unite to build anything but more consumption.

Armageddon Approaching?

Most US citizens remain ignorant of our true history and the effect of our government's present military and economic actions. The world is one of increasing inequity and violence, led by the US and supported in many instances by the nations of the OECD. The US public is inundated with stories of evil Arabs who are denying us access to oil. During the buildup to the Iraq war a picture of a woman bearing a sign with the words "Kick their Ass and Take their Gas" circulated on the Internet. The attitude of the average American is that he or she is good — and that Arabs are ripping us off. The Arab world has come to hate and fear the US for past and present exploitation.

When an American president says "our way of life is not negotiable" it is a clear and frightening threat. People in the Middle East recognize the menacing US media spin now directed toward Iran, calling that country a supporter of terrorism, a builder of nuclear weapons and unfair to women. Iran and other nations in the Middle East consider this propaganda to justify a possible American military invasion.

History, including that of the US Revolutionary War, shows that colonized nations do not give in to colonization and that people are willing to die for freedom from control and exploitation. The example of Vietnam is not too far in the past, and the current example of Iraq verifies this principle. Because of the vital need of every nation for oil, it can be expected that major powers such as China and Russia, and possibly India, will eventually support countries with oil and natural gas resources. As the situation becomes ever more desperate, these nations and maybe others could begin increasing their defense expenditures and joining together to counter US hegemony. If the US were to attempt to fully control the oil and gas resources of the Persian Gulf countries, other nations which also need oil might support Arab resistance. Supply lines from the Middle East to the US are long, and fighting alliances between countries like Iran, Russia and China would not be the same as invading a weakened country like Iraq.

Hannah Arendt, in her book *Eichmann in Jerusalem: A Report on the Banality of Evil*, noted how Nazi leader Adolf Eichmann was not evil incarnate but an average bureaucrat interested in furthering his career. The evil he did came from the seductive power of a totalitarian state and unthinking adherence to the Nazi cause.[10] The American way of life was not intended to create massive poverty and violence along with environmental devastation. It evolved from people seeking a life of ease, convenience and comfort. But the American way of life is now characterized by infatuation with material possessions and electronic toys. This lifestyle does not desire violence and exploitation — but it does require them. The US essentially gained control of the world in 1945 and chose consumption of material goods as the national priority. To meet this priority, it chose dependence on fossil fuels. And today it must continue to control the world to maintain its huge disparity in resource use, leading to more violence and now the official use of torture. Furthermore, the US has recently committed to a policy that is in the worst tradition of evil: first strike attacks with nuclear weapons against non-nuclear countries. The enemy is evident: the mostly Islamic nations that contain most of the oil reserves of the world. The strategy requires that the US use propaganda to attack the religion of Islam, making that religion and its followers appear to be raving, irrational madmen.

US control of oil rich nations is not possible without enormous violence and suffering. The US could not defeat the Vietnamese because people will always fight to the death to defend their homeland, particularly when — like the Vietnamese — there is nowhere else to turn. We need to ask ourselves how many people are we willing to have our government kill to obtain cheap energy? And even if enough are killed, how long can the oil last with the US's prodigious use?

Could the US Lose the War?

Science fiction writer Kim Stanley Robinson, in his 1984 book *The Wild Shore*, imagined a United States which had been destroyed by the other countries of the world working in concert, as a defensive measure against US dominance, arrogance and disproportionate consumption of the world's resources. The country is kept in an unreconstructed state with Canada controlling the northern border, Mexico the south, Japan the west, and Russia the east. With satellite surveillance and advanced weapons systems, these countries destroy any attempts by Americans to rebuild infrastructure which might enable them to regain any power in the world.[11]

Couldn't happen, you think? Then consider the situation with Iran. The US continues to threaten that country. But it is questionable if China and Russia would allow a repeat of the Iraq invasion. They might instead choose to go to war to protect their access to Middle Eastern oil. These other countries also have a way of life to protect and particularly in the case of China, a rapidly growing desire for more and more oil. Should China and Russia decide to protect Iran from invasion, nuclear war might occur, particularly if the US, following its latest stated policy of using nuclear weapons against a non-nuclear nation in a preemptive strike, attacks Iran. This could lead to retaliatory attacks by Iran against the oil fields and shipping terminals of Saudi Arabia — possibly with borrowed nuclear weapons. World War III would have begun.

Views in the US become more extreme daily with deliberately cultivated hatred for Islamic countries as well as other oil producers such as Venezuela. On August 23, 2005 Pat Robertson, founder of the Christian Coalition of

America and a former presidential candidate, suggested on television that the US government assassinate Hugo Chavez, the president of Venezuela, saying "We have the ability to take him out, and I think the time has come that we exercise that ability....We don't need another $200-billion war to get rid of one, you know, strong-arm dictator....It's a whole lot easier to have some of the covert operatives do the job and then get it over with....I don't know about this doctrine of assassination, but if he thinks we're trying to assassinate him, I think that we really ought to go ahead and do it....It's a whole lot cheaper than starting a war...and I don't think any oil shipments will stop."[12]

Of course, not everyone agrees with the US government's actions and goals. Former president Jimmy Carter, in a November 14, 2005 editorial in the *Los Angeles Times*, described his concerns with the current direction of the US.

> In recent years, I have become increasingly concerned by a host of radical government policies that now threaten many basic principles espoused by all previous administrations, Democratic and Republican. These include the rudimentary American commitment to peace, economic and social justice, civil liberties, our environment and human rights. Also endangered are our historic commitments to providing citizens with truthful information, treating dissenting voices and beliefs with respect, state and local autonomy and fiscal responsibility. At the same time, our political leaders have declared independence from the restraints of international organizations and have disavowed long-standing global agreements — including agreements on nuclear arms, control of biological weapons and the international system of justice. Instead of our tradition of espousing peace as a national priority unless our security is directly threatened, we have proclaimed a policy of 'preemptive war,' an unabridged right to attack other nations unilaterally to change an unsavory regime or for other purposes. When there are serious differences with other nations, we brand them as international pariahs and refuse to permit direct discussions to resolve disputes. Regardless of the costs, there are determined efforts by top U.S. leaders to exert American imperial dominance throughout the world.[13]

In his book *Our Endangered Values*, Carter reviewed a number of key points.

- Powerful lobbyists …have distorted an admirable American belief into the right of extremely rich citizens to accumulate and retain more and more wealth and pass it on to their descendents."

- American children are sixteen times more likely than children in other industrialized nations to be murdered with a gun, eleven times more likely to commit suicide with a gun and nine times more likely to die from firearms accidents.

- American girls are five times as likely to have a baby as French girls, seven times as likely to have an abortion, and seventy times as likely to have gonorrhea as girls in the Netherlands.

- In the 1970s only one in a thousand Americans was in prison.…More than seven Americans out of a thousand are now imprisoned — most of them for nonviolent crimes.

- [T]he greatest challenge we face is the growing chasm between the rich and poor people on earth… At the beginning of the last century, the ten richest countries were nine times wealthier than the ten poorest ones. In 1960 the ratio was 30:1. At the beginning of this century, average per person income in the twenty richest nations was $27,591 and in the poorest nations, only $211, a ration of 131 to 1.

- Our entire society is becoming increasingly divided, not necessarily between black, white, or Hispanic but primary between the rich and the poor.

- Americans … believed that our government gives as much as 15% of our federal budget in foreign aid. But we are, in fact, the stingiest of all industrialized nations. We allot about one thirtieth as much as is commonly believed

- [T]he minimum wage …has been held at only $5.15 per hour for eight years and not indexed to accommodate inflation. In comparison in US dollars and based on currency

values in April 2005, the minimum wage in Australia is
$8.66, in France $8.88, in Italy $9.18, in England $9.20, and
in Germany $12.74.[14]

Making Choices, Moving Forward

Colin Campbell has designated the period of human history from the birth of
Christ to 1850 as the period of Sustainable Man, the period from 1850-1950
the time of Industrial Man, and the period from 1950-2050 the time of
Hydrocarbon Man. He says the end of Hydrocarbon Man marks the end of
consumerism and the beginning of the period of New Sustainable Man.[15] Our
culture is best described as one devoted to consumerism. This is a far cry from
the values that are core to our religious traditions. We have moved from the
idea that "the love of money is the source of all evil" to the concept that greed
is good. Our way of living is not sustainable — which ultimately means it is
not survivable. Only economic growth (which is income growth) is important
to us, and that growth is totally based on consuming fossil fuels. In our case,
the love of fossil fuels may be the source of all evil, an evil that is destroying the
climate necessary for the survival of all life. It is the love of big houses, jet
travel, SUVs and industrial agriculture that is bringing the nation and the
world to possible ruin.

Five

Peak Technology and the Private Car

THERE ARE NO APPARENT NEW BASIC TECHNOLOGIES we can rely upon to avoid the crisis of depleting fossil fuels. As energy supplies become scarcer and more expensive, numerous technical solutions are being proposed. Most are not new and were researched extensively during the energy crisis of the 1970s. This chapter analyzes key machine and energy options, their histories and their limitations. History can give us a sense of the possible speed and cost of implementation, as well as the limits of the technologies themselves. There are few new creative solutions being offered by governments, corporations and scientists, not because they are failing to make the effort, but because energy production and use itself is a very mature industry. It would seem that — in addition to peak oil — the world is reaching a time of peak technology.

The Private Car

There are many exemplars of modern life's commitment to energy consumption and CO_2 generation but undoubtedly one of the most destructive is the private automobile. At the same time the automobile is one of the most attractive benefits of modern life. The car is more than a mode of transportation — it defines North America's homes and communities. The car has formed our physical communities through suburban sprawl and to a great extent destroyed our social communities. Although the car supposedly represents freedom and independence, it may be the greatest creator of alienation between humans that has ever existed. James Kunstler, in his book *The Geography of Nowhere*, succinctly describes the results of a 100-year love affair with the automobile.

Love affairs, exciting though they may be, tend to destroy fidelity; and the fidelity and integrity of our communities is almost gone.[1]

Americans are often quoted as saying that they would die before giving up their car. We would rather destroy the environment than share a vehicle. Simply put, we have used up our own oil to drive cars so now we want the oil from other nations to support our habit. And we will take it if we have to, even attacking and killing other people to maintain our motoring lifestyle. The private car has cost us not only our communities but to some extent our souls. And should a tipping point in climate change occur unexpectedly, it may also cost *us* our lives.

The Fuel Cell Mirage — 30 Lost Years

According to Jeremy Rifkin, the term hydrogen economy (including its core technology — the fuel cell) was first floated by General Motors in 1970.[2] Joseph Romm gives credit to Australian electrochemist John Bockris.[3] Whoever used the term first, the idea was that hydrogen could take the place of oil and other fossil fuels, allowing the US to continue its growth economy. It seems appropriate that a new idea would be proposed in the same year (1970) that Hubbert's peak oil theory was verified in the US. Given the enormous amounts of funding in the years since the concept was announced, there has been notably little progress made; we need to question the continuing hype around this now discredited concept.

The fuel cell was invented by William Grove in 1839, and the first practical fuel cells were developed for the US space program in the 1960s. In the 1970s many alternative fuel programs for cars were funded. The US Department of Energy (DOE) hydrogen program website shows the key milestones relating to hydrogen and fuel cell federally-supported research and development (R&D) over the following decades.[4] In 1974, President Richard Nixon announced Project Independence stating, "in the year 1980, the United States will not be dependent on any other country for the energy we need to provide our jobs, to heat our homes, and to keep our transportation moving."[5] He proposed ending American reliance on foreign oil through a series of energy programs, among them hydrogen-fuelled vehicles that could be developed "to enable a shift away from oil." In 1993, President Clinton launched the $1 billion Partnership for New Generation Vehicles with the big three automakers, aiming to produce a prototype car that was three times more fuel-efficient than conventional vehicles by 2004. The Hydrogen Future Act of 1996 considered integrating fuel cells with photovoltaic systems for hydrogen production along with producing hydrogen from solid fuels e.g. coal via gasification.

In 2002 the *Founding Agreement for FreedomCAR and Fuel Partnership Energy Security for America's Transportation* was signed. This was a partnership between the Department of Energy and United States Council for Automotive Research, which included the major US automobile manufacturers. Its objective was to advance research and development of affordable hydrogen fuel cell vehicles and a national hydrogen infrastructure. The FreedomCAR defined five American transportation freedoms.

> Freedom from petroleum dependence.
> Freedom from pollutant emissions.
> Freedom to choose the vehicle you want.
> Freedom to drive where you want, when you want.
> Freedom to obtain fuel affordably and conveniently.[6]

President Bush said in his State of the Union Address, January 28, 2003, "With a new national commitment, our scientists and engineers will overcome obstacles to taking these cars from laboratory to showroom so that the first car driven by a child born today could be powered by hydrogen, and pollution-free."[7] The Energy Policy Act of 2005 directed the Secretary of Energy to conduct a research and development program — in consultation with other federal agencies and the private sector — on technologies related to the production, purification, distribution, storage and use of hydrogen energy, fuel cells and related infrastructure."[8] In the president's State of the Union speech on January 31, 2006 the Advanced Energy Initiative was redefined with an increase of funding to $250 million for hydrogen fuel cells.[9] President Bush's words on hydrogen and fuel cells were similar to those of Richard Nixon in his original Project Independence speech as well as speeches by Gerald Ford, Bill Clinton and the first president Bush. The results have been and still are disappointing. Joseph Romm notes "By 2003, more than 160 years after the first fuel cell was built, and after spending more than $15 billion in public and private funding, only one fuel cell with significant commercial sales existed, and purchases of that product received a government subsidy to buy down the cost."[10] The dream of hydrogen replacing gasoline has not been realized.

Disinformation and Hype

There has been an enormous amount of hype and disinformation about hydrogen, not just from car companies and government agencies but also consultants and energy experts. Consider the following comments from Amory Lovins, referring to commitments made in 1997: "Daimler pledged annual production of 100,000 of such [hydrogen fuel cell] vehicles by 2005" and "The president of Toyota said he'd beat that goal." He later tells us the same president of Toyota predicted "...hybrid electric cars would capture one-third of the world car market by 2005."[11] Jeremy Rifkin is another popular proponent of the hydrogen economy and the fuel cell. In *The Hydrogen Economy* he notes that Daimler would produce 100,000 fuel cell cars by the end of the decade (1990s) and that GM would have fuel cell cars ready by 2010.[12] None of the numbers quoted were realized, and GM no longer quotes a date. Yet both men continue to lobby for a hydrogen miracle.

The man who is sometimes given the title *father of the fuel cell*, George Ballard, founded one of the world's leading fuel cell companies, Ballard Systems of Canada. He tells the story of his company's first fuel cell bus, displayed onstage at a press conference in Canada. When the bus could not be driven off the stage, a group of Ballard staff, standing behind the bus and invisible to the audience, pushed the bus off, giving the impression that the bus drove itself off the stage. To Ballard, this is an amusing anecdote. But it shows that truth has never been given a high value in the hydrogen world. The stock of Ballard Systems, funded partially by over $100 million in investments from Ford and Daimler Chrysler, has declined from a price of $115 in 2001 to around $5 in 2007, representative of the declining fortunes of the fuel cell car industry.[13]

J-Cast Business news observed, "What is putting the brake on the development of fuel-cell cars, first of all, is that the device itself is very costly. It has been found out also that the building of infrastructures, such as the networks of filling stations that would provide hydrogen needed for the fuel cell, would take a long time. It is expected to take at least 20 years before the fuel cell can be widely used."[14] What does the article mean by "...the device itself is very costly"? According to James Woolsey the price is about $1,000,000 per car.[15]

There are three hydrogen myths constantly repeated. The first is that hydrogen will provide unlimited energy supported by the claim that 75% of the matter in the universe is hydrogen.[16] Although this is true, it is deliberately misleading. Hydrogen must be obtained from this planet, not from the sun.

The percentage of hydrogen on earth is much lower and must be extracted.[17] The second fallacy is that hydrogen is *clean* energy. In a similar way one could say electricity is a clean, non-polluting source of energy. But the methods of producing both hydrogen and electricity are potentially extremely polluting. The major source of electricity is burning coal, which releases carbon dioxide, nitrogen oxides and sulfur oxides. Most hydrogen is produced from fossil fuels; 94% is manufactured directly from natural gas, oil or coal, and 6% is manufactured by electrolysis, a process that uses electricity generated mostly by fossil fuels. The hydrogen manufacturing process pollutes the environment, just as do power plants which produce electricity.

The third fallacy is that the energy cost of making hydrogen is low. Hydrogen is not an element that can be gathered; it must be extracted from some other material. It can be made from water, but only by expending huge amounts of electrical energy for electrolysis; or it can be made from natural gas or other fossil fuels by steam reformation. Steam reformation uses fossil fuels (mostly natural gas) both as a hydrogen feed stock (or raw material) and as a source of energy to run the reformation process. But the quantity of energy contained in the manufactured hydrogen is much less than the energy contained in the fossil fuels used as feed stock and for processing.

Ulf Bossel shows that, regardless of whether renewable or conventional power sources of electricity are used, the electrolysis approach to creating

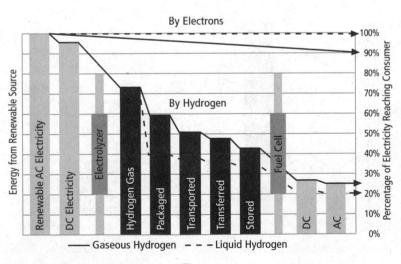

5.1: *Electricity Transport via Hydrogen or Electrons*

hydrogen is extremely costly.[18] In Figure 5.1, the two columns on the left illustrate the original generation of electricity. Although this figure uses a renewable source of energy, the same argument applies if the source is conventional fuels. The third column represents the electrolysis process, which creates hydrogen from water using the generated electricity. Note that the fourth column, labeled hydrogen gas, is much smaller than the original column representing generated AC electricity, indicating a sizable loss of energy. Next, hydrogen gas is packaged in some way (possibly as a liquid), transported by pipeline or truck, then transferred to a fueling station of some kind, and finally stored until needed by the consumer. At each step in the process, some of the energy is used or lost, as represented by the declining heights of the subsequent columns.

Eventually, hydrogen may be used in a fuel cell as a source of electricity generation. The fuel cell column represents this second machine. The first machine, the electrolyzer, has converted electricity to hydrogen and the second machine, the fuel cell, now converts the hydrogen back to electricity. The last two columns show the final amount of electricity produced. The declines in energy from the original AC electricity to the hydrogen gas and from the hydrogen gas back to electricity are due to the second law of thermodynamics. The amount of energy left for powering a device in a home or a car is about 20% of the original amount.

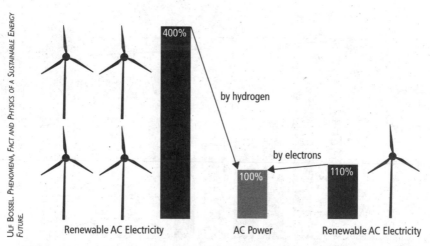

ULF BOSSEL. PHENOMENA, FACT AND PHYSICS OF A SUSTAINABLE ENERGY FUTURE.

5.2: *Four Renewable Energy Generators Needed for Hydrogen Energy Transport vs. One for Electrons*

In other words, it would take at least four power plants or wind turbines to get the same amount of electricity via the hydrogen method as can be provided by a single power plant shipping electrons directly to your home, as shown in Figure 5.2. This is a four-to-one difference in efficiency — one method (hydrogen) requires four times as many equivalent sources as the other. It makes no difference if these are coal or natural gas power plant sources or if they are wind turbines or photovoltaic cells — there is a four-to-one ratio. The fuel cell mirage is just that — a mirage. It has been 10 years away for 35 years.

The Electric Car Option

The fuel cell is not the only technological product with a long dubious history — a history whose length and failures are known only to a tiny group of people. The electric car or electric vehicle (EV) also called the battery electric vehicle (BEV) is another example. The difference between the EV and fuel cell vehicles is that the EV actually worked! Far less time and fewer dollars were expended to build about 5,500 of these cars in the late 1990s. Many were recalled and destroyed by corporate policy, but some remain and their utility can be measured.

In the early days of the automobile industry, the EV was sold in similar numbers to the internal-combustion engine. A temporary resurgence of the EV occurred in California in the late 1990s. In 1990, California established a Zero Emission Vehicle (ZEV) Mandate which required that by 1998 2% of vehicles sold in California would have to have zero emissions, increasing to 10% by 2003. Any automobile manufacturer that sold cars in California was required to develop and offer such vehicles for sale. Since California is such a large market, no manufacturer could fail to respond; several EV models were developed and sold by GM, Ford, Toyota and Honda.

Among them was the General Motors EV1, a two-passenger electric vehicle. About 1,100 were built. 800 of these were leased to consumers during the period from 1997 to 2003. GM invested more than $1 billion to develop, design and build the car. Another example was the RAV4 EV manufactured by Toyota. Toyota built about 1,400 electric vehicles from 1997 through 2003, close to the number of EV1s. Smaller volumes were produced by Honda and Ford and a few other manufacturers in the same time range, roughly from 1997 to 2003. About 5,500 EVs were leased or sold.[19]

In 2001 California granted companies credit for low-emission vehicles, rather than just zero-emissions vehicles, particularly the hybrid cars from

Honda (Insight) and Toyota (Prius). Changing the rules gave the auto industry the opportunity to challenge the entire regulation. General Motors and DaimlerChrysler sued the state of California and the California Air Resources Board (CARB), alleging that the newer zero emission vehicle (ZEV) rules violated a federal law barring states from regulating fuel economy in any way. They argued that the new rules amounted to a regulation of fuel economy since they covered hybrids which burn traditional fuel. In late 2002, the Bush Administration filed an amicus (friend of the court) brief, claiming that the state, by regulating emissions, was setting a gasoline mileage standard, which was the province of the federal government. As a result of these actions CARB dropped the requirement that automakers produce battery-powered electric cars and instructed the industry instead to produce more fuel-cell electric vehicles and hybrid vehicles. With agreement that the rules would not be changed again, the auto industry dropped its suit in late 2003.[20]

There was great enthusiasm by people who leased EVs in California. Many protested strongly when GM took back the leased cars and scrapped them. Toyota began to do the same but later sold some of the cars to their owners. A film released in June 2006 entitled *Who Killed the Electric Car* suggests a plot by oil companies, car companies and politicians to withhold a promising technology from the market.[21] There may be elements of truth in this, but the fact remains that batteries limited the range of the cars. The concept of the Electric Vehicle is decades old, and the main problems with EVs have always been battery weight, time to charge the battery and distance traveled on a battery charge.

The Hybrid Car

Technologies generating interest today are not necessarily revolutionary breakthroughs but continuations of long-term R&D investments and research. Victor Wouk and Charlie Rosen created a prototype hybrid gas-electric vehicle in 1974 under contract from the Environmental Protection Agency, using a Buick Skylark body. Toyota and Honda decided to pursue the hybrid about the same time that the US formed the Partnership for a New Generation of Vehicles in 1993. In December 1995, Toyota announced that the hybrid vehicle would go on sale in Japan in two years' time and on December 10, 1997, it did.[22] By the end of 2007, cumulative sales for hybrids in the US from 1999 through 2007 were about 1 million units out of about 217 million cars.[23]

Partnerships between US car companies and the Departments of Energy (DOE) and Transportation (DOT) have produced little. While Toyota and Honda focused on the hybrid car, US companies, in agreement with the government, made fuel cells a priority. Unfortunately the hybrid was not the only lost opportunity. Japanese and European manufacturers have made major improvements to the diesel engine as well, and almost half the cars in Europe are now sold with high mileage diesel engines.

Another US Automobile Error — Flex Fuel Vehicles

Auto companies, supported by the government, go to great lengths to avoid basic change in the kinds of cars produced. One way this is achieved is by running cars on a fuel called E85, a mix of 85% ethanol and 15% gasoline. However, E85 cannot be used in all automobiles. Currently there are about 4.4 million flex-fuel (dual fuel) vehicles on the road, out of some 217 million cars and SUVs.[24] Auto companies get a Corporate Average Fuel Economy (CAFE) credit for every flex-fuel vehicle they produce; this allows them to lower the actual average fuel economy of their remaining fleet, based on the dubious assumption that gasoline use will be offset. But of the 4.4 million flex fuel vehicles, 99% run on regular gasoline because E85 is rarely available to the everyday driving public.[25] There are only about 1,200 of the nearly 200,000 gas stations that sell E85 — that is about one of every 170 stations.[26] Rather than improving fuel economy, auto companies have chosen to produce flex-fuel vehicles since it only costs $50 to $100 to convert an ordinary car into a flex-fuel one. And manufacturers will still get CAFE credit even if alternative fuels are not used in the vehicles.

Changing Horses Again — From Fuel Cell to the Plug-in Hybrid (PHEV)

Fuel cells and Electric Vehicles did not work, and now the country is adopting another quick techno fix — the Pluggable Hybrid Electric Vehicle or PHEV. The proponents of the PHEV, like advocates of the fuel cell, began their program by misrepresenting their offering. They overstated potential mileage, quoting numbers like 100, 250 and 500 mpg. The fact that the electricity that replaces the gasoline comes mostly from coal, a fuel more polluting than oil, is never discussed. In a talk in 2005, Senator Joseph Lieberman said plug-in hybrids are "just now on the threshold of commercialization." He said, "These vehicles could be in your garage within a couple of years."[27]

The PHEV is a marriage between the older technologies of an electric vehicle and a gasoline fueled one. In contrast to the hybrid car, which uses the battery and electric motor to provide some acceleration assistance allowing a smaller gasoline motor to be used, the PHEV is both an electric car and a gasoline car in that it can drive on the battery only or use the gasoline engine. This implies it must carry the weight and space penalty of an electric engine, a gasoline engine, batteries and a gas tank. Its disadvantages are ignored based on the misleading hype of hundreds of miles per gallon.

CO_2 Emissions — Electric Engines vs. Gasoline Engines

It is necessary to technically compare the electric car to the gasoline car in terms of its thermodynamics as well as its power source to expose misleading arguments. A first step is to compare the known statistics of a car that has an electric and a gasoline version — the 2003 Toyota RAV4. Toyota made two versions of this car, one a gasoline version with the designation RAV4, and the second an electric version with the designation RAV 4 EV (EV standing for electric vehicle). We will use the designation RAV4 IC (Internal-Combustion) for the gasoline version. The car mileage website maintained by the US Department of Energy and the US Environmental Protection Agency provides a side by side comparison of the two cars.

Popular wisdom says that Electric Vehicles (EVs) get 3-4 miles per kilowatt hour (kWh). Figure 5.3 shows that annual fuel costs for the EV version of this vehicle are $362 based on an electricity cost of $.08 per kWh. Dividing $362 by $.08 gives 4,525 kWh. The DOE data was based on driving 15,000

US DEPARTMENT OF ENERGY. FUELECONOMY.GOV/FEG/BYMANU.HTM

2003 Toyota Model	RAV4 EV	RAV4 IC
Mpg (miles per gal)	112	22
Annual Fuel Cost	$362	$2,116
Annual Petroleum Consumption (barrels)	.3 barrels	15.6 barrels
Annual Tons of CO_2 Produced	3.9	8.3
Electricity Price (kwh)	$.08	
Gasoline Price (gallons)		$2.71
Gallons/barrel		42
Mileage driven	15,000	15,000

5.3: 2003 Toyota RAV — Electric (EV) vs. Gasoline (IC) engines miles. Dividing the 15,000 miles by 4,525 kWh gives a mileage for the RAV4 EV of 3.3 miles per kWh, within the popular wisdom range. The next step is to verify the 22 mpg for the IC. Annual petroleum consumption for the EV is .3 barrels of oil and for the gasoline version (IC) 15.6 barrels of oil (655 gallons). Dividing this number into 15,000 miles gives 22.9 mpg, close to the 22 mpg in the original data. We can assume the .3 barrels for the EV (the equivalent of 12 gallons) is for oil changes and lubrication.

Next we will verify the CO_2 emissions. The annual tons of CO_2 for the RAV4 IC is 8.3 tons. Each gallon of gasoline that is burned generates 20 pounds of CO_2[28] so 655 gallons will generate 13,100 pounds per year, about 6.6 tons. This is about 20% less than 8.3 tons but close enough. Next we must determine the CO_2 generated by the electric car. Two pounds of CO_2 are generated per kWh from coal.[29] If the car was powered by coal-generated electricity, then CO_2 generated would be 4,525 kWh times 2 or 4.5 tons. Natural gas generates 1.3 pounds of CO_2 per kWh.[30] If the power for the car was from natural gas, the CO_2 emitted would be 4,525 times 1.3 or 3 tons. A mix of $2/3$ coal and $1/3$ gas would emit 4 tons of CO_2. The annual tons of CO_2 listed in Figure 5.3 for the RAV4 EV is 3.9 tons. It is not a simple calculation to determine CO_2 emissions since electricity comes from coal, uranium, oil, natural gas, hydroelectric, wind and other sources. A complete study would require finding the CO_2 generated by each fuel type. But the CO_2 numbers I have calculated are similar to the original data provided.

Figure 5.3 shows a two to one difference in CO_2 generated. It also shows a five to one difference in miles per gallon. The mpg difference is caused by a common oversight. A kWh provides 3,413 Btus and a gallon of gasoline provides 125,000 Btus. Using the 3,413 Btus from a kWh, a gallon of gasoline contains 36 kWh. The RAV 4 EV gets 3.3 miles per kWh; multiplying this 3.3 times 36 (kWh per gallon) gives 119 miles per gallon, very near the 112 mpg in the table. But this does not take into account the loss of energy that takes place in burning petroleum to make electricity. Gasoline is not normally converted into electricity except in small generators in places like construction sites. But there are power plants that use oil (from which gasoline is derived) so a comparison can be made. In such power plants, as well as in coal plants, 65% of the energy in the fuel is lost in heat generation.[31] Using fuel oil which contains 138,000 Btus and assuming 35% can be converted to electricity then the electrical energy provided in kWh is .35 times 138,000 Btus divided by

3,413 Btus or 14 kWh, not 36 kWh. Thus the miles per gallon would be 3.3 (miles per kWh) times 14 kWh or 52 mpg. This is about 2.4 times the regular gas RAV IC, and the ratio of the carbon emissions are 2:1, showing the expected balance. This is far from a 5 times improvement in mileage.

Supporters of EVs and PHEVs do not make this form of calculation. Once more we are faced with misleading statements from advocates and car companies, a repeat of the fuel cell fiasco. In the book *Plug-in Hybrids*, for example, one reads comments such as "The simplest plug-in hybrids can get 100 miles per gallon, but they might get 500-1,000 miles per gallon of gasoline if the primary fuel that backs up the hybrid is .....a biofuel......" and "Upgrade that car to a plug-in hybrid that runs 20 miles on electricity before tapping the liquid fuel, and it might get 1,000 miles per gallon of gasoline."[32] With quotes of 1,000 miles per gallon one can expect that the PHEV fascination may delay fundamental change a few more decades — with possible disastrous consequences.

In a major research report, The American Center for an Energy-Efficient Economy compared a PHEV to a hybrid car. The report predicted that, on average, a typical American driver is expected to achieve about a 15% greater reduction in net CO_2 emissions with a PHEV compared to the driver of a regular hybrid. The hundreds of miles per gallon claims were not substantiated.[33] An American Solar Energy Society report showed a similar reduction when comparing a PHEV with electricity from a modern coal fired power plant to a gasoline engine.[34] Figure 5.4 illustrates the comparison along with carbon from a natural gas plant. One should use the coal fired plant numbers since natural gas plants will decline as peak natural gas approaches.

Continuing to push fuel cell cars, EVs, flex-fuel vehicles and now PHEVs is a prime example of an ignorant and foolish nation religiously believing in technological salvation. We can blame government, science and business, but in the final analysis Americans have elected officials

Charles F. Kutscher, Editor. Tackling Climate Change in the U.S.: Potential Carbon Emissions Reductions from Energy Efficiency and Renewable Energy by 2030.

Technology	Carbon*	
	Per Gallon	Per Mile
Gasoline Engine	6.6 lb.	.22 lb.
PHEV/Modern Coal-Fired Power Plant	5.6 lb.	.19 lb.
PHEV/Gas Combined-Cycle Power Plant.	2.5 lb.	.08 lb.

* Assumes 10 kWh of electricity is required to drive the same distance (30 miles) as on one gallon of gasoline; includes 10% transmission loss.

5-4: *Carbon Emission Reductions — PHEV Coal Electric vs. Gasoline Vehicles* who have given them what they want — more consumption. They have also accepted the somewhat trivial unproven tenet coming from the dominant religion of economics: "The market will provide." Yet there is more to this. Energy companies and car companies have not prospered in silence. They cannot argue that they merely serve the wishes of the consumer. At each suggestion of change or limitation, lobbyists descend on Washington and ad budgets are increased. To a great extent, the public are pawns in the economic growth game being played by energy companies, car companies, scientific institutions and government. It is these elite groups who decide what will be built and when.

It is vital that we understand the limits of technology. Although science has provided an amazing variety of new products, it has also provided an amazing variety of problems. And these problems are not simply a matter of political will but include limitations of technology itself. There are resources or natural barriers that apparently cannot be overcome. Science is also limited by the problems that science itself causes. Treatment of cancer has progressed significantly since Richard Nixon declared a *war on cancer* in the 1970s. But overall cancer has increased rapidly on a worldwide basis. One reason might be that while one set of scientists is trying to cure cancer, another set is busily developing new products (mostly based on some version of fossil fuels) that are extremely toxic and which may cause cancer. Oddly enough, the cure for cancer may be to stop certain scientists from continuing their work. In terms of the science of fossil fuels, one set of scientists has discovered a wide variety of new technologies which allow the extraction of fossil fuels faster and more completely than ever before, while those scientists looking for new sources lag far behind.

The great tragedy is the continued apathy and ignorance of people who are waiting for another technical solution. As a nation, we Americans cling to our current lifestyle, one that must and will change as oil and natural gas decline. This attitude, with its foundation in the idea of technofix, is best illustrated by a quote from a 2003 *New York Times* article on the hydrogen economy. A 37-year-old lawyer who owned a Hummer said "The way I think about it, we're close today to switching to a hydrogen economy, so it won't matter what mileage we get on cars now. I think that will happen soon."[35]

Six

Peak Technology and Electric Power

THE MEDIA FREQUENTLY TELLS US that "we must find a new source of energy," preferably one that is both clean and inexhaustible. This seems reasonable but it is somewhat equivalent to saying that "we must find a new continent." It is unlikely that some new mineral combination will be found to replace the vast volume of hydrocarbons being rapidly consumed. Minerals were found over the course of several centuries. But like continents, there are a fixed number of them. Twelve of the basic elements listed in the Periodic Table of Elements were known in ancient times. One was added in the period 1650-1699. In the 18th century; 18 were found, and 49 in the 19th century. Many found in the 20th century are manmade — created in atomic processes in tiny amounts that last for a few seconds.[1] Just as the discovery age for finding new continents and new kinds of basic elements is past, so it may be with fossil fuel burning machines. In the previous chapter we pointed out that automobile technology has not fundamentally changed since the internal-combustion and battery-based vehicles of the late 19th century. In thirty years, electric power plant efficiency has only increased from 30% to 35%.[2] Buildings are the greatest users of energy, but construction technology and materials have also changed little in the last century — major building energy — consuming processes are still heating, air conditioning and lights. Few significant technological advances have been made in those applications. Even the more recent improvements — heat pumps and fluorescent lighting — are decades old.

Renewable Energy and Power

If the fuel burning technology used in cars, power plants and buildings is dated with few prospects for real improvements, can we find new fuel sources? There are several options to consider including solar energy (both thermal for hot water and photovoltaic for electricity), wind energy, energy from plants such as corn and soybeans, energy from woody plants and agricultural waste, as well as increasing use of old standbys — oil, natural gas, uranium and coal. Other options that were tried in the 1970s and are still available include tar sands from Canada, oil shale from Colorado and heavy oil from Venezuela. Today's options are mostly variations on previous themes — no breakthroughs are on the horizon. Like automobile technology, the fuel sources are the same as they have been for many decades.

This is evident in the *Energy Independence and Security Act of 2007* passed by Congress and signed by President Bush in December 2007. Key provisions included a long overdue increase in car mileage standards as well as increased production of biofuels — both corn ethanol and cellulosic ethanol. Other provisions support research and development for carbon capture and storage, recognizing the need to protect the atmosphere from the growing use of coal in the US.[3] In Chapter 1, I described the decline of oil and natural gas production in the US. Within a few decades, oil and gas will be less and less available to North America as Asia, Africa and Europe compete for oil and gas from the Middle East and Russia, the areas where 70% of the world's remaining oil and natural gas reserves are located. Nuclear power is being reconsidered; there are proposals to build new reactors in the US. But supplies of domestic uranium will limit that option. Thus the continent's future energy resources will likely be biofuels, solar, wind and coal.

It is useful to review recent trends for these energy sources. Figure 6.1 shows US energy consumption during years when energy awareness dramatically increased.

Coal and oil consumption grew while natural gas use declined. (It is much harder to import natural gas since the gas must be frozen and transported in special ships.) Nuclear power consumption changed little. Hydroelectric (dams) and geothermal numbers increased slightly, reflecting the limitation of sites. Biofuels and wind energy both grew at the same rate — 145% between 2002 and 2006. Solar PV increased only 9.4% in the same period. Coal consumption increased 2.8%. Although the percentage of growth in coal consumption was small, the growth in total energy produced from coal was .6 quadrillion Btus, the same as the total combined growth in energy produced from biofuels, wind and solar PV. This emphasizes the low increase in total renewable energy relative

Energy Source	2002	2003	2004	2005	2006
Total	97.927	98.280	100.413	100.756	99.960
Fossil Fuels	83.994	84.386	86.191	86.451	85.307
Coal	21.904	22.321	22.466	22.785	22.511
Coal Coke Net Imports	0.061	0.051	0.138	0.044	0.061
Natural Gas	23.628	22.967	22.993	22.886	22.518
Petroleum	38.401	39.047	40.594	40.735	40.217
Electricity Net Imports	0.072	0.022	0.039	0.084	0.060
Nuclear Electric Power	8.143	7.959	8.222	8.160	8.208
Renewable Energy	5.893	6.151	6.261	6.404	6.844
Biomass	2.706	2.817	3.023	3.114	3.277
Biofuels	0.309	0.414	0.513	0.594	0.758
Waste	0.402	0.401	0.389	0.403	0.404
Wood Derived Fuels	1.995	2.002	2.121	2.116	2.114
Geothermal Energy	0.328	0.331	0.341	0.343	0.349
Hydroelectric Conventional	2.689	2.825	2.690	2.703	2.890
Solar/PV Energy	0.064	0.064	0.064	0.066	0.070
Wind Energy	0.105	0.115	0.142	0.178	0.258

US ENERGY INFORMATION ADMINISTRATION, RENEWABLE ENERGY CONSUMPTION AND ELECTRICITY

6.1: *US Energy Consumption by Energy Source, 2002-2006 (Quadrillion Btu)*

to the increase in fossil fuels. Wind and biofuels may grow at double digit rates but from such a low initial amount that less rapid conventional fossil fuel growth such as coal still predominates in terms of new energy production.

Many people concerned with climate change lament the relatively slow growth of renewables in government planning documents, hoping for a massive shift to wind and solar. Figure 6.2 shows future growth projections for different kinds of fuels from the Energy Information Agency (EIA) report *Annual Energy Outlook 2007*. The forecast for 2030 includes a relatively small amount of energy from renewables compared to the standard CO_2 generating fossil fuels of oil, coal and natural gas. Since most people would prefer to use fewer fossil fuels, it is necessary to understand the nature and limits of renewables. So even with these new sources growing at a 30-40% annual rate, significant growth will take decades. Figure 6.2 shows the small size of the initial base for renewables. This slow growth does not imply a deliberate government policy to limit renewables. Nor does it imply that the government is doing as much as it can to develop renewables.

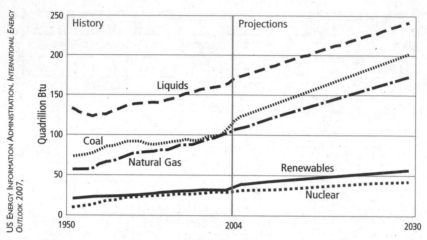

US Energy Information Administration, *International Energy Outlook 2007,*

6.2: *World Marketed Energy Use by Fuel Type, 1980-2030*

Biofuels

The *Energy Policy Act of 2005* provided tax incentives and loan guarantees for energy production of various types. It increased the amount of biofuels (usually ethanol) that must be mixed with gasoline sold in the United States to triple the current requirement (7.5 billion gallons by 2012). The law included a government ethanol subsidy via a 51 cent per gallon excise tax credit that refiners receive for meeting the federal Renewable Fuels Standard (RFS) mandate. It also placed a 54 cent per gallon tariff on imported ethanol.[4]

The issue of ethanol is a controversial one. As reported in *The Energy Balance of Corn Ethanol: an Update*, the energy returned on energy invested (EROEI) for ethanol made in the US from US corn is 1.34, which means that ethanol provides only 34% more energy than it takes to produce it, a much smaller percent than we are used to with fossil fuels (closer to 1000% for Middle East oil).[5] But other researchers report that ethanol production actually consumes more energy than it yields. David Pimentel has analyzed the EROEI for many different plants and reports that corn, switch grass and wood biomass take respectively 29%, 45% and 57% more fossil fuel energy to produce ethanol from than the energy supplied by the ethanol from these plants.[6]

The side effects from this highly subsidized fuel program are not trivial. Corn prices have almost doubled in two years, affecting food costs. *The Economist* notes that ethanol subsidies in America have ended a long era of falling food prices. The magazine's food-price index is now at its highest since it began in 1845, having risen by one-third in the past year. These record food prices are occurring at a time of abundance as the US now uses more of its corn crop for ethanol than it sells abroad for food. In the past the US exported 70% of world corn, and many nations have depended on American corn for food and for animal feed. Thus the increased production of US ethanol limits food availability in other nations, both in terms of direct food like tortillas and in terms of livestock and poultry feed. And according to the International Food Policy Research Institute, the expansion of ethanol and other biofuels could reduce Calorie intake by 4-8% in Africa and 2-5% in Asia by 2020.[7]

As gasoline-hungry consumers become more interested in ethanol, more tropical forests are cut down and replaced with palm trees or other plants that can be converted to auto fuels. Ethanol and biodiesel can be produced from a variety of crops including maize, soy, rapeseed, sunflower, cassava, sugar cane, palm and jatropha. As the price of petroleum rises, many farmers in the developing world are finding that they can earn more income by growing bio-fuel crops than they can earn by growing food crops either for their local community or for export. The competition for grain between the wealthy car drivers of the world and the poorest people who are trying to survive is a moral issue that we should not ignore. The continued increase in biofuels pro-duction will result in a continued decrease in food availability, which we could someday consider to be a crime against humanity. And the continued destruc-tion of forests in the developing world for land to grow crops for biofuels exacerbates the problem of climate change as it removes the natural sinks for CO_2.

After years of massively subsidized production increases, it is still not clear if ethanol can provide more energy than it consumes. This has lead to a search for a new source — cellulose ethanol. In theory ethanol could be derived from a variety of woody plant foods or even crop residues such as corn stover, the remnants of the corn plants in the fields left after harvest.[8] Unfortunately there is no proven technology to do this economically. In 2007 the US Department of Energy granted six contracts totaling $385 million to do research in cellulosic ethanol.[9] We may be fortunate that the craze for this kind of fuel is far ahead of our actual ability to produce it because if cellulosic fuels were to become feasible, there could be even more damaging effects on the environment. Every kind of plant in any place in the world could become a potential fuel for our automobiles. Taking even more plant material from fields and forests could lead to massive soil degradation.[10] Unfortunately the US government made a major commitment to cellulosic ethanol in the *Energy Independence and Security Act of 2007.*[11]

Solar Photovoltaics (PV)

Willoughby Smith discovered the photovoltaic effect in selenium in 1873. In 1876, William Adams discovered that illuminating a junction between selenium and platinum has a photovoltaic effect. These discoveries were the foundation for the first selenium solar cell built in 1877. Albert Einstein provided the most comprehensive theoretical work about the photovoltaic effect in 1904, for which he was awarded a Nobel Prize in 1921. In 1954, AT&T Bell Laboratories designed a solar cell with 4.5% efficiency. In 1957, Hoffman Electronics introduced a solar cell with 8% efficiency. In 1958, the first satellite powered by solar cells, Vanguard I, was launched. In 1960, Hoffman Electronics introduced another solar cell with 14% efficiency. Originally most PVs were used in the space program, but in 1970 Solar Power Corporation was established for applications of photovoltaic technologies on Earth. In 1980 ARCO Solar became the first company to produce photovoltaic modules with peak power of more than 1MW per year and built a 105.6kW system in Utah. In 1983, the Solar Trek vehicle with photovoltaic system of 1kW drove 4,000 km in twenty days in an Australian race. On April 29, 2003 the world's largest photovoltaic plant (4MW) was connected to the public grid in Hemau near Regensburg (Bavaria), Germany.[12] In 2006 PV shipments worldwide were $20 billion.[13]

The solar cell is over a century old in concept and half a century old in implementation. Costs have dropped significantly, but at a far slower rate than comparable technologies such as computer chips. More PV systems are being installed each year — in recent years PV shipments have increased at the rate of 25-35% per year. But solar PV electricity provides only a tiny part of total energy in the US.

Figure 6.3 shows a reversal of the long term decreases in PV prices. Improvements in materials and yields, along with an increase in the amount of sunlight per square inch converted, have been marginal. Much of a PV system consists of basic commodity materials such as aluminum, glass and silicon. The rising costs of these materials are canceling out the relatively small improvements in the efficiency of converting sunlight to electricity.

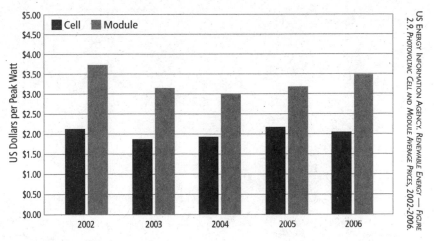

US Energy Information Agency. Renewable Energy — Figure 2.9, Photovoltaic Cell and Module Average Prices, 2002-2006.

6.3: *PV Recent Price Trends*

Wind

The first large windmill which generated electricity in the US was a system built in Cleveland, Ohio, in 1888 by Charles F. Brush. In 1891, a Danish scientist, Paul La Cour, developed the first electrical output wind machine to incorporate the aerodynamic design principles used in the best European conventional windmills. By the close of World War I, 25kW electrical output machines were used throughout Denmark. The development of bulk-power, utility-scale wind energy conversion systems was first undertaken in Russia in 1931 with the 100kW Balaclava wind generator. Subsequent experimental wind plants in the United States, Denmark, France, Germany and Great Britain during the period 1935-1970 showed that large-scale wind turbines would work, but failed to result in a practical large electrical wind turbine. In Denmark, the 200 kW Gedser Mill wind turbine operated successfully until the early 1960s, when declining fossil fuel prices once again made wind energy non-competitive with steam powered generating plants.

US government support of wind energy began within two years of the Oil Crisis of 1973. Funding was allocated to the development of multi-megawatt turbines in the belief that US utilities would not consider wind power to be a serious power source unless large, megawatt, utility-scale systems were available. During the years between 1973-1986, the commercial wind turbine market evolved from domestic and agricultural applications of small machines in the 1 to 25kW range to utility-interconnected wind farm applications of intermediate-scale machines

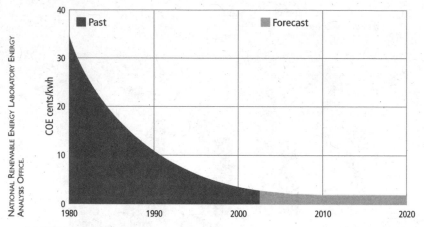

NATIONAL RENEWABLE ENERGY LABORATORY ENERGY ANALYSIS OFFICE.

6.4: *Wind Energy Cost Trends*

of 50 to 600kW. A federal energy credit of 15%, a federal investment credit of 10% and a 50% California state energy credit were key economic factors stimulating the early development of wind farms. These tax breaks, together with attractive rates offered by utilities for power produced by alternative sources (mandated by state regulations), were packaged into an attractive investment product by private financial firms and investment houses.[14] Wind installations also grew overseas. In Germany, Denmark, Spain and India, wind turbine installations increased steadily through the 1980s, 90s and into the 2000s. In 2006 total world wind generation capacity installed was 74.3GW. The percentage of installations was Germany (28%), Spain and USA (16% each), India (8%), Denmark (4%) and the Rest of World (28%). World growth in shipments from 2006 to 2007 was 25%.[15] The total number of gigawatts installed is impressive, but is only about 2% of the total worldwide installed electrical generating base of 3,872GW.[16]

Like many technologies that are reaching the point of diminishing returns, the rate of improvement is decreasing (Fig. 6.4). In recent years the prices of wind turbines have actually begun to increase from $31/MWh for projects built in 2002- 2003, to $35/MWh for projects built in 2004-2005 and to $49/MWh for 2006 projects.[17]

Wind and PVs fatal flaws — Capacity Factor and Dispatchability

Wind generation of electricity has a long history — over 100 years. In the future when fossil fuels are depleted, wind energy may well be the most cost-effective source of electrical power available. But the major technology advancements in wind power commercialization have already been made, and although there will be many refinements and improvements, it is doubtful any breakthrough improvements will be made which would dramatically reduce costs. There have been enough installations worldwide to accurately measure wind availability and the effectiveness of turbines at various wind speeds.

It is important to be cautious about wind and PV claims. Often the media reports that wind is as cost-effective as fossil fuels; sometimes these statements include the caveat *at the best sites*. But there is a big difference between a conventional fossil fuel plant and a wind or solar farm. If one builds a hundred identical coal power plants, the last plant built will generate the same amount of electricity as the first. It might take a thousand wind turbines to match the energy output of one large coal power plant. But the last turbine installed will not generate as much electricity as the first one installed. The windiest, most productive sites (or in the case of PVs the sunniest sites) are always developed first, followed by the less windy (or sunny) sites. This makes it harder to project the effectiveness of potential wind and solar production worldwide.

Any electrical generating device has a *capacity factor* which represents the percentage of the maximum turbine rating (called the *nameplate factor*) it can actually achieve. A coal or nuclear plant has a capacity factor of 80-90%, which means that most of the time it is generating close to the maximum rate possible. But a wind turbine's capacity factor is in the 20-30% range. Thus at the end of a year a coal plant will have generated 80% of its possible capacity while a wind turbine will have only generated a quarter or so of what it is capable. This capacity factor is often overlooked when comparing wind to conventional generating systems. Because media reports typically discuss only the nameplate factor and ignore capacity factors, most comparisons of wind to conventional power plants are misleading. Solar PV capacity factors are even lower than wind systems.

The electricity generating industry uses the term *dispatchability* to describe the ability to generate electricity, or dispatch it, as soon as the need arises. A major disadvantage of wind and solar power is that they are intermittent and thus cannot be counted on to produce a constant level of electricity. Wind can die down for days, and solar PVs cannot generate electricity at night. The variable nature of wind and solar means electricity cannot be dispatched with the consistency of a coal or natural gas power plant. On a large scale, wind turbines will require backup fossil fuel power plants which must always be idling — running at a low speed — so that they can be brought online quickly if wind speeds decline. Some experts suggest that wind and solar electricity can never completely replace fossil fuel plants to meet the world's electricity needs.[18] The most likely estimate is that wind and solar can replace about 20% of total fossil fuel-based electricity generation, and that will take decades to achieve.

Wind speeds are higher in the winter while solar PV cells are more effective in the summer when more sunlight is available. This suggests the use of photovoltaic arrays to provide power in the summer when the wind is low. However, solar cells are much more expensive than wind turbines for the same number of kilowatt hours generated. During the times when neither solar PVs nor wind turbines can generate electricity we will still need coal plants that can be moved from an idling condition to full generation. In fact, we may need almost as many coal plants in the future as we have now. The largest utility provider of wind energy in the world, E.on Netz, notes that backup fossil fuel plants must provide 90% of the capacity of the wind turbines and PV panels.[19] Fortunately these plants would not be burning large amounts of coal most of the time. A vital perspective on wind and solar, missing from the consciousness of the average person, is that wind turbines and solar PV cannot replace coal plants if we want uninterrupted electricity for our homes and businesses.

Ted Trainer, an Australian researcher, is one of the few people who have attempted to analyze the variability and dispatchability of wind and solar. He gives an example of an Australian wind farm whose capital investment cost was 13 times that of a comparable coal plant. Adding the lifetime cost of the fuel to the capital costs of the coal plant gives a ratio of 4.2 times. The wind turbines are still several times more expensive. A similar example for a solar PV alternative gives a cost figure of 12-14 times the cost of the coal plant including the cost of the coal it consumes. Trainer points out that wind turbines and solar PV should actually be built to supplement conventional power plants, not to serve as replacements or alternatives to building future conventional power plants. Their virtue is in reducing the amount of coal burned, not in avoiding building coal plants.[20] Howard Hayden, author of *The Solar Fraud*, has done a similar analysis.[21]

Renewables and an Electric Economy

The US was enamored with the so called *hydrogen economy* for three decades. With its demise, a new term is starting to appear — the *electric economy*. This implies that most energy would be provided in the form of electricity — thus the pluggable hybrid automobile. It would be useful to estimate the approximate capital cost of an electric economy based on renewables. Let's use wind as an example. The Energy Information Administration reports that US annual energy use is about 100 quads (quadrillion Btus). Part of that is nuclear and part hydroelectric (a total of about 15 quads), leaving (for this example) 85 quads to be replaced by a renewable electric economy. We will presume that all 85 quads of renewable electric energy would heat all electric homes and power electric cars.

The equivalent of 85 quads of Btus is 25,000,000,000,000 (25 trillion) kilowatt hours (kWh). A one-mega-watt capacity wind turbine with a capacity factor of 25% and a price in the range of $1,670 per kilowatt (a $1,670,000 cost for a one mega-watt turbine is the basis of calculation) will generate 2,190,000 kWh per year (1,000 kW wind turbine rating times 24 hours per day times 365 days per year times the 25% capacity factor). Dividing 25 trillion kilowatt hours by 2,190,000 kWh gives 11,415,525 wind turbines. At $1,670,000 per turbine, total cost would be in the range of $19 trillion. This is the true scale and cost of an electric economy: that is, the number of turbines necessary to provide electricity directly from turbines to point of use.

If hydrogen is used to make a hydrogen economy equivalent to the suggested electric economy, it would be necessary to multiply the number of wind turbines by a factor of 4, resulting in 45 million turbines dotting the landscape and near $80 trillion in cost.[22] Operational costs and allocations for the replacement of the wind turbines after 30 years are other key factors not included in these calculations.

Coal

In the near term, the future fossil fuel used in the US will undoubtedly be coal. Coal generates 50% of electricity in the US and its use for power generation is expected to grow to 57% by 2030.[23] Natural gas is the second major fuel used to generate electricity (about 20%); unfortunately it will be the next fossil fuel after oil to peak. It's also very valuable for other products like fertilizer. The result will likely be a decline in the use of natural gas for generating electricity and an increase in the percent of electricity generated from coal. Coal's role will be dominant because new hydroelectric sites are no longer available, and nuclear plants are dependent on shrinking sources of uranium. Wind and solar will contribute about 20% or so.

Coal supporters offer two options for fueling the automobile. One is to convert coal to a liquid fuel. This process was used extensively by Germany in WWII and is still popular in South Africa. Unfortunately the energy consumed to produce liquid fuel from coal generates CO_2 , adding to the CO_2 generated from burning the fuel in car engines. So using liquefied coal could double current automobile CO_2 emissions. (On an energy to weight basis, coal is less efficient than natural gas and oil. In addition it generates more CO_2 than oil or gas. Coal produces 2.08 lbs of CO_2 per 10,000 Btus compared to 1.17 lbs of CO_2 per 10,000 Btus from burning natural gas). For this reason, few people are seriously proposing to move the US auto fleet to burning liquids from coal. The second option is to use the coal as a source of electricity for electric vehicles or pluggable hybrids (PHEVs). This is an important component of the current government strategy. It means a huge increase in coal consumption.

The Risk of Clean Coal — Carbon Sequestration

A popular idea called *clean coal* proposes to burn coal to generate electricity using a supposedly clean technology called Carbon Sequestration or Carbon Capture and Storage (CSS). For either term, the use of the word Carbon actually means Carbon Dioxide (CO_2), the greenhouse gas generated from fossil fuels that is primarily responsible for climate change. One may wonder how coal can go from something fairly dirty to something clean. It can't. The terminology *clean coal* is a misnomer — nothing is done to the coal to make it clean. The actual meaning is that the noxious products of coal burning are not released into the air as is done at present. Just as many damaging compounds are created when the coal is burned, but presumably they will not be allowed to enter the atmosphere. This is termed *capturing* the CO_2. After capture, noxious chemicals and dangerous CO_2 are somehow removed from the power plant site and placed somewhere.

In theory, the dangerous products can be captured either before combustion or after combustion. If captured before (pre-combustion), the coal will first be gasified, which converts solid coal into gaseous components by applying heat under pressure in the presence of steam. Part of the coal is burned to provide the heat for this process. Most of the coal is chemically broken apart by the heat and pressure, producing a gas called *syngas* composed primarily of hydrogen, carbon monoxide and other gaseous constituents. A few experimental power plants in the US and Europe use a technology called Integrated

Gasification Combined-Cycle (IGCC) to achieve this. Presumably the CO_2 that is removed in this process can be liquefied and pumped into the ground or the ocean. The first experimental plant (referred to as FutureGen) was to be built in Illinois beginning in 2008, hopefully to be completed in 2012. But in January 2008 the government removed its financial support for FutureGen due to complexity and cost overruns.[24] The after combustion option (post combustion) involves removing the CO_2 from the flue gas of a conventional coal, oil or gas burning power plant by a chemical process. A few experimental power plants have begun testing this concept as well. Both pre and post combustion options are essentially research projects. The costs to capture and the percentage of CO_2 that can be captured are unknown. Both processes will require extra energy to capture the CO_2, meaning more coal must be burned to get the same amount of kWh delivered to the consumer.

Of course this leaves the disposition of the captured CO_2 in question. Where will the CO_2 be placed? Since the idea is to keep it out of the atmosphere, obviously that leaves only the land or oceans. Both are being proposed as so called *sinks* for CO_2. There are many suggested ways of doing this. One is to store the CO_2 in old oil reservoirs. This would mean transporting it around the globe as oil is transported today. Another option is to store the CO_2 in old coal mines (which will require transportation of the CO_2 by surface (truck, train or pipelines). Presumably it can also be stored in aquifers deep under the surface of the earth. Finally, burying CO_2 in deep sediment layers of the ocean beneath the water is potentially possible. However, placing it directly into the oceans may change the acidity of the water, and this is less frequently recommended (Fig. 6.5).

The potential amounts to be buried or sequestered are unbelievably large. There will be tens of thousands of power generators around the globe, each providing a steady stream of CO_2 twenty four hours a day, seven days a week, 52 weeks per year, feeding into a huge infrastructure of trains, pipes and ships delivering the gas to places where it will be pumped into the earth. Consider the CO_2 to be sequestered from a single US resident. The average American already generates about 40,000 pounds of CO_2 per year.[25] When his or her energy comes from coal generated electricity (the natural gas having been replaced with coal) he or she will generate even more CO_2. For the US this will mean about 33 billion pounds of CO_2 per day must be captured and buried. And that's just for the US. Probably the better term for Carbon Sequestration

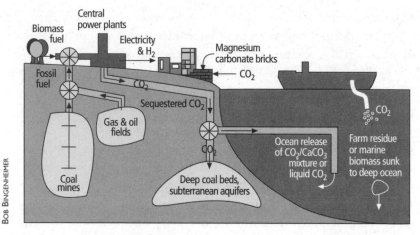

BOB BINGENHEIMER

6.5: *Carbon Sequestration (Carbon Capture and Storage)*

is Carbon Bequestration. A bequest of destruction to future generations may more realistically reflect the dubious nature of this technology. Consider writing this clause into your will: "To my darling children. I, being of unsound mind, leave to you my personal legacy of 3,000,000 pounds of CO_2, and a few hundred thousand pounds of plastic, glass and miscellaneous toxins. Guard them well. And I also leave you a few hundred pounds of plutonium. Be particularly careful with the plutonium. Think of me and remember I loved you even though it may not look that way."

Will sequestered CO_2 stay in place for centuries? How can that be known? So far, only a miniscule amount of CO_2 has been buried for a few years at a site in Norway's Sleipner natural gas field in the North Sea and at the Weyburn Project in Canada just above the US-Canadian border.[26] In the years since those projects began they have pumped about 20 million *tons* of CO_2 deep underground. This is an average of about 15 million *pounds* per day, which is about .0005% of the possible load discussed above. The CO_2 has been stored in these locations for five to 10 years. What is a good test period to determine if it will stay buried for a thousand years? 50 years? Longer? Shorter? Or do its proponents even care? Is it enough that it would stay buried for the lifetime of the scientists proposing it or maybe the lifetimes of their children? How can any scientist with integrity claim that a substance stored in the earth for 10 years in miniscule amounts (monitored principally by oil companies) is justification for storing thousands of times that amount for thousands of years?

What if it were to be released? In 1986 in Cameroon, central Africa, the volcanic crater-lake Nyos released bubbles of CO_2 into the night air. The gas settled around the lake's shore, where it killed 1,800 people and thousands of animals.[27] Could we possibly have disasters thousands of times greater?

Risking the Future of Life

Professor Ian Lowe, emeritus professor, former head of the School of Science at Brisbane's Griffith University, and president of the Australian Conservation Foundation, succinctly described the desperate situation: "Parents in today's western societies are cheating their children by funding their own lifestyles from the future." In a presentation at the Global Mind, Global Soul, Global Action conference at Tamkang University in Taiwan, Professor Lowe emphasized that the future is not some destination but rather something that is being created. "There are many possible futures. We should be trying to establish a future that can be sustained, even if not for the four to five million years that the earth is expected to last."

He then described how one might go about destroying a planet by destroying its future.

"How could we do it? We could start with exponential population growth. Then we could increase the rate of consumption per person. We could base our economy on consumption, stimulating consumption that is not necessary. In fact, we could stimulate consumption by appealing to the seven deadly sins. Then we could deplete significant mineral resources, starting with oil. We could over-use potentially renewable resources like fisheries and forests and groundwater. And we could disrupt the global climate. In the social dimension we could widen inequality between rich and poor, ensuring that the future is less socially stable. And we could replace traditional spirituality by promoting materialism. A visitor from another galaxy would see these strategies as deliberate, would see that we were intelligent and would assume that for some reason we wanted to destroy life on Earth."

Professor Lowe noted that there have only ever been three models of change over time in a species population. These are: (1) increase population over time until it naturally comes into balance and remains in balance; (2) increase population and exceed the sustainable level, collapse, increase again or (3) grossly exceed the resources and collapse. He listed some of the problems with population expansion and then discussed oil: "Our most crucial resource is petroleum. Production will decline, price will increase, we will have to make fundamentally different decisions about personal transport and the provision of food, which are currently predicated on the presumption of cheap transport." Professor Lowe then gave his estimate of peak oil production as 2009 and his estimate of peak natural gas production as 2040, similar to the ASPO estimates.[28]

Americans may well commit to coal and hope Carbon S(B)equestration works. But if this technology fails it is unlikely that the coal plants, once built, will be dismantled. If this is the choice the US makes, then its fate is assured. By this choice the living world could be destroyed in the not so distant future, so that cars can be driven a little while longer and air conditioners can continue to run 24 hours a day. Humanity has been quietly destroying the world by burning fossil fuels. Our willingness to consider risking all life to drive big cars fast and consume more and more shows the level of ignorance and depravity to which Americans have sunk. The hope for a renewable-energy future in which Americans can live just as profligately as they have in recent decades is simply the blissful fantasy of children.

Seven

Corporations, Media and Disinformation

BY PLACING OUR HOPES ON UNSUBSTANTIATED TECHNOLOGICAL CLAIMS for the future we risk a major economic depression as fossil fuel availability declines. Or, as coal burning increases, a climate tipping point might occur. Why are these major crises upon us? King Hubbert predicted peak oil in 1956,[1] environmental degradation was foretold by Rachel Carson in 1962 in her seminal work, *Silent Spring*,[2] climate change warnings were first heard at the 1970 Earth Day,[3] and in 1972 The Club of Rome's *The Limits of Growth* described the planet's limited resources.[4] In 1971 US President Nixon took the first step towards globalization by removing the gold backing of the dollar, beginning the global increase in inequity.[5] These predictions and Nixon's action occurred decades ago, but few Americans understand their implications.

US citizens have more college degrees per capita than any other nation. Yearly expenditures for higher education are approximately $277 billion dollars, almost $1,000 per person in the US.[6] The country produces thousands of magazines, offers hundreds of channels of television and the Internet contains millions of websites. Tens of thousands of new books are published yearly. We view ourselves as well educated and well informed people, yet we are still unaware that our world is in danger. How is it that we are fundamentally ignorant of the seriousness of our situation? Why can't we grasp simple curves like Hubbert's Peak, the "hockey stick" of global warming or the Gini index of inequity? Is it possible that our main providers of information, corporate controlled media, are deliberately misinforming us?

91

Core Ignorance and the Media

There are four main areas that are so critical that peoples' lack of knowledge or understanding could result in a tragedy of unimaginable horrors: militarism, global climate change, peak oil and inequity. With increased militarism the chances of global nuclear war, and possibly the end of human life, increases. As the climate changes due to ever increasing amounts of greenhouse gases, global warming accelerates, threatening all life on earth. Peak oil and the end of cheap abundant fossil fuel bring a realization that the basis of our economic system is not sustainable. And inequity describes the widespread injustice under which the vast majority of the people on the planet live. I contend that the media and the corporations that run it, are to a large extent, to blame for Americans' lack of understanding of these issues.

Militarism

Each year the US grows increasingly stronger in military might. Figure 7.1 shows the annual military expenditures per capita with the US at over $2,000 per person. The US and its main allies — UK, France, Germany and Japan — spend far more than the rest of the world including Russia. Of the $1,100 billion spent on arms in 2005, the US spent about $623 billion and the rest of the world spent about $500 billion.

The Bush Administration withdrew from the Anti-Ballistic Missile Treaty between the US and Russia in 2002 and adopted a policy of preemptive use of nuclear weapons. The country prides itself on its war making capability, and media constantly supports this view. Americans are ignorant of history in general, particularly the types of violence the US uses abroad and the results of that violence.

The current upsurge in the US's use of torture is an example. In 2006, the Dean of West Point, Brigadier General Patrick Finnegan, along with experienced military and FBI interrogators and representatives of Human Rights First, met with the creative team behind the hit Fox Television show "24." 15 million viewers watch "24" each week. Its programs feature counter-terrorism agents who have just 24 hours to foil a terrorist plot. These agent heroes torture suspects so that they divulge critical information. Torture tactics on "24" include drugging and electrocution. General Finnegan asked the team to stop creating torture scenes for their TV show because American soldiers in Iraq were practicing the show's tactics on prisoners.

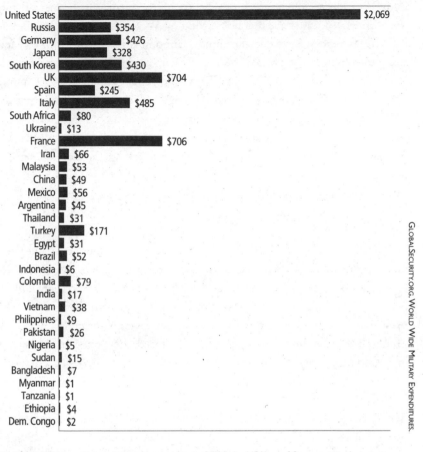

7.1: *World Military Expenditures per capita in 2005 (in US$) — 33 most populous nations containing 80% of world population*

In five seasons of the show, there were sixty-seven torture scenes (more than one per show) according to the Parents Television Council. Before 9/11 there was an average of about four scenes of torture on prime time per year. Since 9/11 that number has increased to more than 100. Formerly villains (such as Nazis) were the ones who tortured. Now American heroes use torture, and it is shown to always be effective. Teachers of interrogation both at West Point and elsewhere state that their students refer to the show "24" when suggesting there are times when torture should be used. One interrogator noted that the idea that torture is needed to combat terrorism is coming from the media, a chilling indictment.[7]

US citizens are often manipulated through the media. In the case of Iraq, the US invaded under the pretense of finding Weapons of Mass Destruction (WMD), a euphemism especially for nuclear bombs. The media, with very few exceptions, religiously printed every comment made by the administration. After the invasion, no WMDs nor chemical or biological agents were found. The *New York Times* later apologized for its bad reporting,[8] yet has continued reporting similar fabrications about Iran's supposed development of nuclear weapons. Armed with tens of thousands of nuclear weapons, the US invaded Iraq on the unproven charge that it was undertaking the development of nuclear weapons, and the same false charge has been used and magnified through the media to justify a future invasion of Iran.

Global Warming

American media have contributed significantly to the almost criminal ignorance of our role in the climate catastrophe facing the planet. Media's major contribution has been the policy they call *a balanced view*. The very small number of climate scientists who deny global warming get the same amount of press space and air time as the large majority of reputable scientists who have predicted it.[9] By this policy, the media confused the public by giving the impression that scientists in general were divided on global warming theory.

Peak Oil

The third example of media induced ignorance is America's unreasonable belief that technology which is based on finite fossil fuel resources can solve any problem that may arise. *The Limits to Growth*, a book much maligned by the media, pointed out that infinite growth is simply not possible in a finite world.[10] This concept strikes hard at the American view of infinite growth based on technical innovation. The initial response from those who hear about peak oil is to immediately ask questions about alternatives. I call these the "what about" questions — what about hydrogen, what about bio-fuels, what about nuclear, tar sands, oil shale, methane hydrates or thermal depolymerization? Most people in the US believe that there is a plethora of available options, so there is no need to worry. Articles and advertisements in our media from the proponents of energy products suggesting that their particular products are clean, safe, locally available and infinite in supply (or at least close to infinite) support this view. So our media reinforces our core fantasy that the

American way of life, based on a cheap and supposedly infinite supply of fossil fuels, can continue indefinitely. Americans do not know that the depletion of fossil fuels will be a death sentence for our wasteful lifestyle.

Inequity

The fourth significant American ignorance is not understanding the allocation of power and wealth in the nation and in the world. The American economic system unfairly favors the rich. For over 230 years, from 1779 on, income distribution remained relatively steady. In the 1970s income and wealth were relatively fairly distributed among all people in the US, within the equity perspective of those times. But in recent decades inequality has grown and is now at its highest level in US history.[11] This growing gap reflects the fundamental competitive philosophy of the nation — few winners and lots of losers. American media rarely publish income and wealth trend lines or charts that show these changes in inequity. Rather, they delight in rags to riches stories. Barbara Ehrenreich, who wrote *Nickel and Dimed* about holding working class jobs, noted that many of her co-workers actually believed they had a chance to attain the American dream of great wealth if they kept at their part time, minimum wage jobs.[12]

Corporatism

US history text books fail to point out that after the American Revolution the new country was not inclined to be completely democratic but rather replaced the English monarchy with an oligarchy. Immediately after the 1776 revolution, only male property holders were allowed to vote. Women, indentured servants and others — the majority of the population — could not vote. It took 144 years until the 1920 ratification of the Nineteenth Amendment gave American women this basic right. Abraham Lincoln wrote in a letter to Colonel William F. Elkins on November 21, 1864.

> We may congratulate ourselves that this cruel war is nearing its end...but I see in the near future a crisis approaching that unnerves me and causes me to tremble for the safety of my country. As a result of the war, corporations have been enthroned and an era of corruption in high places will follow, and the money power of the country will endeavor to prolong

> its reign by working upon the prejudices of the people until all wealth is aggregated in a few hands and the Republic is destroyed. I feel at this moment more anxiety for the safety of my country than ever before, even in the midst of war. God grant that my suspicions may prove groundless.[13]

A similar sentiment was expressed by Henry Adams in 1870.

> The belief is common in America that the day is at hand when corporations ... after having created a system of quiet but irresistible corruption — will ultimately succeed in directing government itself. Under the American form of society, there is no authority capable of effective resistance. ... Nor is this danger confined to America alone. The corporation is in its nature a threat against the popular institutions which are spreading so rapidly over the whole world... and unless some satisfactory solution of the problem can be reached, popular institutions may yet find their very existence endangered.[14]

The US has been moving towards *corporatism* for more than 100 years. Under corporatism industrial and professional corporations exercise political control over people and activities within their jurisdiction.[15] Corporate power in the US has increased over a long period of time. During the first phase from 1820–1900 many state governments gradually revised laws to limit liability for shareholders. Legislatures were primarily responsible for these changes, which included switching from custom charters to general incorporation in the late 1800s. Legislators allowed corporations to have virtual locations so that a corporation could be located anywhere. Corporations were also made infinite so that corporations, unlike humans, can live forever.

Between 1886 and1986 rights that had been given to people in the US Bill of Rights were extended to corporations. The most important judicial event was the Supreme Court decision in the 1886 case of *Santa Clara v. Southern Pacific Railroad*. In this case the Supreme Court declared that corporations were persons and thus protected by the Fourteenth Amendment to the US Constitution. This led to many other legal decisions granting more individual rights to corporations: due process (also in the Fourteenth Amendment) was granted in 1890, due process for federal legislation (part of the Fifth Amendment) was granted in 1893, freedom from unreasonable searches was granted in 1906. Other rights of people that were granted to corporations were: jury trial in a criminal case (Sixth Amendment – 1908), compensation for government takings (Fifth Amendment – 1922), freedom from double jeopardy (Fifth Amendment – 1962), and jury trial in a criminal case (Seventh Amendment – 1970). Various extensions to free speech under the First Amendment were given to corporations by judicial decisions in 1976, 1978 and 1986.[16]

In recent years even more power has been given to corporations.[17] The powers of transnational corporations now exceed the sovereign powers of any particular nation, enabled by international free trade agreements such as NAFTA, GATT, and FTAA. International trade committees, particularly those of the World Trade Organization (WTO) can overrule laws of any nation that limit the powers of transnational corporations.

The history of industrialization is the continuous growth in the power of corporations — a power growing faster than in the past and one that is causing great physical and financial suffering to people everywhere. Just as the aristocracy in earlier times controlled the US economy by its ownership of land resources so do the corporate aristocracies of today control the economy by their ownership of financial resources. Corporatism is also growing in ex-communist nations such as China and Russia. In a comparison with Mexico, China's Gini index of inequality has increased from about 0.28 in 1983 to about 0.48 in 2005 while Mexico's Gini index increased from about 0.42 to 0.47 over the same period.[18]

It may seem surprising and shocking that the shift of political control from party or people to corporate institutional control could have taken place in both democratic and non-democratic societies. One wonders why people in democratic societies like the US vote for politicians who gave their basic rights to these legal entities. It is surely only possible where mass media are controlled by corporations.

Corporatism and the Control of Democracy

The true purpose of corporate media was explained in a seminal work *Taking the Risk Out of Democracy — Corporate Propaganda versus Freedom and Liberty* by Alex Carey.[19] In the book's introduction, Noam Chomsky quotes Carey.

The 20th century has been characterized by three developments of great political significance; the growth of democracy, the growth of corporate power, and the growth of corporate propaganda as a means of protecting corporate power against democracy.[20]

Chomsky lists the media functions Carey identified including

1. Advertising devoted to creation of artificial wants;
2. The huge public relations industry with its goal of diversion to meaningless pursuits and control of the public mind;
3. The increasing concentration of media in fewer people who make it taboo to criticize the contemporary media enterprises.[21]

Carey begins his analysis of media and its relationship to corporatism by noting that business interests are never described overtly as special interests dedicated to protecting their assets. Instead such business interests are linked to national interests. Together they are described with phrases like *freedom of the individual, free enterprise* and the *free market*. In almost every sphere of government and in all political parties in recent decades, the free market has taken precedence over public and community interests. Thus, in a culture with an almost religious worship of the free market, corporatism supported by media dominates.

Carey illustrates US media's use of propaganda with an analysis of the role of the National Association of Manufacturers (NAM) early in the 20th century. A massive propaganda campaign had been initiated against the Germans to prepare Americans for entry into World War I. Because this effort was so successful, NAM began to use wartime propaganda techniques to solve business problems in peacetime. In 1934 NAM initiated a media blitz to counter a drift toward socialism and other liberal ideas. These ideas were popular because ordinary people had become disillusioned with American business during the Great Depression. After WWII media propaganda took up two fundamental themes: identification of the American free enterprise system with family, church, freedom, harmony and democracy, and the identification of government regulation of business with communism, subversion and lack of patriotism. Influenced by this massive public relations effort, the US populace turned more to the political right while Europe was becoming more liberal.

Today, corporate media continues to foster its view of the American dream and the superiority of America — not to strengthen democracy but to foster corporate power. According to Carey, Daniel Boorstin says that the corporate image is the most elaborate and costly constructed image of this age. Boorstin also notes that the rise of image making and its displacement of ideals has come about through the rise of advertising; this has meant not just an increase in untruthfulness but a reshaping of the country's very concept of truth.[22] Carey's work explains the increasing level of ignorance in an increasingly educated but propagandized population.

Education and Corporate Propaganda

Our ignorance should not be blamed on the US educational system but rather on the unacknowledged incessant propaganda from our media. To educate is to provide schooling for, or to train by formal instruction especially in a skill, trade or profession. Propaganda spreads ideas, information or rumors for the purpose of helping or harming an institution, cause or person.[23] For example, it is to an oil corporation's advantage to damage an opposing cause (for example, environmentalism) by funding reports which debunk global warming. This is propaganda. It is the purpose of a university's environmental department to give an objective evaluation of the global warming issue; this is education.

One might say that the purpose of American media is to persuade while the purpose of American education is to inform or teach. Although the US spends 100s of billions of dollars on education annually it also spends 100s of billions of dollars on various forms of advertising, public relations and general media. While the country's educational system is controlled by school districts in local communities, higher educational institutions may not be free of propaganda, particularly if they accept contributions from corporations. Thus, in parallel with its educational system, the US has a propaganda system consisting of advertising, public relations and controlled content which is broadcast through mass media and managed and directed by the richest and most powerful people in the world, the heads of global corporations.

Controlling Democracy Today — Manipulation vs. Reason

In his 2007 book *The Assault on Reason*, Al Gore quotes US Senator Robert Byrd of West Virginia, "Why do reason, logic and truth seem to play a sharply diminished role in the way America now makes important decisions?"[24] Gore notes that even in the face of massive and well-understood evidence to the contrary falsehoods are endemic. Five years after 9/11 about 50% of Americans still believe the falsehood that Saddam Hussein was connected to the attack. Gore also questions why free speech and the free press have failed the nation. He then points out that

> TV is dominated by obsessional programs with celebrities (O.J. Simpson, Michael Jackson, Britney, Paris, etc.).
>
> The Senate is sparsely populated for debates since the members need to be fundraising for expensive TV ads.
>
> The high cost of television ads has radically increased the role of money in politics.
>
> The massive flow of information from TV is in one direction only. Individuals can hear but cannot speak.
>
> Image on TV is everything — ideas play an ever diminishing role.[25]

Gore points out the manipulative power of visual rhetoric and body language in media — far more significant than the logic and reason in what a person says. The control of mass opinions and feelings, initially discovered and used by commercial advertisers, is now being exploited by a "new generation of media Machiavellis" who, using powerful computers and opinion sampling techniques, tailor individual media appeals, further magnifying "the power of propagandistic electronic messaging."[26]

Gore reviews Marshall McLuhan's description of television as a cool medium as opposed to the hot medium of print, hot representing the mental work required in reading. McLuhan recognized that the passivity (coolness) associated with watching TV was at the expense of the activity of the parts of the brain associated with abstract thought and reasoning (heat). Gore quotes from an authoritative global study that concludes Americans now watch television an average of *4 hours and 35 minutes every day* — 90 minutes more than the world average and says, "When you assume eight hours of work a day, six to eight hours of sleep and a couple of hours to bathe, dress, eat and commute, that is almost three-quarters of all the discretionary time the average American has."[27] Gore's analysis of media is well considered and thought provoking.

Time Using Machines

TV and other electronic media are time consuming not time saving. Avner Offer, author of *The Challenge of Affluence*, points out that the time saved in the household due to time *saving* machines (washing machine, vacuum cleaner, water heaters) has just about been canceled out by time *using* machines (TVs, radios, VCRs).[28]

Time *saving* machines tend to reduce or ease physical labor, while time *using* machines provide sensual arousal. Prior to modern machines, the printing press contributed to time use by providing sensual arousal (Avner Offer's term) through novels. Other early arousal time using machines include the gramophone, cinemas and radio. Now sensual arousal comes from CDs, DVDs, Walkmans, iPods, TV, video, computers and the Internet. TV is the most ubiquitous, being instantly available and possibly the least demanding source of arousal — that is, the least mental energy is required to watch it. It is also the cheapest way of averting boredom. Reading, sports and conversation might be cheaper but they require much more mental and physical effort. Of all household pastimes, watching TV requires the lowest level of concentration, alertness, challenge and skill. Thus saving time with an automatic dishwasher and using that time to watch TV is making people less active.

Avner Offer's use of the term sensual arousal has a sexual overtone, and sexuality is fundamental to visual media. Both content and advertising show sexually attractive men and women in a wide range of activities, from a simple ad for hair toner to a drama involving seduction, violence or murder. Thus the American viewing public spends hours per day in a subconscious world of sex and violence. That the United States has the highest per capita rates of most forms of violence should be no surprise.

TV — The Ultimate Time Using Machine

Jerry Mander in his seminal work *Four Arguments for the Elimination of Television* pointed out that most Americans believe that any technology is merely a benign instrument or tool which could be used for good or evil depending on the user. Technology determines its interaction with the world, the way it will be used, the kind of people who use it and to what ends. But TV and other electronic systems are not neutral.[29] TV is a compelling product providing vivid and highly visual experiences of immediate gratification, often substituting for social interaction and as an antidote to feelings of loneliness, as well as a baby sitter for children. TV watching can be addictive. Viewers tend towards habituation, desensitization, satiation and an increasing level of arousal is required to maintain satisfaction. Viewers have no control over what is available to them on TV, what effects it will have on their lives or what advertising will be shown. The effect is to drastically confine all human understanding within a rigid channel, useful for creating pliant consumers.

The Internet — Dr. Jeckle or Mr. Hyde

Americans seem to accept the negative aspects of TV. Heavy watchers are known as *couch potatoes* and people often lament the time they waste. People use the popular descriptor *vegging out* to describe their own TV behavior, affirming the brain scientists who continually report on research that verifies the low level of activity associated with TV watching. But Americans hold a different view toward the Internet, a form of media with a popular mystique and power normally reserved for god-like beings. Presumably sufficient time spent *surfing* could make the viewer omnipotent (all powerful) and omniscient (the quality of having infinite awareness, understanding, and insight). With the Internet one can presumably possess universal or complete knowledge. But a writer cannot obtain information by analyzing tens of thousands of hits on a topic. More often, he or she quickly turns to a set of well written books with a good index. Books are associated with communities of writers, printers, proofreaders and a host of other people with whom the writer interacts. A good book comes from this kind of human interaction between qualified people. Granted there are some websites that provide well written and researched articles and information. Unfortunately, many are not. The Internet may be more of a time using machine than TV. And its usage is not always positive. *HomeNet*, a research project at Carnegie Mellon University, has been studying Internet usage since 1995. Their research shows that greater use of the Internet is associated with declines in the size of participants' social networks, declines in communication within the family and, for teenagers, declines in social support. Greater use of the Internet is associated with increases in loneliness and symptoms of depression. These declines are especially strong during the first years online.[30]

Wasted lives and wasted minds

How can the media be so effective in convincing people to live in ways that are not in their best long term interest? How is it that media can change people's

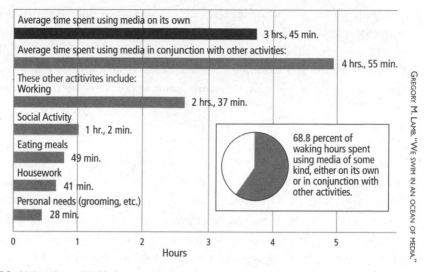

GREGORY M. LAMB, "WE SWIM IN AN OCEAN OF MEDIA."

7.2: *Multitasking with Media*

values, creating a different world view than that of the education system, the culture at large or religions? For this to happen, people must receive massive amounts of information with themes that can be repeated over and over again. Thus a population which immerses itself in media receives an extremely high volume of manipulative data.

The *Christian Science Monitor* noted that Americans use media of some kind for 68.8% of their waking hours (Fig. 7.2).

Another report on media in the lives of 8-18 year olds points out that American young people today spend an average of 6 hours and 21 minutes each day imbibing media, an amount of time equivalent to slightly more than a full-time job (44 hours and 30 minutes a week); 26% of that time young people are using more than one medium at a time (reading and listening to music, for example). Thus they are actually exposed to the equivalent of 8 hours and 33 minutes of media content, concentrated into the 6 hours and 21 minutes. In comparison the average American school age child spends

2 hours and 17 minutes with parents,
1 hour and 25 minutes in physical activity
50 minutes doing homework
32 minutes doing chores. [31]

Spending such a large part of our time consuming or imbibing media is unprecedented in the history of humanity and in fact is unprecedented even in recent history. For the industrialized world, this trend began in the latter half of the 20th century and accelerated in the last few decades. However, in many parts of the world people do not live with media as the dominant influence in their lives.

Media Fantasy

We never experience an actual event unless we are present and participating. Media may claim that they place everyone at the scene, but this is never true. What we see or hear on TV, radio or the Internet is selected and scripted by media experts. The eyes, ears and all the other senses of someone present at the scene would be taking in much more than media recording devices. In fact a person present at the scene might notice that the camera operator was viewing a miniscule part of the actual scene. The camera presumably never lies, but the camera can have a severe case of tunnel vision. Yet this is only the beginning of the story. Video or audio tapes are sent to editors who further reduce the length or size, possibly change the sequence, maybe intersperse comments and add music to create a particular emotional impression. A media editor may even tell the story using a scene from some other event that is more riveting. Then the result is reviewed by management to insure that it supports the policy of the producing organization. Finally the whole piece may be eliminated entirely for business reasons.

The important thing to realize is that we never see the actual events which media present. We see a very tiny snapshot taken out of context which is then modified to create an impression. This is recognized by media terminology like *infotainment* (a television program that presents information as news in a manner intended to be entertaining), *infomercials* and *advertorials* (blends of advertisement, information, editorials and entertainment). Most media productions can be described in those terms. Our need for information about the world is obvious. But adding entertainment, advertisements, editorials and public relations releases changes basic information so that impartial and objective reporting is not possible. The result is always propaganda.

Thus through media we live vicariously, sharing mythical characters' experience through our imaginations or emotions. Our senses are captured in an artificial environment created for the purpose of controlling minds. This media environment consists of sound bytes, billboards and clips from professional writers interspersed with commentaries or brief appearances by a few thousand highly paid celebrities. And tragically, the stories selected appeal to people's base emotions — particularly fear.

Corrupted Values

Advertisements present values and goals that are in conflict with traditional values. They have reversed traditional values by recommending indulgence in the Seven Deadly Sins. In Figure 7.4 the *Traditional Saying* column reflects the values of community, cooperation and conservation while the *Modern Advertisement* column supports selfishness, individualism and consumption.

In these ways the commercial world has systematically corrupted the values of religion and community, restating them to support consumption and greed.

Media Costs

Media and advertising are used to create artificial needs that are then satisfied by corporations' products. This is not an inexpensive undertaking. Americans pay for *free* media by purchasing products from corporations who advertise. Corporate advertising expenses are factored into the price of every product. So our media are not free but subsidized by corporations. Since media's purpose is to deceive, describing it as free is an appropriate tactic. The cost for advertising in the US is about $276 billion per year compared to $284 billion for the rest

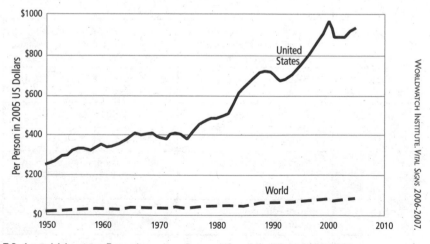

7.3: *Annual Advertising Expenditures per Person, US and the World, 1950-2005*

The Seven Deadly Sins		
The Sin	**Traditional Saying**	**Modern Advertisement**
Pride	Pride goes before a fall	You deserve it; have it your way; you are unique; we do it all for you
Anger	Don't let the sun go down on your anger	Get revenge, kick some butt
Avarice	Don't be greedy	Get rich quick; stock up now; collect them all
Gluttony	Stop eating while you are still hungry	All you can eat; indulge yourself
Lust	Chastity is a virtue	Get lucky
Envy	Envy is a green-eyed monster	You'll be the envy of your friends; don't be left out
Sloth	The early bird gets the worm	Pretend you're working

The Seven Virtues		
The Virtue	**Traditional Saying**	**Modern Advertisement**
Prudence	Look before you leap, study to be wise	Just do it; why wait; act now
Temperance	Moderation in all things	Too much is not enough; get all you can
Justice	Do unto others as you would have them do unto you	Look out for number one; get them before they get you; crush the competition
Fortitude	Be brave, courage is noble	It's not my fault; call us and sue
Faith	Faith is the evidence of things not seen; have faith in God	You can believe in this product; believe only in yourself
Hope	God holds the future	Live for today; hurry before it's too late; get it while you can
Charity	Love your neighbor as yourself	Charity begins at home

ROBERT HARRIS, THE SEVEN DEADLY SINS AND SEVEN VIRTUES IN ADVERTISING.

7.4: *The Seven Deadly Sins and The Seven Virtues*

of the world. On a per capita basis the US spends about $900 per person annually (Fig. 7.3), while the per capita expenditure for the rest of the world is about $50 per person.[32] Corporations also spend massive amounts of money to control the hearts and minds of people and politicians through public relations and lobbying.

Media and Addiction

Food, food additives, alcohol, tobacco and drugs are materials that affect our bodies and our minds. If taken to excess or taken at all, these substances can lead to health problems. All are, or can be, harmful addictions. People become addicted in other ways as well — to gambling, pornography or the OJ Simpson trials to name a few. Mental addictions are analyzed less frequently than physical ones. Mental addiction to media can be as great as a physical addiction. Is it legitimate to say that there is such a thing as media addiction? It appears so — withdrawal from television often leads to anxiety and suffering. The BBC reported that 15% of those surveyed would not give up television for a million pounds. 20% would not give it up at 500,000 pounds, and a third would need a bribe of 100,000 pounds. In 1977 the *Detroit Free Press* offered $500 to 120 families to give up television for one month before it found five who would agree.[33]

The Greek philosopher Plato, the most influential of Socrates' disciples, wrote in *The Republic* a story of people in a cave, chained to face a wall on which they viewed shadows of actual experiences occurring behind them. These shadows were projected on the wall by a continuous fire.[34] Today Plato might replace the cave with a movie theater, the fire with a projector, film replacing the objects which cast shadows and the projected movie on the screen replacing shadows on the cave wall. The important point is that the prisoners in the cave are not seeing reality, but only a shadowy representation of it. In Plato's tale, when people were unchained and shown the real experiences occurring behind them, many refused to believe what they were seeing and wished to return to their habitual viewing of shadows, which had been their reality for such a long time. Do modern Americans spend so much of their time viewing false shadows of reality that they have no wish to see things differently? It might be said that corporations rule us through our addictions to media. To change this we will have to remove ourselves from the electronic cave.

PART II

Eight

Plan C — Curtailment and Community

THE TRIPLE THREATS OF PEAK OIL, climate change and increasing inequity are worsening each year. We are told that China is a threat to US survival because China wants a North American lifestyle. Al Gore's movie *An Inconvenient Truth* suggests that our very survival is at stake from global warming.[1] Jimmy Carter in his book, *Our Endangered Values*, says the greatest challenge we face is the growing chasm between the rich and poor people of the earth.[2] And globalization is like an economic plague injuring billions of people. The handwriting is on the wall — massive change is in the offing — but most people are totally unprepared. Four plans, labeled A, B, C and D, describe the current responses to these threats. The proposal I advocate, Plan C, addresses the energy reductions that are needed in the areas where each person has control: the food we eat, the cars we drive and the houses we live in.

Plan A — Business as Usual

Plan A is the most widely discussed option concerning energy depletion and climate change. It is the growth-oriented paradigm obsessed with scientific technology; this model has driven industrialized societies for 60 years, and much of the rest of the world more recently. Individual self-interest is its underlying philosophy, and one of its key theses is the capitalist doctrine of substitution. Substitution means that the world will never run out of resources because the free market will always find an alternative i.e. technology always finds a solution to every problem. Under this philosophy we treat the natural world as a garbage dump. The free market is successful only because it dumps the refuse, toxins and waste of manufactured goods and services into the air and water as well as on and under the land. Extreme Plan A proponents advocate using anything that will burn to generate energy, regardless of environmental consequences or concern about the availability of resources for our descendents. Proponents of this plan include leaders of most major manufacturing corporations, fossil fuel companies, utility companies and recent presidents of the United States. The fuel sources for Plan A are largely nonrenewable oil, natural gas, coal and uranium. In this plan future non-renewable fuels include lower quality versions of oil extracted from tar sands and oil shale in the US and Canada, and the heavy oils of the Orinoco region of Venezuela. A sizable majority of the US population has put its trust in Plan A and a continuing flow of oil from the Middle East. Some Plan A proponents even believe that humanity has little to do with climate change and global warming.

Plan B — Clean Green Technology

Plan B advocates are content with the status quo, particularly their lifestyle, and hope to simply replace non-renewable energy products with renewable ones.[3] Plan B supporters generally accept the capitalist system with its underlying values of competition and infinite growth. They argue that cleaner technology is available; it just needs to be deployed. Sometimes Plan B advocates suggest that corporations and governments have deliberately held new technologies off the market. Representatives of this group include former US Vice President Al Gore, wilderness organizations and many environmentalists as well as solar, wind and biofuels manufacturers. Mr. Gore, in his film *An Inconvenient Truth*, promotes carbon sequestration as a way to shift the economy to *clean coal*, a concept popular with utility and coal companies.[4] Biofuels are a major component of Plan B and are supported by agribusiness companies such as Arthur Daniels Midland and Cargill, large suppliers of ethanol and biodiesel. The environmental movement is the largest identifiable population that supports some version of Plan B. Although this plan also includes efficiency as a key component, its proponents typically ignore Jevons' Paradox, which says that consumption increases as efficiency improves.[5]

The overriding majority of US citizens believe in either Plan A or Plan B. They share basic consumer values, and their preferred green energy projects sometimes overlap. Plan A and B supporters do not see the need for citizens to take any particular action. They do not hold themselves accountable for the energy crisis and climate change. For them, it is the responsibility of government and corporations to make the necessary changes — *a guilty producer – innocent consumer* perspective.

Plan D — Die Off

Those who endorse Plan D (die off of the race or a drastic population decline) believe it is too late to avoid catastrophe. These people tend to assume there is no viable solution to peak oil and climate change; that economic growth, population and consumption will increase unabated and that humanity can expect economic collapse, chaos, wars and other forms of violence — possibly even mass starvation. Plan D proponents tend to focus on individual and family survival and the need to defend whatever sustainable communities can be formed. Some people dismiss Plan D advocates with flippant remarks or critical labels, but there is reason to take this view seriously, as we may have already passed the carrying capacity of the planet and major population die off is not out of the question. Wars over dwindling fossil fuels, possibly involving nuclear weapons, could occur. The effects of climate change on agriculture, exacerbated by the loss of fossil fuel inputs, could cause widespread hunger and unrest. With our business as usual attitude, Plan D's negative perspective is not unfounded.

Plan C — Curtailment and Community

Plan C assumes that the relatively recent availability of fossil fuel energy (a blip in geological time) has caused a temporary detour in the evolution of humankind. Its view is that fossil fuels have led to a two-century long addictive fascination with oil-based machinery and excessive consumption; and this has led to massive global inequity and potentially catastrophic climate change. Under Plan C, the first priority for society as a whole is to drastically reduce consumption of fossil fuel energy and products derived from fossil fuels. The key action is to *curtail.* That means buying less, using less, wanting less and wasting less. To curtail means to cut back or to downsize. *Curtail* reflects the seriousness of the current situation more than the politically acceptable word *conserve.* Conservation can imply a relatively small reduction in consumption: recycling, buying compact fluorescent lights or maybe a hybrid car. If conservation were used as a synonym for curtailment, it would be appropriate to preface *conservation* with some modifier such as *radical, extreme, deep* or *rapid.* Plan C people are conservers rather than consumers but they view current conservation efforts as insufficient. This plan implies permanent societal change to reduce consumption of dwindling natural resources in order to control and mitigate climate change. It calls for a resurgence of small local communities as the alternative to the American way of life that must be abandoned. And it accepts a reduced standard of living as part of being a global citizen.

Plan C and Thinking Globally

The popular phrase *Think Globally, Act Locally* is catchy, but it's important to consider the context in which the phrase is used. Corporations and media have a way of taking concepts that were developed at a grass roots level and using them to manipulate people. Some commercially promoted global thoughts are meant to stimulate frivolous and largely irrelevant local actions, such as buying stylish clothing and new model cars. Other thoughts — such as choosing between paper and plastic bags — are well-meaning but are relatively ineffectual; they mostly just make us feel better.

Globalization, one widely discussed global thought, is basically a process where large corporations move manufacturing facilities around the world to obtain cheap labor rates while avoiding as much as possible the environmental and labor constraints imposed by elected governments. Globalization contributes to environmental degradation, increasing inequity (the breeding ground of terrorism) and excessive use of energy. A corporation's global thoughts have little to do with the well-being of people anywhere and a lot to do with shareholders' profits. Thus, corporate global thought is largely contrary to the interests of local communities, a key component of Plan C. In terms of corporate globalization, a good local action might be to avoid purchasing goods from international corporations as much as possible.

Thinking globally, Plan C advocates might develop awareness of these topics.

1. Increasing economic inequity
2. Increasing climate deterioration
3. An unsustainable world population
4. Excessive use of declining fossil fuels

Awareness of global economic inequity means knowing that the majority of the world's people are living in poverty and that a significant number are near death from starvation. These are more important global thoughts than, for instance, what country fields the best soccer team or even who should be allowed to join the World Trade Organization. Increasing climate deterioration is simply the result of massive consumption of fossil fuels; and it is fossil fuels that have fueled the growth of globalization. The solution to this is obvious. Population is illustrated in Figure 8.1 which shows the correlation between increasing consumption of fossil fuels and the population explosion which began in 1945. This is the year when the two began to increase in lock step. Declining fossil fuels probably means a lock step decrease in population. Avoiding a too rapid decrease in population is a significant challenge.

A global view should also include a historical perspective. People need to think comprehensively in both space and time. Human beings lived on the earth in a sustainable manner for many millennia. A few centuries ago new sources of non-renewable energy were discovered, starting with coal, followed by oil and natural gas and then by uranium. The standard of living increased rapidly for a very small part of the world's population. And world population began growing rapidly. When cheap and easy fossil fuels became available, the value system of affluent humanity moved from an orientation of community relationships toward the acquisition and consumption of material goods. We were no longer citizens — we became consumers. Plan C brings us back to a focus on community. A needed global thought for today is that we must change from a growing economy to a contracting economy — first because we

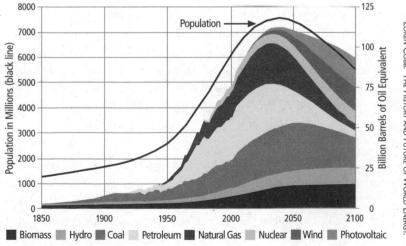

8.1: *World Energy Production and Population*

are running out of fossil fuels and second if we continue to burn the fuels we have, climate chaos will result. Plan C accepts the need to contract, while at the same time offering a new way of living in community where economic success is not the principal motivation of society. It seeks to mitigate the worst of possible suffering from the inevitable decline of fossil fuels and population.

The Psychology of Curtailment

There is a strong psychological resistance to curtailment. To Americans, consuming more products and services is the critical measure of both national and personal success — even freedom. A growing economy means affluence, abundance, success and progress; these are the core values of the current society. Curtailment means the economy stops growing and begins contracting; and a contracting economy means fewer goods and services and more limited choices. For Americans this is the opposite of success — it is failure. Changing this perspective will be extremely difficult. But if we look at the big picture — if we think globally — then we will realize that we have been and still are the major nation causing global climate change. We are living in such a profligate way that we are destroying the habitability of the planet and pushing the poor of the world to the edge of survival. Surely making the planet uninhabitable for everyone is the ultimate failure.

What would it take for us to view success differently? As energy supplies peak, the model of economic development that depends on perpetual growth, increased consumption of fossil fuels and other resources will no longer be viable and will have to be abandoned. If we choose to consume less, is there a way to manage and measure such curtailment in positive terms? Even more importantly, are there models of what curtailment might be like? If we were to curtail to Europe's standard — a 50% cut in energy consumption — our cars would get 42 mpg instead of the American average of 21 mpg. Our average house size would be 1,000 square feet rather than 2,400. Instead of mostly single family homes, many houses would be multi-family — much more common in the rest of the world and a style that uses much fewer resources both in construction and operation. Eating more locally and seasonally would be the norm, as would more public transportation, biking and walking. And most of Europe has national health care and excellent public schools, so social systems need not suffer.

However, even Europe's 50% less is still producing too much CO_2 for the planet. NASA scientist James Hanson says that "the safe upper limit for atmospheric CO_2 is no more than 350 parts per million." He further says we are already past that level.[6] Much deeper cuts are needed to reverse climate change and avoid Plan D. All developed countries will need to make dramatic reductions in their consumption — towards the level of the majority of the world's people — the 85% of the world's population who live on one-seventh the per capita consumption of people in the US. These people have lived much more frugally, within a world of limits, than have the US or Europe. It is not that they chose curtailment as an alternate path; most would prefer to adopt US consumption standards. In reality, many people in the rest of the world are destitute, with minimal access to basic needs. There are two notable exceptions, places which provide adequate food and housing and high levels of education and health care for all citizens. They are the state of Kerala in south India and the country of Cuba.[7] In the past their achievements have been at best curiosities to the rich world, but in the time to come Kerala and Cuba may be invaluable models. Cuba is an especially powerful example, as they already experienced an over 50% cut in fossil fuels in the early 1990's. In spite of the devastating economic collapse that resulted, they maintained basic social services for all sectors of society (particularly important were free health care, education and a basic level of food supplies), and began rebuilding their society on a more agrarian model.

To make the choice to curtail before it is forced upon us (as happened in Cuba) will require an enormous change in our consciousness, both at the government and the personal level. We must go through the kind of transition that Germany did after World War II when faced with the knowledge of its war crimes. People in the US will need to face the damage done by our culture of greedy consumption of limited resources and disregard for other people and future generations.

Giving Up Technology Worship

Plan C advocates are not Luddites, attacking technology and its benefits without discrimination. We are skeptical of the unfounded technology claims that are constantly being sold through the media and are aware of the damage caused by technology and consuming — including the massive amount of greenhouse gases that result. We see the worship of technology as an invisible religion in this historical time — perhaps more fundamental than any other belief. We must question this belief and come to understand and accept that there is no new invention, technology or fuel on the horizon that can bail us out of our current dilemma. Consumption as a way of being is doomed by the realities of peak oil and climate change. As stated earlier, the material prosperity we are used to (and its related technologies) is simply fossil fuel energy prosperity. The US high energy infrastructure is no longer viable. A reduction in energy means a reduction in technology use and our material standard of living. Any attempt to delay this, in the hope of some miracle that will eliminate the need to curtail, simply delays the actions that all must take to consume less. The cost in human suffering will increase the longer action is delayed.

We naturally hope for some breakthrough technology. But most current machine technologies are quite mature. There are research labs with experts that have been addressing energy shortages for many decades. Oil, natural gas and coal companies have massive research staffs. So do governments and universities. In 2006 Research and Development (R&D) for the top six car companies (Toyota, Ford, Daimler-Chrysler, General Motors, Volkswagen, Honda) was $38 billion.[8] These researchers have been seeking new options in the past decades and will continue to do so in the future. But improvements in efficiency over several decades have only been 1.5 to 2% per year.[9] Car design is mature. Cars of the future will have four wheels, an engine with a transmission and a steering wheel. The same holds true for all transportation vehicles. This technological reality has been obscured by much more rapid developments in electronics whose performance and efficiency have improved at a dramatically faster rate. But electronics has little to do with the ordinary consumption of energy for food, homes and cars. A PC that is a hundred times faster than yesterday's or an MP3 player which holds 10,000 songs will not allow us to continue America's high-energy lifestyle. In spite of the advent of the so-called information economy and all the hype about a knowledge society, Americans continue to consume energy at an unprecedented and unsustainable level. New technology has not helped. We are in a quandary. We can either assume a technological fix will be forthcoming and so choose to do nothing, or begin the personal process of changing our lifestyle. This is truly thinking globally: choosing a healthy planet and a sustainable lifestyle over the short-term pleasures of excessive consumption. Innovative use of current technologies and improvements in machine efficiency will aid us, but must be used to support the necessary decision to give up machine fascination and curtail consumption.

Personal Change and Community

We at Community Solutions have long advocated for small local communities, where towns and villages are interspersed with reasonably sized cities — cities far below the scale of the current ones. As noted earlier, there has been a continuous population movement from rural areas to urban cities. The world urban population has increased four fold from 732 million in 1950 to 3.15 billion in 2005. According to a Worldwatch report, in 2007 almost as many people will live in cities as will live in the country. Urbanization has been sold as one of the benefits of economic growth and globalization. Yet the report notes that roughly one billion of the 3.15 billion city dwellers (one in three urbanites) live in slums.[10] The article "The Second Coming of the American Small Town" suggests the suburb is harmful to children and is not the best place to raise them.[11] A Gallup pole conducted in the US in 1989 asked, "What kind of place do you want to live?" The answers were

> Small town – 35%
> Suburb – 24%
> Farm – 22%
> City – 19%.[12]

The 22% who chose *farm* is close to the percentage of the workforce that would be required to provide locally grown organic food under Plan C. Thus many people who have been unable to pursue their preferred vocation of farming could thrive on small farms in the future. Currently only 2% of the US workforce is involved in industrial food production.

Developing small local communities and local economies have become popular concepts among those seeking a new future after peak oil. Books and conferences abound on these topics. But this localization movement must be careful not to fall into the trap of the Plan B option, an option which lacks a perspective of the need for limits and which hopes for a solution to support the current lifestyle. There is a risk that people will focus on municipal use of fossil fuels and ignore their own personal consumption of energy. But the energy consumed by a town or city is small compared to the energy consumption of its citizens. It matters little what kind of bus or police car is purchased. A small town will have a dozen public vehicles but thousands of commuter cars. Big changes must begin with personal change.

Household Sector Personal Consumption

The US is consuming far more energy (and other goods) than any other nation. Most people feel helpless to change this. Planning strategies for change requires that we understand fully what part of the total energy consumed in the US is under the direct control of each individual. For example, each person can choose the type of car to drive and the kind of home in which to live. One could buy a Honda Insight that gets 60 miles per gallon or a GM Hummer that gets 10 mpg. Or one might decide to only use mass transportation. One could buy a large home with lots of glass and appliances or a small home designed to conserve energy — or even live in a small apartment. One can eat manufactured foods and foods that have been transported long distances, some by air, or eat foods that were grown close to home.

To be able to make any change, we must know our current level of consumption. For this reason I have elected to concentrate on the energy associated with housing, personal transportation and food, commonly referred to as the household sector of the economy. To begin, I emphasize again the importance of a global view by repeating this Chapter 2 data in Figure 8.2.

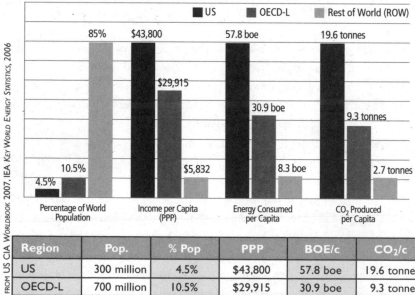

Region	Pop.	% Pop	PPP	BOE/c	CO₂/c
US	300 million	4.5%	$43,800	57.8 boe	19.6 tonne
OECD-L	700 million	10.5%	$29,915	30.9 boe	9.3 tonne
ROW	5,700 million	85.0%	$5,832	8.3 boe	2.7 tonne

8.2: Income, Energy and CO_2 per Capita — US, OECD-L and ROW

Of the US total annual energy consumption of 57.8 boe/c (barrels of oil equivalent per person), housing consumes 15.4 boe/c, personal travel consumes 13.5 boe/c and food consumes 10 boe/c — 67% of the total.[13] This is the amount of energy consumed annually that is under each person's direct control.

Figure 8.3 shows the annual per capita consumption of energy for the world. The left three columns show the total amount of energy used yearly by each citizen of the US, each citizen of the subset of the OECD nations I label OECD-L and by each citizen of all the rest of the world's people (ROW). The four columns on the right break down US energy consumption per capita into food, cars, homes and other. The *other* column includes US energy consumption that is not under each individual's personal control, mostly industry, commercial and education. US food, cars and homes account for about 67% of total US energy consumption. Note that energy consumed by US housing (15.4 boe/c) is almost twice the per capita energy that 85% of the people of the world consume for every purpose.

The categories of *other* and personal energy consumption are not independent of each other. Personal levels of energy consumption help to set corporate and governmental levels of energy consumption. For example, suppose every car owner immediately purchased the most energy efficient car possible — a 50-mpg vehicle — replacing his or her 22 mpg car. If we were to combine these purchases with lowering the speed limit to 45 mph (which would provide a

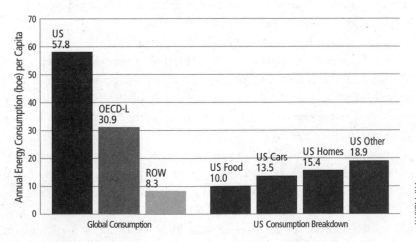

8.3: *Annual Per Capita World Energy Consumption with US Breakdown*

further 25% improvement in fuel economy), per capita gas consumption in the US could drop from 15.4 boe/c to 4-5 boe/c.[14] A 50-mpg car would be half the size of a large car, so the energy expended in its manufacture would be reduced. This reduction would curtail the energy used to mine and smelt iron ore for steel. Driving more slowly would extend the life of highways. Better highway conditions would reduce government energy expenditures for road maintenance.

Similarly, choosing to ride a bus rather than drive a car would impact the transportation industry. Likewise, if we reduce our consumption of household furnishings and a host of other manufactured goods, there will be an impact on the industries that produce those goods. Living in smaller houses would shrink the construction industry, and eating locally grown, unprocessed organic food would shrink the food manufacturing industry and its heavy fossil fuel use. I don't think we can expect government and industry to lead in reducing. A personal reduction in consumption may, in fact, be the only way to shrink government and reduce the power of corporations. People cannot now vote on products that are made, and energy-intensive products mean more corporate revenue and more taxes for government so there will always be powerful forces that counter any attempts at conservation or curtailment. Simply put, by concentrating on the areas within our control and reducing what we consume for food, transportation and housing, we will cause a corresponding reduction in the industrial sector of our society. A commitment to *walking lightly on the earth* could lead to a saner life, with a focus on family, friends and community instead of wealth, consumption and deal-making.

In a few generations, total availability of fossil fuels may be much less than 5 boe per person on the planet — far less than the current US annual per person consumption of 57.8 boe. Yet the vast majority of people in the US are unaware of the magnitude of changes they can make or of the huge disparity of energy consumption between the US and the rest of the world. Nor have we given any consideration to the implications of declining fossil fuels for other people or even for our children. Because of climate change, the long term consumption reductions necessary in the US are not in the range of 5-10% or even 20-30%, but in the range of 70-80%! How can a US citizen continue consuming at the current level in light of this information? Radical management of fossil fuel resources, for an order of magnitude reduction, is the long term requirement. But since North Americans cannot count on the government and corporations, we must begin by focusing on the energy consuming categories where we have personal control.

Plan C and Food

In the local, high-labor form of agriculture which was practiced for centuries and is still practiced in many parts of the world, one Calorie of labor produced more than one Calorie of food. David Pimentel points out that we now require ten fossil fuel Calories for one food Calorie requiring each person to consume an average of ten boe annually for food.[15] Other research shows that the US spends 17% of its total energy on food,[16] which is also ten boe/c per year for food. This is not sustainable and we must change. Six steps to begin that change are:

1. *Eat less.* Pimentel notes that the average person in the US consumes 2,200 pounds of food in a year, which provides about 3,600 Calories per day. However, humans only need about 2,500 Calories per day, so US food consumption could be reduced by one-third.[17] A side benefit of eating less would be better health. Overeating leads to obesity which can lead to a variety of other diseases. The costly US medical system treats many diseases that are caused by a fossil fuel-rich lifestyle. In a contracting economy, maintaining good health will reduce dependence on expensive medical care.

2. *Change our diet.* This means eliminating foods that are very energy-intensive. Good examples are beverages and snack foods which use inordinately high amounts of fossil fuel in their manufacture. Avoid fast foods and pre-packaged, highly processed foods. The manufactured food industry also contributes to high fuel costs for refrigeration since the North American lifestyle requires that liquids be chilled and food kept frozen. Consider 100 million refrigerators connected to thousands of power plants spewing CO_2 into the atmosphere just to keep hundreds of millions of cans of soft drinks or beer at a constant low temperature! Food corporations play several significant roles in our health. Large food manufacturers can provide extremely dangerous products. Part of wise purchasing is to determine the corporations behind the brands, examine their actions and motivations and purchase accordingly.

3. *Reduce meat consumption* — Meat production creates high amounts of greenhouse gases, so reducing both the volume eaten and eating meat raised in a

different way is important. The consumption of meat per capita in developed countries is almost three times the consumption in the developing world.[18] Unfortunately, the developing world, following our example, has doubled its per capita meat consumption since 1990, leading to more fossil fuel consumption. An industrial meat-based diet takes twice as many fossil fuel Calories as a plant-based one. However, this does not mean the complete elimination of meat. Meat can be provided without using high-energy feeds like corn and soybean meal. Locally grown meats using natural forage are not energy-intensive and are better for our health.[19]

4. *Purchase local organic food.* Buy food produced by local organic producers to the maximum extent possible. Joining a Community Supported Agriculture (CSA) group is important. There are three benefits. First, you are supporting local production and that means less fossil fuel is used to transport your food. Second, CSAs help to convert agriculture from a corporate-based, high-energy consuming model to a more efficient one. Third, CSAs support new farmers, in many cases young ones desiring a farming career. Buying organic food raised locally offers a major reduction in fossil fuel consumption.

5. *Preserve and store food.* Canning or drying reduces the energy used to keep products frozen for months in commercial storage. Combining this with buying local produce for winter storage (like winter squash, onions and carrots), will support local food production rather than buying food grown hundreds of miles away. Preserving and storing your own local food further reduces dependence on large corporations and helps develop local food security. It also allows you to begin to participate personally in how food gets to your table. Learning to can and preserve is easier than learning to farm.

6. *Create a garden and/or a henhouse.* Americans are not as far from the soil as is popularly assumed. Gardening, even if for flowers and not food, is a pastime many people enjoy. Producing your own food or keeping a few hens allows you to actually experience the miracle of food growing on the land. Start small and find what it takes to make a piece of your lawn grow organic tomatoes, or some other vegetable you love. Cuba is a good example. When food and fertilizer shipments stopped, they turned to composting and backyard gardens. By doing this, the people themselves kept starvation at

bay as their economy recovered. It is important to raise our consciousness about food production and counter the ignorance that currently colors the US view of nature and its bounty.

In short, people need to eat differently — not just for the planet but also for health reasons — particularly if medical costs continue to rise. We can eat less and reduce meat consumption of industrial animal products. We can buy locally, eat locally and store locally grown produce. We can avoid manufactured and pre-packaged goods to the fullest extent possible. Finally we can replace our fossil fuel intensive lawn with a back- or front-yard garden.

Plan C and Transportation

Thinking out of the box is a mantra of the techno-fix society, but getting too far outside the box is not popular. Every innovative proposal relative to the car is acceptable for discussion except getting rid of it. Owning a private car is a core American value; some would say the car is an American addiction. The US has 5% of the world's population, and 25% of the cars. But US citizens use 44% of the gasoline.[20] The style of private transportation is a major issue in the United States. US manufacturers make large cars in their native land but offer complete lines of small efficient cars to other countries. Americans think that new technology (such as fuel cells, hybrids, electric vehicles or combinations like pluggable hybrids) will be available soon. This rationalization lets consumers continue to buy wasteful cars while lambasting auto companies for making them. At the same time, television's nightly news extols high performance hybrids that get only 24 miles per gallon! There is little political interest in change. The energy bill passed by Congress in December 2007 mandated a mere 40% improvement, which only brings us to 35 mpg.[21]

A step each of us can take is to change to an efficient car — whether new or used — at the earliest opportunity. Hybrid prices and limited availability cannot be used as an excuse; there are many small cars available and more are being introduced every year. These small cars such as the Honda Civic VX (made from 1992 through 1995, which averaged over 40 mpg) or the 60-mpg Honda Insight have been available for a long time. Unfortunately these particular cars are no longer marketed because of lack of customer interest.

The second step is to share rides wherever possible. In 2001, the average trip in the US carried 1.63 persons, including the driver.[22] Increasing the number of people in a car directly reduces energy consumed and also congestion. By adopting sharing as a value, the huge reduction in energy consumption needed could be quickly achieved. Driving less and more slowly as well as bicycling and walking as much as possible are also important. Developing the Smart Jitney system described in Chapter 11 could reduce energy consumption for automobiles by the 80% needed to help stop climate change.

Plan C and Housing

Like everything in the US since World War II, the *bigger is better* value system has affected housing. In 1950 the average new house size was approximately 1,000 square feet; today it is about 2,400 square feet. At the same time the average family size has decreased from about 3.7 to 2.6 people. Thus the average square feet per person has increased from 270 square feet to 815 square feet, a factor of three times.[23] Style changes have raised the average ceiling height and added more windows, further increasing energy consumption. New appliances have been added to the household, increasing fuel consumed in operating the home. Even though improvements in efficiency have occurred in building structures, in heating and cooling systems as well as in appliances, energy consumption has continued to increase.

The first energy saving step is to live in a smaller space. Smaller homes, particularly multi-family units, use less energy to maintain the same level of heating and cooling. Like food (eat less) and cars (drive smaller cars shorter distances, or walk and bike), living in a smaller space is not an easy change. Each person must begin reducing consumption as she or he sees fit. As the average home lasts more than 60 years, it will take a very long time to convert to more efficient buildings. Some people may be able to simply build a new, smaller, more efficient dwelling. Major home manufacturers do not focus on providing such homes, which means a custom home might be required. It should be super efficient and small.

To date, most so-called green residences are very expensive, one-of-a-kind, architect-designed homes. Green building, like new technology for cars, obscures the fact that it is not technology but personal will that is needed to bring about change. Like our cars, our homes are too big. The cars get lousy gas mileage, and houses are too poorly insulated for today's energy reduction requirements. But new buildings alone cannot provide the energy savings required to stop global warming. A more important need is for retrofits of existing homes and buildings to dramatically reduce energy use for homes by 80% using the German Passive House techniques. This may call for another New Deal as the cost to do this nationwide will be massive.

Values and Actions for the Future

A basic societal transformation is needed. At present the US is choosing war and the use of military power to continue consuming fossil fuels. To reduce the threat of resource conflicts and save ourselves and the planet, the US needs to change its three principal values of competing, hoarding and consuming to values of cooperating, sharing and conserving (or curtailing). These latter values are easier to implement in small local communities where people know each other and have a history of working together. To usefully *think globally, act locally* Americans must cooperate both at home and abroad in finding just and equitable solutions to the challenges of peak oil, climate change and inequity. By thinking this way, we can choose to bring life systems on the planet back into balance so that humanity and other species can survive. The first steps are personal ones — changing the American way of life to one that uses as little energy as possible, keeping in mind the welfare of our children and generations to come.

Post-Peak — Change Starts with Us

I HAVE PREVIOUSLY COMPARED ENERGY CONSUMPTION, income and CO_2 generation between the rich and poor world, pointing out that the average American consumes about seven times the energy and generates about seven times the CO_2 of the average person in the Rest of the World.[1] My next step is to analyze energy consumption and CO_2 generation at the personal level. Many individuals and groups are beginning to understand that peak oil offers a unifying perspective on war, inequity and pollution. It is important for such people to make the personal changes needed to live in a post peak oil world, providing authentic leadership for those who will follow. These visionaries can model ways to live on a severely reduced energy budget.

Energy availability and consumption present complex problems. It is not easy to understand as it is a massive subject and complicated by many differing opinions and ideas. Often it is difficult to decide what to do. Should one recycle plastic bags? Is changing light bulbs really a good idea? Is burning wood the right choice? We need new skills to wisely formulate responses to the energy crisis. These skills include thinking numerically about energy, understanding per capita analysis and grasping the difference between embodied energy and operating energy.

Numeracy Skills

Many people lack the ability to understand the numbers that measure energy and thus can't grasp what the figures imply. This makes it hard for people to understand the significance of peak oil and climate change. Lester Milbrath says, "We used to think a person was educated if he was literate. We later came to see that mere literacy was insufficient, people also need numeracy. We should expect people to develop the ability to handle numbers and the habit of demanding them."[2] More recently, Edward Schreyer said, "To be a responsible citizen in a world where nonrenewable fossil fuels are put to ever increasing and 'ever faster track' depletion requires that ultimately citizens band together to demand reanalysis and redirection. We used to say that good citizenship requires *literacy* and that democracy requires a literate population. That remains true but it becomes obvious that to understand energy and environmental sustainability in this Modern Era now also requires a pervasive *numeracy*."[3]

Adding to our difficulty and confusion is manipulation of data by special interest groups. For example, consider responses to the now well known Association for the Study of Peak Oil (ASPO) curve (Chapter 1 Figure 3) which illustrates the volumes of oil consumed in the past and shows projected future consumption diminishing. Frequently economists counter this chart with statements such as, "This is ridiculous. We are not running out of oil. We have enough oil to last 30 years at today's rate of consumption." A person skilled in numeracy will quickly see that the ASPO chart and the economist's response are not contradictory, understanding that both parties concur on the amount of oil remaining. But the economist is putting a positive spin on an agreed-upon fact to counter ASPO's warning of a peak in production. ASPO has never said that we are running out of oil.

Understanding critical numbers is a prerequisite for any major change. To begin, we can study how we allocate and use energy, so that our energy decisions are based on good accounting principles. We need to understand our energy budget (what we are consuming) and then determine how to reduce it. Millions of people have gone through a similar process with their financial budget after an unexpected layoff or accident that stopped or reduced the family income. In countries like Argentina and Cuba that have gone through financial collapse, the whole society has made such readjustments.

Using Per Capita Numbers

It's important to learn per capita calculations for energy consumption. Without a per capita perspective it's difficult to understand the implications of peak oil personally. Our leaders sometimes take advantage of Americans' ignorance. We are informed that China now uses more energy than Japan. But China has ten times the population of Japan! The average Chinese citizen actually uses ⅓ the energy of the average Japanese citizen.[4] As this example shows, until we are able to think clearly on a per capita basis and ask for the numerical data, the significance of worldwide energy problems may elude us.

Using per capita analysis, we can make clear comparisons concerning consumption. This understanding is vital in our effort to find ways to reduce the US's excessive use of fossil fuels. Many of the ways we have of talking about energy stir up emotions but leave us uncertain about the implications. For example, a recent article noted that changing a particular way of building would save enough wood to build a picket fence across the country and back. This is colorful but useless information. A more meaningful comparison would note that the change in the building process would reduce the wood used by each person in the US each year by a certain percentage.

An example worth studying is the per capita consumption of minerals and fuels in the US. Figure 9.1 shows the minerals that an American uses during his or her lifetime. Adding up these numbers and dividing by the average US life span shows that a citizen of the US consumes 47,769 pounds of minerals and fuels each year.[5] This includes coal (7,442 lbs), oil (7,544 lbs), natural gas (7,323 lbs), cement (965 lbs), iron ore (420 lbs) and clays (263 lbs). The total weight of the three fossil fuels consumed per person each year is 22,309 pounds. For comparison, US annual food consumption is only 2,200 lbs per

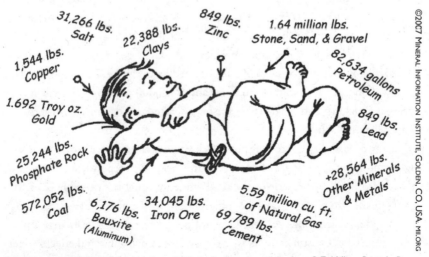

9.1: *American Lifetime Consumption of Minerals, Metals and Fuels – 3.7 Million Pounds Per Capita*

person. These figures show dramatically what is needed to maintain an afflu-ent American lifestyle. A citizen of Bangladesh annually consumes $1/46^{th}$ the energy that a US citizen consumes.[6] Yet that nation's people survive on this limited amount, living a simpler, more sustainable lifestyle that is easier on the earth. In fact, most of the people in the world live in a simpler manner, much less dependent on fossil fuels, than US citizens.

Pollution Numeracy

We Americans consume an enormous amount of materials — but we gener-ate even more waste. In his 1997 book *GeoDestinies*, Walter Youngquist noted, "The child from birth to death will generate 13 tons of waste paper, 10,355 tons of waste water, 2.5 tons of waste oil and solvents, 3 tons of waste metals, and 3 tons of waste glass. From manufacturing processes, mining and agricul-ture used to support this individual, there will be 83 tons of hazardous waste, 419 tons from mining (not including coal mining), 197 tons from manufactur-ing in general, 1,418 tons of carbon dioxide, and 19 tons of carbon monoxide. Consumption of materials during a lifetime will include 1,870 barrels of oil, and 260 pounds of pesticides used to produce the food to sustain the individ-ual."[7] Using this slightly dated information and converting the data to pounds per year (assuming a life span of 77.3 years) we arrive at the following amounts of waste materials per US citizen per year: carbon dioxide (36,668 lbs), man-ufacturing general (5,097 lbs), hazardous waste (2,147 lbs), carbon monoxide (492 lbs), paper (336 lbs), waste metals (78 lbs), glass (78 lbs), and waste oil/solvent (65 lbs). Note that the US 2007 CO_2 generation per capita of 43,232 lbs is well above the 36,668 lbs derived from the 1997 Youngquist data. The volume of these waste materials (about 50,000 pounds per person each year) is shocking, and the invisible waste generated in a gaseous form is threat-ening life on earth.

Lack of visibility contributes to a lack of awareness; many are unwittingly ignorant about the impact of their consumption. We respond to a plastic bag (made from oil) by the side of the road while ignoring the invisible emissions (also made from oil) from the tailpipe of our vehicle. The US Energy Information Agency has warned, "One important category of costs that is often not reflected in consumers' bills is energy-related environmental effects. These unwanted effects can be thought of as the tail end of the energy cycle, which begins with extraction and processing of fuels (or gathering of wind or solar energy), proceeds with conversion to useful forms by means of petroleum refining, electricity generation, and other processes, and then concludes with distribution to, and consumption by, end-users. Once the energy has rendered the services for which it is consumed, all that is left are the byproducts of energy use, i.e., waste heat, mine tailings, sulfur dioxide and carbon dioxide gases, spent nuclear fuel, and many others. ..."[8]

Our *out-of-sight out-of-mind* system of solid waste disposal helps people ignore the massive burden our lifestyle places on the environment. Solid waste is at least temporarily visible before it is hauled away. Gaseous pollution, on the other hand, is also a product of the average North American's lifestyle, but it is invisible and thus very easy to discount. Yet gaseous pollution is extremely dangerous, leading to a possible climate cataclysm. When North Americans burn coal, natural gas or oil to generate electrical power or use oil as fuel for transport, CO_2 (carbon dioxide, which causes global warming) and other pollutants enter the atmosphere. For every pound of fossil fuel burned, between two to three pounds of CO_2 is created and spreads into the environment.[9]

Americans tend to feel virtuous about recycling their garbage. In her book *Garbage Land*, Elizabeth Royte explains, "Of all the waste generated in the United States — including mining and agricultural waste, oil and gas waste, food processing residues, construction and demolition debris, hazardous waste, incinerator ash, cement-kiln dust, and other categories too rarefied to describe — municipal solid waste represented a mere two percent."[10] She points out that the average person in the US throws out 4.3 pounds per day of municipal solid waste (1,570 lbs per year). She notes that only 27% of the 1,570 pounds — 423 pounds (less than 1% of all the annual waste per person) — is recycled.[11] But the 1,570 pounds of trash per year per person is miniscule compared to the approximately 43,000 pounds of CO_2 per year per person generated from burning fossil fuels in the process of heating and cooling homes, driving cars and other fossil fuel uses in the US.

Americans spend a lot of time and energy arguing about the merits of paper versus plastic bags and what kinds of containers should go in what recycling bins, as if this was the most pressing environmental issue. Big as the post consumer solid waste problem is, it is insignificant compared to pollution, toxins and hazardous waste from manufacturing of everyday products. These are usually unseen or, as noted, if seen for a while they are quickly buried in landfills. North Americans need to learn to weigh the embodied energy costs of products including the total energy cost of recycling. Today recycling simply eases our consciences as we continue consuming.

Embodied Energy and Operating Energy

Embodied energy plus operating energy equals the total energy cost of an object or a material over its lifetime. Understanding the difference between the two is important in order to make wise choices about energy use. Simply put, embodied energy is the amount of energy required in all phases of the production of a material or product — its energy cost. This includes extraction and refinement of raw materials, transportation, manufacturing, installation and later disposal. Though fairly simple in concept, the actual quantification of embodied energy is an inexact and challenging science with many complex variables. Nevertheless, it is important that the embodied energy factor become part of our decision making.

MATERIAL	EMBODIED ENERGY		MATERIAL	EMBODIED ENERGY	
	MJ/kg	MJ/m³		MJ/kg	MJ/m³
Aggregate	0.10	150	Glass	15.9	37,550
Straw bale	0.24	31	Fiberglass insulation	30.3	970
Soil-cement	0.42	819			
Stone (local)	0.79	2,030	Steel	32.0	251,200
Concrete block	0.94	2,350	Zinc	51.0	371,280
Concrete (300 Mpa)	1.3	3,180	Brass	62.0	519,560
Concrete precast	2.0	2,780	PVC	70.0	93,620
Lumber	2.5	1,380	Copper	70.6	631,164
Brick	2.5	5,170	Paint	93.3	117,500
Cellulose insulation	3.3	112	Linoleum	116.0	150,930
Gypsum wallboard	6.1	5,890	Polystyrene insulation	117.0	3,770
Particle board	8.0	4,400			
Aluminum (recycled)	8.1	21,870	Carpet (synthetic)	148.0	84,900
Steel (recycled)	8.9	37,210			
Shingles (asphalt)	9.0	4,930	Aluminum	227.0	515,700
Plywood	10.4	5,720	NOTE: Embodied energy values based on several international sources — local values may vary.		
Mineral wool insulation	14.6	139			

Canadian Architect: Measures of Sustainability — Embodied Energy. canadianarchitect.com/

9-2: *Building Material Embodied Energy by Weight and Volume in Megajoules (MJ)*

Some materials need to be measured in one way and others in a different way when calculating embodied energy. For example, minerals are normally sold by weight while lumber is sold by volume. Figure 9.2 shows the embodied energy in a variety of materials measured both in millions of joules per kilograms (weight) and millions of joules per cubic meter (volume).

Operating energy is the energy used over the lifetime of a material or product after it is manufactured. If product A requires 20 units of energy to make (its embodied energy) and uses 6 units of operating energy per year over its projected 10 year life, its lifetime energy cost will be 80 units (6 times 10 plus 20). If product B requires 25 units of embodied energy and does the same job for 10 years on 3 units of operating energy per year its lifetime energy cost will be 55 units (3 times 10 plus 25). So even though product A has less embodied energy when compared to product B, the total energy use over its lifetime is much greater than product B. Thus, product B would use less total energy.

Later in this chapter we determine the amount of embodied energy for a car — about $\frac{1}{6}^{th}$ of the total energy used by that car during its lifetime. Buildings also have an embodied energy cost as well as operating energy costs. And, as in the case of a car, the embodied energy cost of constructing a building is small compared to its operating energy cost. Figure 9.3 shows that the

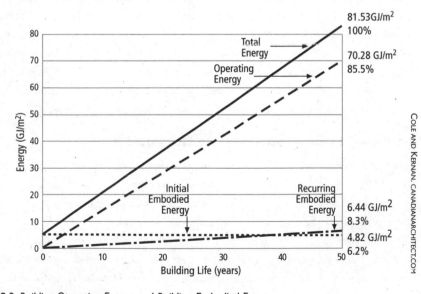

9.3: *Building Operating Energy and Building Embodied Energy*

embodied energy cost of construction, remodeling and maintenance is about 15% of the total energy consumed by a building in its lifetime. Other sources suggest that 10% is a more reasonable figure for residential buildings. I use the figure of 14% (see chapter 10 for details).

Unfortunately we are all too often unaware of the implications of numerical calculations as the authors of one report note: "While the cost of the [operating] energy used in our typical houses is about 10 times the energy used in the structure, maintenance and demolition, the present value of *annual* energy bills over the life of these virtual houses represents only 13-15% of the cost of the structure. As a consequence there is resistance to spending large sums for better energy efficiency in order to lower the environmental burden. In effect, the low cost of energy is a major factor contributing to its use."[12]

Food embodied energy increased with industrialization and manufacturing, just as did transportation, housing and the many products and services the modern era provides. Interestingly, some of our modern energy intensive food products are not as healthy for us as those that use less or no fossil fuel. Modern agribusiness uses excessive amounts of energy, as will be discussed more in chapters 12 and 13. It requires 10 fossil fuel Calories to provide one food Calorie. (A Calorie is a measure of a less well known form of embodied energy.) Unfortunately in our culture people have learned to calculate payback time in money so that we reject more efficient products (which typically are more expensive) as too costly if that payback time exceeds what we expect from investments. Some people can't afford the up-front cost to buy more energy-efficient products unless government lends a hand. But government has been promoting growth (not conservation), whatever the cost. This will likely change as peak oil boosts the costs of fuel and agricultural additives.

Personal Consumption — The Bottom Line

Let's consider an average American's daily activities and energy use in some detail.[13] For simplicity I will use she, but our average citizen could as easily be a man. Starting with the alarm from a coal-powered electric clock, our average person turns off the coal-powered electric blanket, turns on the coal-powered light and goes to the bathroom where the use of the sink and toilet trigger the actions of coal-powered electrical pumps that move water and sewage into and out of coal-powered energy-intensive treatment plants. Possibly she adjusts the thermostat upward a bit, and in the basement a furnace begins burning natural gas or baseboard electric heaters draw energy from the mostly coal-fired power grid. Taking a shower will trigger burning natural gas or coal depending on whether the house has a gas or electric hot water heater. If it is summer our householder may adjust the air conditioner, causing puffs of coal CO_2 from some remote power plant to enter the atmosphere.

Next she opens the kitchen cabinets and refrigerator and brings out some food. While she slept and while she was at work, the refrigerator was constantly turning itself on and off, each time drawing amps from the electric power grid. As she turns on the kitchen range to cook breakfast, natural gas from buried pipes which are part of the country's natural gas grid or electricity from a coal or nuclear powered electricity generating plant cooks her meal. As she eats she might consider that on average, each food morsel traveled 1,500 miles in diesel-powered trucks before reaching her plate. If she reads food labels while she eats and adds up the Calories she consumes, she could multiply that figure by 10 to know how many Calories of natural gas, coal and oil were consumed to produce and deliver the meal. Comparing her oatmeal to bacon, she could see that producing the bacon took many more fossil fuel Calories. After breakfast our average person might use the electricity-driven garbage disposal and dishwasher to clean up the kitchen before she steps into her car and drives to work, leaving the furnace, refrigerator, water heater and possibly some lights on — consuming electricity while she is gone. Small heaters in her TVs and other appliances will continue running all day to make sure there is no delay when she next turns on the machine. If she has a typical car and drives the typical distance, by the time she goes to bed that night she will have burned three gallons of gasoline. As she enters her workplace she may begin to operate her tools of work — personal computers for some, saws and welders for others — mostly powered by coal-produced electricity. In most office environments, heating and air conditioning keep the building at a constant temperature day and night. Each person at their workstation or in their office (most with a computer) sits beneath a bank of fluorescent lights, drawing power constantly from the electrical grid.

Throughout the day we use energy to provide materials for our standard of living: the car, the house with its appliances, the airplane on which we fly to conferences, the hundreds of millions of computers that manage the nation's enterprises. Other people in the world are going about their daily business as well — in Europe, Asia, Africa and Latin America. Each person will do the same thing — rise up, eat, go to work, return home — and each will use different amounts of material and their energy use will vary tremendously. Some will ride in cars, others on buses or trains, still others on bicycles and many will walk. The quantity of energy consumed for ordinary life is dramatically different. At the end of the day the average US worker will have burned seven gallons of oil equivalent while the average Bangladesh citizen will have used two cups.[14]

Personal Choice and Boe

Ultimately there is little energy use that does not come down to the individual, either using energy directly or via products that are made from or use fossil fuels. On average, people in the US spend most of the day (90%) in buildings or in cars, both of which are heavy energy users.[15] Industries and businesses make cars and buildings and provide the appliances (more energy consuming machines) and furnishings for the buildings. By looking at our personal way of living, we will be able to begin to understand energy flows, how energy is being expended and what has to be done to use less. The next step in this process is to convert the different types of energy into their equivalent in barrels of oil. This is called boe for *barrels of oil equivalent.*

Boe and Food

According to Cornell researcher Dr. David Pimentel, the average person in the US consumes 2,200 pounds of food per year; this provides 3,800 Calories per day or 1,387,000 Calories per year.[16] Since 10 Calories of fossil fuels provide only one Calorie of food, 13,870,000 fossil fuel Calories are used per year to produce the food for one person.[17] A gallon of gasoline contains 31,000 Calories.[18] Dividing personal Calories used per year by the Calories per gallon gives 447 gallons of gasoline (or the fossil fuel equivalent). In barrels, 447 gallons is about 10 barrels of oil equivalent (boe). Thus our food energy budget is about 17% of the 57.8 boe each person in the US uses yearly, or 10 boe/c. This detailed analysis indicates that changing what we eat could reduce the energy used in agriculture and food production. This could provide significant energy savings. The energy used is not just on the farm but also in the manufacturing and distribution networks. Dale Pfeiffer has analyzed the allocation of fossil fuels in the different components of the total food system in detail.[19] Folke Gunther, Swedish energy researcher, has modeled a program for reducing energy inputs in agriculture by a factor of ten.[20] Considering that fossil fuels are finite and that it currently takes ten fossil fuel Calories for one food Calorie, then Gunther's 90% reduction is the ultimate requirement for sustainability.

Boe and Transportation

The private automobile is the largest single energy-using machine in our energy budget. There are over 800 million cars, trucks and busses in the world.[21] There are 217 million cars and personal trucks in the US.[22] Worldwide, 75 million new cars (or car equivalent units — CEUs) are built each year, 20 million as replacements and 55 million as new additions to the world passenger vehicle fleet. The growth of automobile fuel consumption worldwide for CEUs has been about 8% annually. The CO_2 produced by America's cars and CEUs is 45% of the total automotive CO_2 generated worldwide.[23]

The average vehicle occupancy in the US is 1.63 persons per vehicle per trip. Car occupancy is 1.58 and van occupancy rates are slightly better at 2.2 persons per trip.[24] In general US citizens have chosen to drive large cars, most of the time alone. A great quantity of fuel is wasted when driving vehicles that could contain more passengers. Unfortunately the average occupancy is decreasing.[25] In 1950 each person traveled 3,029 miles while in 2005 they traveled 10,087 miles.[26] Today, each car (not passenger) in the US travels an average of 12,000 miles per year, while every person (not car) travels an average of 17,000 miles per year.

The average material consumption for the manufacture of one domestic automobile made in 2004 included: various kinds of steel (1,859 lbs.), other metals including iron (308 lbs) and aluminum (289 lbs), other materials including plastic and plastic composites (257.5 lbs), fluids and lubricants (198 lbs), rubber (152 lbs), glass (99.5 lbs), copper and brass (51.5 lbs), powder metal parts (41.5 lbs), magnesium parts (10 lbs), zinc die castings (8.5 lbs) and other materials (133 lbs) for a total weight of 3,391 pounds.[27]

The 217 million cars and light trucks in the US use 9,100,200 boe daily, which equates to an annual 11.1 boe per capita.[28] Manufacturing a car consumes about 18% of the lifetime energy use of the vehicle (assuming a 13-year life span).[29] Combining manufacturing (embodied) energy with per capita operating energy cost of a car gives a total yearly energy cost of 13.5 boe per car per person in the US.

Hybrid sales are growing but at a relatively small rate. Sales for all hybrids in 2007 climbed 38% to almost 350,000 units. This represented 2.15% of the new vehicle market-share for the year. There are less than 2 million hybrids on the world's roads, about .25% of the 800 million cars in the world. Considering the seriousness of the climate situation this amount is minuscule.[30] The highest mileage car (60 mpg) in the US, the hybrid Honda Insight, had total sales of about 600 cars in 2004. The GM Hummer — which received the 2004 award for most flaws in a car, weighs more than three times the Honda Insight, and gets about 10 miles per gallon — had sales of 25,000 cars in the same year.[31] In a time of looming energy crisis, a large number of Americans rejected a 60 mpg car for one that gets 10 mpg.

Buildings, Energy and Waste

The private residence is the largest energy consuming complex in an individual's energy budget. Within the house a host of energy consuming machines constantly draw electricity and natural gas from utility networks and add heat and pollutants to the environment. As part of understanding energy, people must become conversant with the machines in their homes. Houses contain a much wider range of energy consuming devices than cars. The furnace is the part of the house that is analogous to the engine of a car, burning more fuel than any other household device.

Houses require an enormous amount of energy intensive construction materials. In 2000, the materials used in the construction of a 2,272-square-foot single-family home included 13,837 board-feet of lumber, 13,118 square feet of sheathing, 19 tons of concrete, 3,206 square feet of exterior siding material, 3,103 square feet of roofing material, 3,061 square feet of insulation, 6,050 square feet of interior wall material, 2,335 square feet of interior ceiling material, and 2,269 square feet of flooring material for the basic structure. It also required 226 linear feet of ducting, 19 windows, 4 exterior doors (3 hinged, 1 sliding), 12 interior doors, 6 closet doors, 2 garage doors, 1 fireplace, 3 toilets, 2 bathtubs, 1 shower stall, 3 bathroom sinks, 15 kitchen cabinets, 5 other cabinets, 1 kitchen sink, 1 range, 1 refrigerator, 1 dishwasher, 1 garbage disposal, 1 range hood, 1 washer, 1 dryer and 1 heating and cooling system.[32]

There is also tremendous waste in the process of building. Typical construction waste for a 2,000 square foot home includes: 1,600 lbs. of solid wood, 1,400 lbs. of engineered wood, 2,000 lbs. of drywall, 600 lbs. of cardboard, 150 lbs. of metal, 150 lbs. of vinyl, 1,000 lbs. of masonry, 50 lbs. of hazardous materials and 1,050 lbs. of miscellaneous materials. An average of four pounds of waste per square foot is generated during construction of a single family home. Each year, US builders produce between 30 and 35 million tons of construction, renovation and demolition (C&D) waste which accounts for roughly 24% of the municipal solid waste stream.[33] Time and space do not permit a detailed analysis of other factors, such as air transportation or surface freight. We also need to know the energy costs of commercial and industrial buildings; this is discussed in Chapter 10. The home analysis of building embodied and operational energy provided in this book does not cover the energy cost of manufacturing the building's appliances, furniture or carpets.

Personal Change is Critical

The United States with between 4% and 5% of the population consumes about 25% of all fossil fuels and generates about 25% of CO_2. Figure 9.4 shows the per capita consumption of Americans as compared to the most populous 33 nations of the world containing 80% of world population.

Of the 57.8 boe consumed per person in the US, the usages under our personal control take about 39 boe — 10 boe for food, 13.5 boe for cars and 15.4 boe for homes. This is about 67% of total per capita US energy consumption. The vast majority of houses and cars are very inefficient since for decades designers and builders have sacrificed energy economy for style and size. Building energy use and CO_2 emissions are not a technology issue but rather a question of how we are choosing to live.

Making change requires skills of numeracy and analysis which will enable us to create an energy budget to help manage and reduce our energy consumption. Changing personal habits should come first, or at least go hand in hand with lobbying for government and institutional change. For it will only be with the experience that comes from personal change that people will develop the wisdom to make the proper societal changes. Every energy-wasting square foot of house or pound of car built today lowers the energy options of our children to meet basic needs for food, shelter or transportation. We need people to act on the basis of hope for the future. This means downsizing as quickly as possible, doing a deep retrofit of your house if you can, walking, biking and sharing rides and eating locally grown and unprocessed organic food — possibly even growing your own. It could be agonizing or it could be exciting — our attitude towards a new future is also a choice. Automobile companies have done a great job promoting the idea that driving small cars risks children's lives. Parents who face this and downsize their vehicle may reduce the odds that someday their children will look at them with anger or disgust for squandering the resources needed for basic survival.

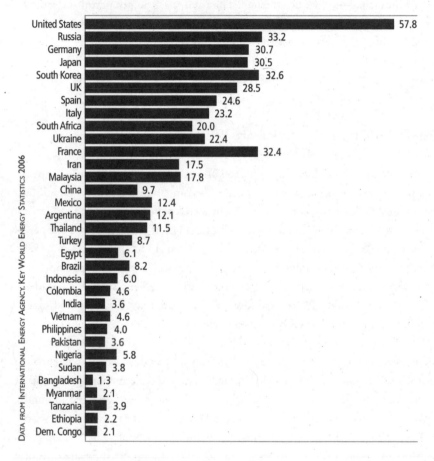

9.4: *Barrel of Oil Equivalents (boe) per Capita — 33 most populous nations containing 80% of World Population*

Ten

The Energy Impact of Buildings

Peak oil and climate change require a revolutionary change to all aspects of our lives. The energy used and CO_2 generated by the automobile or from food production is much less than the energy consumed by US buildings. Furthermore, building energy consumption has been continually increasing in spite of improvements in building efficiency. This is a reminder that we cannot solve the nation's problems simply by improving technology. It is important to understand the current buildings infrastructure and the choices made in past decades which resulted in the particular kind of home and commercial structures we now occupy. It is also important to apply the concepts of embodied and operating energy to these buildings. We must not forget that a building is a container for a large number of machines that use energy. This chapter is not intended to convey a set of tips but rather an understanding of the depth and seriousness of the problem. Until the scale of the building problem is grasped, we will not be able to develop adequate solutions.

Buildings and Per Capita Energy Consumption

The US Department of Energy's *2007 Buildings Energy Data Book* shows that in 2005, the operation of buildings in the US consumed nearly 40 quadrillion British Thermal Units (Btus) or 40 quads (a quad is an abbreviation for quadrillion Btus). This is about 40% of the total energy (100 quads) consumed annually in the US.[1] The *Data Book* also reports that carbon emissions from building operations were 630.3 million metric tons or 39% of the total carbon generated in the US.[2] (630.3 million metric tons of carbon is the equivalent of 2,332 million metric tons of CO_2.)

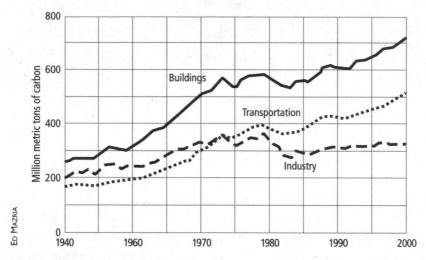

ED MAZRIA

10.1: *US Carbon Emissions by Sector*

Figure 10.1, based on the work of Ed Mazria, compares carbon generated from buildings, transportation and industry in the US. Mazria estimates that buildings consume 48% of US energy annually. His estimate includes energy consumed in construction (often referred to as embodied energy) and suggests that, over the lifetime of a building, ⅙ of the total energy consumed is used in the construction of buildings (embodied energy), and ⅚ of the total energy is consumed in operating buildings.[3]

Gil Masters of Stanford University uses 39% as the amount of operating energy (21% for residential buildings, 18% for commercial buildings). He adds an additional 2% for industrial buildings, giving a total of 41% and then adds an additional 7% for the embodied energy in construction materials,[4] giving a ratio of about ⅐ to ⁶⁄₇ between embodied energy and energy used to operate buildings. The *Canadian Architect* organization estimates 85.5% for building operating energy and 14.5% for building embodied energy, the latter divided into initial embodied energy and recurring embodied energy.[5] Over the life of the building, this gives the same ratio of ⅐ to ⁶⁄₇ between the embodied energy and the operating energy estimated by Masters. By taking the operating energy from the 2007 *Buildings Energy Data Book* (40%), adding the 2% for industrial buildings from Masters and applying the derived ⅐ ratio of embodied energy to operating energy, I obtain an approximation of the building energy portion of total yearly energy consumption of 48%, the same as Mazria. So if total building energy use is 48 quads, 40 quads is from building operation and 8 quads of embodied energy for construction. I conclude from this summary that embodied or construction energy uses 14% of building energy and operating energy uses 86%. Thus constructing, operating and demolishing buildings accounts for almost half the energy consumed yearly in the US.

I have chosen barrel of oil equivalent (or boe) per person as a common measure for energy use. Sometimes I use boe/c as an abbreviation for boe *per person or per capita*. To determine boe/c we must first convert quads of energy (measured in Btus) to barrels of oil equivalent. There are 5,800,000 Btus per barrel of oil, and the US population in 2005 was 296 million people. Dividing total building energy used (48 quads) by Btus/barrel and population gives 28 boe/c per year for building energy. Total building energy is divided 55% for residential and 45% for commercial.[6] As noted above, building energy is also divided 14% for embodied energy and 86% for operating energy. Thus total residential energy consumption is 15.4 boe/c (13.2 boe/c operating energy and 2.2 boe/c embodied energy) and total commercial energy consumption is 12.6 boe/c (10.8 boe/c operating energy and 1.8 boe/c embodied energy).

Embodied energy is not as obvious as the operating energy measured in our utility bills. However, it is apparent when one moves from a small house to a larger one. The higher cost of the larger house to a great extent represents the energy embodied in the house, including the energy used at the time of initial construction as well as energy used for remodeling or repairs over the life of the home.

Like its cars, US buildings consume far more energy than equivalent buildings in the rest of the world. In the US 39% of CO_2 emissions are from buildings (operating energy) while on a worldwide basis 9% of emissions are from buildings.[7] This is an example of extremely excessive consumption relative to the rest of the world. The country's buildings are bigger than they need to be and are often inefficient and wasteful. Designers have for years designed energy-consuming buildings under principles like "bringing the outdoors inside" requiring large areas of glass; but many large windows makes buildings very energy wasteful.

Building Energy Consumption Trends

In 2005 the US had about 5 million commercial buildings totaling about 75 billion square feet.[8] In the same year there were about 113 million households living in about 83 million residential buildings in the US totaling about 169 billion square feet.[9] Total square footage for commercial and residential buildings

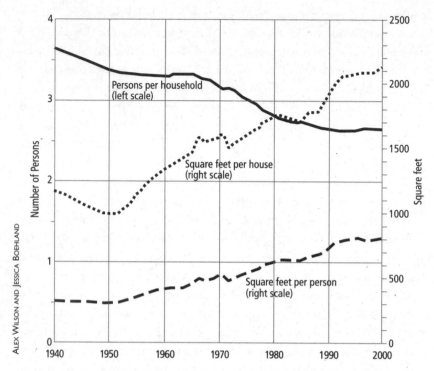

10.2: *Change in Household Size, House Size and Square Feet Per Person – 1940 to 2000*

in the US was about 244 billion square feet. In 2005, average household size was 2.6 people.[10] In 2001, the approximate distribution of types of residences was 69% single family, 25% multifamily and 6% manufactured housing.[11]

A change in building energy consumption over any period of time can be measured by the change in the number of square feet per person (or per capita). Estimates of per capita house area vary. Some methods analyze single family homes only; others consider all units including multifamily housing. All show the same result — a large increase in the square feet of US housing per person since WWII. A detailed study in *The Journal of Industrial Ecology* showed that the average per capita square feet of housing in 1950 was 293 compared to 893 square feet per capita in 2003, a per capita increase of about three times.[12] Figure 10.2 shows the increasing size of houses (from about 1,000 square feet to about 2,200 square feet in the year 2000), the decreasing number of occupants per house (from 3.7 in 1950 to 2.6 today) and the increasing square feet per person (about 300 to 900). Increasing house size and fewer residents is a

Period when built	Per Square Foot 10,000 btus	Per Household (Hh) 1,000,000 btus	Per Hh Member 1,000,000 btus	% of Total Consumption
Prior to 1970	51.6	100.7	40.3	56%
1970-1979	45.5	79.0	31.6	15%
1980-1989	41.4	79.7	31.9	15%
1990-1999	38.5	91.3	31.2	13%
2000-2001	36.6	111.1	32.9	1%
Average	46.7	92.2	36	100%

US DOE, 2007 BUILDINGS ENERGY DATA BOOK.

10.3: *Historical Residential Energy Consumption*

change which means more and more consumption of fossil fuels and generation of CO_2 per person.

Figure 10.3 shows the changes in operating energy use per square foot, per household and per household member in houses built in different time periods. It also shows the percentage of total US energy consumption by the homes built in those time periods. These measures of consumption were compiled in 2002. Houses built prior to 1970 used 51,600 Btus per square foot in 2001. These older buildings now consume 56% of the total energy for residential buildings. Houses built from 2000 to 2001 consume 36,600 Btus per square foot, but use only 1% of the total energy consumed by residential buildings in the US. Decreasing consumption from 51,600 Btus per sq. ft. to 36,600 Btus per sq. ft. is not too impressive over 35 years. People in the oldest homes each use 40.3 million Btus annually while people living in homes built in 2000 or 2001 each use 32.9 million Btus. And even less improvement has been made when measured on a per capita basis as new appliances and building features are added to the household. Thus improvements in building efficiency have not provided significant energy savings because even as we add efficiency features, we make houses larger, fewer people reside in them, and they use more energy-consuming appliances than ever before. This is a good example of Jevons paradox previously mentioned which essentially says that the more efficiency that enters the economy, the greater the consumption.

Longevity of Buildings

Compared to cars, buildings have a much longer life. The average age of a car or light truck is around nine years. Few passenger vehicles last more than 12-16 years. But the average life of a house is more than 75 years.[13] Commercial

LEON GLICKSMAN. ENERGY EFFICIENT BUILDINGS: ISSUES, RESEARCH OPPORTUNITIES.

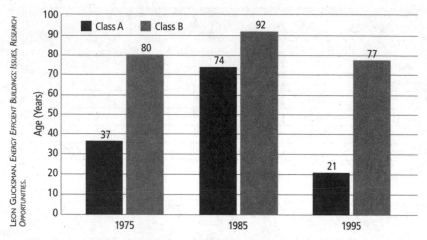

10.4: Median Age of New York City Office Buildings

buildings also have long lives. The Empire State Building is 75 years old and it shows little signs of aging (Fig. 10.4).[14] Commercial and other large buildings can last for centuries. Many existing New York buildings are even older than the Empire State Building. The life span of existing buildings is an important consideration when estimating future energy needs. Building longevity means that new energy conserving building techniques affect only a small number of newer homes. In 2005, there were 113 million households in the US and the country built approximately 2.1 million new household units.[15] At that rate, it will take decades to replace existing homes with energy efficient construction. By that time there may be very little fossil fuels remaining.

Building Operating Fuels

Buildings use a wide variety of fuels including petroleum (fuel oil), natural gas, coal and electricity from coal, natural gas, uranium, dams and other renewable sources. In our cars it is clear that fossil fuels are being used when we fill the gas tank. The smell of the gasoline is obvious. The efficiency of driving can be measured in miles per gallon. The use of energy in buildings is not as obvious. The natural gas that warms the house or the coal that generates the electricity to run its machines is not visible. But nonetheless energy is being consumed constantly in our buildings.

Primary heating fuels are natural gas and electricity although there are still some homes that burn fuel oil for heat. Electricity is mostly derived from coal,

Fuel	All	Residential	Commercial
Coal	38%	36%	41%
Natural Gas	31%	33%	29%
Nuclear	15%	14%	16%
Petroleum	8%	9%	7%
Hydro	5%	5%	5%
Other Renewables	3%	4%	3%

US DOE. 2007 BUILDINGS ENERGY DATA BOOK.

10.5: *Distribution of Fuels Used in Buildings – 2005*

since coal is the most popular fuel for power plants in the US. The small amounts of fuel oil and coal that are burned directly are trucked to the houses. Natural gas and electricity are carried to houses through buried pipes and overhead wires.

Using electricity generated by coal plants to heat a home rather than burning coal in the home does not eliminate pollutants but simply moves them from the place of consumption to the place of generation. Much more coal is used in heating with electricity generated from coal than would be used if the coal were burned directly to heat the house.[16] A coal furnace is approximately 70-80% efficient while coal power plants that generate electricity are 35-40% efficient. Thus, using electricity from coal to heat a home rather than using coal itself will generate about twice as much CO_2. In the future we may be burning coal in stoves again so as to generate less CO_2 using the more efficient techniques of a bygone era.

Note that coal and nuclear combined provide 53% of the energy used in US buildings (Fig. 10.5). The US government currently plans to increase the percentage of energy from these extremely toxic fuels to replace declining supplies of oil and natural gas. Most of the energy designated *other renewables* comes from wood, and there is little hope for growth in the use of that fuel unless the country is deforested. Only a fraction of 1% of the energy consumed comes from photovoltaics and wind turbines, reminding us that although renewable sources are important they are limited.

Indirect Building Energy Uses

Two underground pipes run to buildings and also consume energy. One is the water pipe that brings water to the building, and the second is the sewer pipe that removes the effluent (urine and feces along with the so called grey water from bathing and laundry) from the building.

There is an energy cost for lifting the water from wells, rivers or reservoirs with electric pumps, pumping the water from source to purification plant and from purification plant to building. The purification process is also energy intensive. Then sewage must be pumped with electric pumps, purified and pumped or transported to some dumping site. Most home energy analyses do not include the energy to provide purified water and process waste. This energy expenditure is allocated elsewhere.

Energy Consuming Machines in Buildings

In addition to the energy consumed in construction and maintenance of buildings, there are a large number of energy-using machines contained within buildings. Figure 10.6 shows the distribution of energy consumption for different machines for both residential and commercial buildings as well as the two kinds of buildings combined.

Figure 10.6 shows that the biggest use of energy (26%) in commercial buildings is for lighting. Since the vast majority of commercial lighting uses fluorescent bulbs, major energy savings by changing light bulbs will not be possible. Larger buildings (and most commercial buildings are larger than residences) also have

End Use	Residential		Commercial		All Buildings	
Space Heating	6.7	31%	2.5	14%	9.2	23%
Lighting	2.4	11%	4.6	26%	7.0	18%
Space Cooling	2.7	12%	2.3	13%	5.0	13%
Water Heating	2.7	12%	1.2	7%	3.9	10%
Refrigeration	1.6	8%	.7	4%	2.4	6%
Electronics	1.6	7%	1.1	6%	2.7	7%
Cooking	1.0	5%	0.4	2%	1.3	3%
Wet Clean	1.0	5%			1.0	3%
Ventilation			1.1	6%	1.1	3%
Computers	0.2	1%	0.6	3%	0.8	2%
Other	0.8	4%	2.4	13%	3.2	8%
Adjusted to SEDS*	1.0	5%	1.0	5%	2.0	5%
Total	21.8	100%	17.9	100%	39.7	100%

* State Energy Data System
Energy consumed is shown in quads and % of totals

US DOE. 2007 BUILDINGS ENERGY DATA BOOK.

10.6: *US Buildings — Primary Energy Consumption Distribution*

less exterior surface for each square foot of floor area, so their heating loads decline proportionally with size.

Residential buildings use 31% of their energy for space heating. So, in residential buildings one machine — the furnace — consumes the most energy. A home furnace may burn natural gas, oil, coal or wood. An electric furnace will use electricity to heat water or air to warm the house. A more recent electrical product, the heat pump, operates on the same principle of compression as a refrigerator. Electricity may also heat the house by resistance electric heaters in different rooms, but these are much less efficient than forced-air furnaces. Major energy savings could be achieved if buildings were designed to be smaller, much better insulated with the heat source placed within the conditioned space. However, even if a residential or commercial building used no energy for heat, it will still use energy for everything else.

The data in Figure 10.6 represents national consumption and provides a guide for any program to reduce home energy consumption. Individual homes will use more or less, but the energy distribution will be similar.

Green Building Programs

Americans are fixated on new technologies, and most still think that energy limitations and global warming issues will be resolved by some techno-fix. The media supports this unrealistic view by writing and speaking of new technologies that are supposedly on the horizon or just around the corner, excusing people's prodigious use of energy. In a similar manner, most of the building industry has used the marketing term of *green building* to excuse low energy performance buildings. Green building in the US includes a wide variety of building technologies and programs such as Energy Star, LEED, Zero Energy and Building America.

The media portrays these options as exciting new developments that are ready now, almost here or at a breakthrough point, giving the impression of significant and rapid progress — an impression that only lasts until the numbers are analyzed. Like the automobile fuel cell dream, these ideas make people feel that businesses and government are on top of the problem and that they need to make only minimal personal change. So far green building has done little to reduce energy consumption and CO_2 emissions. A very small number of homes have been built under these designations, about 2% of new building in 2006.[17] This is a minuscule part of all existing homes. A discussion of these energy savings programs follows.

Energy Star

In 1992 the US Environmental Protection Agency (EPA) introduced Energy Star as a voluntary labeling program to promote energy-efficient products and practices to reduce greenhouse gas emissions including CO_2. To qualify for the Energy Star rating, new homes must meet EPA guidelines for energy efficiency. Such homes must be at least 15% more energy efficient than homes built to 2004 International Residential Code (IRC) requirements.[18]

Energy Star labels are now found on major appliances, office equipment, lighting and home electronics as well as new homes, commercial and industrial buildings. Energy Star benefits in 2005 (avoiding 37 million metric tons of greenhouse gas emissions) are said to be twice those of the year 2000, a 15% per year improvement rate.[19] 37 million tonnes is a large number but it represents only ⅔ of 1 % of the total US emissions of 5,782 million tonnes per year.

After 15 years, the Energy Star program has made relatively little progress toward reducing CO_2 emissions by the 70-90% needed to avoid climate calamity. Like the government's Corporate Average Fuel Economy (CAFE) standards for automobiles, its objectives are too low. Energy Star offers a welcome improvement but does not approach the scale of change that needs to be made.

LEED

The US Green Building Council (founded in 1993) originally established a Leadership in Energy and Environmental Design (LEED) Green Building rating for commercial buildings. This has become a nationally accepted benchmark for the design, construction and operation of so called high performance green buildings. The designation does not mean the building is actually a green color, nor is high performance specifically defined. Some LEED buildings are little more energy efficient than traditional structures though they may offer advantages in dealing with water consumption or may use recycled materials.[20] LEED has five ratings with different point values: Certified/Bronze 26-32 points, Silver 33-38 points, Gold 39-51 points and Platinum 52-69 points. Only 17 of the 69 possible points are assigned to Energy and Atmosphere items.[21] From the year 2000 to mid 2005, 430 buildings were LEED certified.[22] Total certified buildings by class as of mid 2007 were Certified/Bronze 936, Silver 293, Gold 266 and Platinum 43, a total of 1,538 buildings.[23] This number is miniscule compared to the total of approximately five million commercial buildings and 83 million residential buildings in the US. Many of the LEED features are not particularly relevant to the building's operating energy use. For example, placing a bike rack near the building earns one point, which is the same value earned if 5% of the building's energy comes from renewable sources. Likewise, installing a metal grate at the entrance to reduce particle count earns one point while increasing energy efficiency, which might cost tens of thousands of dollars, only earns two points. To date, LEED has not contributed significant reductions to energy consumption or CO_2 emissions. This is due to the extremely small number of LEED buildings as well as a not very impressive reduction in energy use (25-30%).[24]

Zero Energy

The US Department of Energy established its Zero Energy program in 2002. The program's name gives the impression of a home that uses no or very little energy. One program slogan is "buildings that generate more energy than they use." But a Zero Energy building is one with an array of solar PV panels on its roof; it is not necessarily energy efficient. (As noted earlier energy expensive materials such as glass, aluminum and silicon wafers are required to produce photovoltaics). A Zero Energy home's excess energy, created by solar panels, is fed into the power grid during daylight hours. When the sun goes down, the house draws power from the grid. It is still dependent on this external power source for an uninterrupted supply of electricity. One study shows that Zero Energy Houses (ZEH) have an average of 32% energy savings from energy efficiency and 19% savings from the PV panels for a total of 51%.[25] This is an impressive reduction, but the term Zero Energy is a misstatement of what has been achieved.

Building America

The US Department of Energy's Building America program focuses on research and development for energy systems to significantly reduce residential home energy consumption. About 40,000 Building America homes have been built to date, a small number when compared to the 113 million households living in 83 million residential buildings.[26] Its research goals are to realize 30%-90% energy savings in existing homes.[27] In a major public relations effort in March 2005, a Building America team of volunteers increased a 1,200-square-foot tract house to a custom-built, 4,200-square-foot, nine-bedroom, six-bathroom, super energy-efficient home, complete with pond, waterfall and Jacuzzi.[28] The result may be a building that uses less energy per square foot but which uses more total energy than the original tract house. Unfortunately, many of the so called green efforts are applied to large homes.

A Review of Passive Solar

Passive solar building began as a grass roots movement in the US during the energy crisis in the 1970s. Most passive solar homes were built by individuals and custom builders. Author Douglas Balcomb notes that passive solar design was the rage in energy efficient architecture in the early 1980s. He estimates that 180,000 passive solar houses were built in that period and further estimates that such homes use about 20% of the heat required by conventional homes.

Balcomb acknowledges that such efforts have declined and now most architects have "only vague memories of passive solar." Estimating another 70,000 were built during the ensuing years, gives approximately 250,000 passive solar homes.[29] This is only about one third of 1% of the total of 83 million residential buildings (including single family and multiple-family). Few, if any, passive solar multi-family home developments exist. Designing and operating a passive solar home is not as easy as designing and operating one with a conventional heating system. The designer must find the right balance between the amount of south facing glass and the thermal storage required. It is difficult to deal with heat loss through long winter nights compared to heat gain during short winter days. If not well-planned and managed, the house can easily overheat in warm weather. And at night and in cloudy colder weather, heat loss through windows can be very high unless one uses window covers.

In addition, a passive solar home costs more than a conventional home since passive features must be added while a heating system is still required for backup. It may be worth it for the projected 80% heat savings (though detailed cost differences are not available). But as energy for heating a house is only 31% of the total energy used in the building, an 80% savings in energy used for heating translates into total household energy savings of about 25%.

Green building programs have realized only small improvements in reducing energy consumption in US building as a whole. Their energy standards are too low to meet the climate change reduction requirements needed and their rate of growth is too small to make the big difference needed. Unfortunately the concept of green building has been oversold in the media. Much more aggressive energy standards are desperately needed. Fortunately there are new programs which offer deep reductions in fossil fuels consumption: High Performance Building and the German Passive House.

High Performance Building and Passive Houses

High performance home building was partially developed by the Building Technology Center (BTC) at Oak Ridge National Laboratory in Tennessee. The BTC, in conjunction with Habitat for Humanity, has built five small high performance homes in Tennessee. These homes have thick Structural Insulated Panels (SIPS) with high R-values — R-40 instead of the more common R-11 — and a very tight building envelope.[30] One of the most significant features in these smaller-than-average houses is the inclusion of the heating system and ductwork within the conditioned space so that the estimated 37% loss of heat through heating ducts in the unconditioned space (unheated attics or crawl spaces) is eliminated. BTC has now begun evaluating ways to retrofit existing homes.[31]

The Northern European concept *passivhaus* (Passive House) used the passive solar concept from the 1970s as a starting point. Designers added a very well insulated and airtight building envelope. Passive houses built in Germany and other Northern European countries typically have no space heating or cooling systems but stay warm in winter and cool in summer. The total energy consumption of a group of passive house multi-unit terrace homes near Goteborg, Sweden is close to ⅓ of that for the standard multi-unit non-passive houses (5,400 kWh per year compared with approximately 15,000 kWh per year).[32] The Swedish buildings have a 19 inch wall thickness compared to the standard US 3 ½ inch wall thickness. Solar panels for electricity are part of the building. Germany has built 4,000 such passive houses in the last several years.[33] As of 2005, 6,000 in total have been built in several Northern European countries.[34] The important thing about the Passive House is that it sets an extremely high performance objective — to reduce energy use 90% in new construction and 80% in existing buildings. This is far ahead of the US objectives of 30-40% which cannot satisfy the necessary CO_2 reductions. It is very important for US builders and home owners to know that the technologies and practices already exist in Europe to achieve the level of cutbacks needed to deal with climate change.

Choices and Values

While these last two examples in particular offer some hope for future building, even they don't represent technical breakthroughs. Nor are there any breakthroughs on the horizon. Rather, there are only a large number of possible small iterative improvements. American homes, like American cars, are basically too big, with energy-wasteful features like high ceilings, excessive lighting, large appliances, thin walls and large expanses of glass. For decades consumers and builders have rejected energy conserving features and have been unwilling to trade floor space for efficiency of operation. During the first energy crisis of the 1970s, a cultural choice could have been made to increase expenditures on efficiency rather than on size. Unfortunately the nation chose differently and now has an enormous investment in large and inefficient buildings where Americans spend 90% of their time.[35] American residences are now at least twice the size of typical homes in Europe and Japan and consume 2.4 times the energy of European homes.[36] This seems to be fundamental to the American character. Often when an opportunity arises to make major improvements for new construction, government and business seem committed to the status quo. In September 2005 the Department of Energy refused to support a bill to increase R-values in walls from R-13 to R-15.[37] The National Association of Home Builders had lobbied against the change. Such examples are tragic.

The American Council for an Energy-Efficient Economy (ACEEE) monitors many high-energy-consuming industries, including housing. The organization has published three reports within a decade that list 198 energy-saving technologies and practices.[38] Each one has the potential to save at least ¼ of 1% of the energy consumed when the specific technology or practice has matured. Perusing these reports, one can see both the depth and breadth of possible reductions in building energy use. However, one also sees how difficult it is to make substantial changes. The difficulties are not merely technical, like changing standard construction practices. They are also cultural, including resistance to giving up our values of convenience, comfort, style and guaranteed economic payoff.

These values are such that even as machines become more efficient, consumption has increased, so that the more improvements are made relative to housing and appliance efficiency, the more these improvements are cancelled out by larger buildings, more lights, more machines and other accoutrements which reflect our consumption orientation. Without a significant change in these cultural values, no technological advances will solve the US's energy and emissions problems.

The Retrofit Option

What can be done with all the large and inefficient houses in the US? Most buildings currently in existence will still remain after oil is gone. It will not be possible to replace them quickly with new energy efficient buildings because of the cost and the amount of fossil fuels required. We could resolve the size issue by doubling up households; if energy prices increase dramatically, this may be done in some cases. We could also use only part of a house during times of the year when heating or cooling is required. This practice is common in less affluent parts of the world. Another less likely alternative would be to actually dismantle buildings and use the components to build more energy efficient replacements. This is extreme, but very rapid changes caused by peak oil and climate change could lead to dramatic shifts in needs. In that case, carefully deconstructing buildings for their materials might become common.

A sensible and practical option is to begin a major retrofit of all buildings to reduce their energy consumption. The principles are simple: make the building as small as possible, make its envelope as thick as possible and make it as airtight as possible, with all furnaces and heating ductwork placed within the conditioned space. Figure 10.7 shows the difference between a simple heating

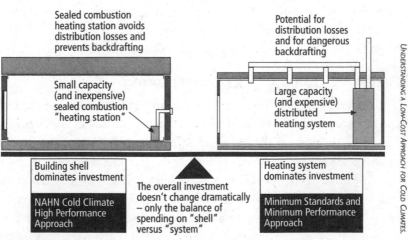

10.7: *Building Shell Investment versus Heating System Investment*

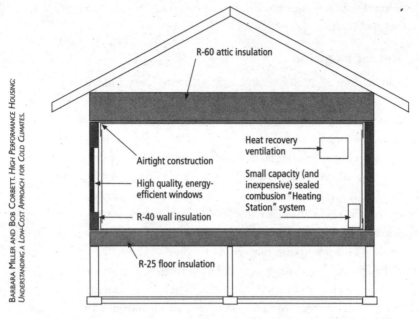

10. 8: *House Section Showing Thick Shell and Heating System in Conditioned Space*

system within the conditioned space and one with the ductwork running above the ceiling, outside the conditioned space. It also shows a thicker envelope.

Figure 10.8 shows detailed features including high insulation values in floors, walls and ceiling along with a heat recovery system (basic to the passive house concept) and a very small sealed-combustion heating system. These principles are simple and practiced in other parts of the world.

Analyzing Home Energy Consumption

To determine how to spend money for retrofitting wisely, we need to consider energy consumption for the machines inside the home as well as energy losses from different parts of the house envelope. Energy for heating and cooling buildings is lost through walls, ceilings/roofs, glass and infiltration (the leakage of air through poorly sealed building envelopes, electrical outlets, ductwork and around doors and windows). Figure 10.9 reflects the different forms of energy consumption in winter and summer for space heating and cooling.

A much higher percentage of energy passes through window glass than through walls. A typical 2,000 square foot house might have 1,400 square feet

End Use	Total Energy % Required	Heating Loss in Winter %	Cooling Loss in Summer %
Space Heating/Cooling	43		
Roof		12	14
Walls		19	10
Foundation		15	
Infiltration		28	16
Windows (conduction)		26	1
Windows (solar gain)			32
Internal Gains			27
Lighting	12		
Water Heating	13		
Refrigeration	8		
Electronics	5		
Cooking	5		
Wet Clean	5		
Computers	5		
Other	4		
Adjustment SEDS	5		

US DOE, 2007 BUILDINGS ENERGY DATA BOOK

10.9: *Energy Distribution by Season — Heating, Cooling, Appliances*

of exterior wall area with about 300 square feet of window area.[39] Figure 9 shows that walls have an energy loss of 19% in winter and 10% in summer. Windows have a 26% loss in winter and a 32% solar gain in summer (which the air conditioner must handle). The average energy loss for walls is about 15% and for windows about 30%. In this example, twice the energy goes out the windows than goes through the walls. But there is about five times as much wall area as window area. So window loss is in the range of several times wall loss on a square foot basis. These national averages can guide home owners planning major or minor retrofits. They show that energy savings must be done in many steps — and that there are more than just one or two things that need to be done.

When making decisions about saving energy, the life span of appliances is also an important consideration. Furnaces, air conditioners and other appliances have a much shorter life than windows and walls. Some average appliance's life spans are:

refrigerator-13 years
freezer-11 years
room air conditioner-10 years
range-14 years
clothes washer-11 years
clothes dryer-13 years
water heater-10 years

Furnaces, heat pumps and central air conditioners typically have a life span of 16-18 years. An appliance's average life span is 11 years.[40] In some cases it may be better to replace appliances first before making changes in the building envelope.

General Retrofit Guidelines

While each home is different, there are some general guidelines for retrofitting.

Lighting

The top five residential energy consuming machines — furnaces, light bulbs, air conditioners, water heaters and refrigerators — use 76% of the total energy in a home.[41] The energy used for lighting could immediately be reduced substantially (by a factor of three) by replacing incandescent light bulbs with compact fluorescents. Improving house lighting would save 8% of total home energy use and should be done without delay. Improving the other four will be more difficult and more expensive.

Infiltration

Leaks account for 8-10% of a house's energy loss, so the second priority should be to find and seal leaks with caulk or weather stripping to make it as airtight as possible. Next, a professional should be hired to conduct a blower door test to find additional leaks. For fresh air, a heat recovery ventilation system is much more effective than uncontrolled leaks and is required when infiltration is mostly eliminated. Tightening the envelope is not an expensive process, but does require some skill and care.[42]

Windows

Windows are a large consumer of energy. If possible, replace single-glazed windows with double-glazed ones — this will cut window energy consumption in half. Storm windows could also be used and are much cheaper. In houses with excessive amounts of glass, some of the window area could be replaced with framed and insulated wall sections. Window covers should be part of the house and used extensively in cold weather, since so much energy is lost through window glass. Window covers are typically made of quilted material or cut from sheets of rigid insulation to fit the window openings. In the summer, shades or awnings can reduce the effects of the sun's heat.

The Building Envelope

Retrofitting a building envelope — the floor, walls and roof — is a complex process. Ceilings can usually be insulated if the attic is accessible, increasing insulation values up to R-50 or R-60. Similarly, floors may be insulated to a greater depth if joists are deep enough. Typically ceiling insulation can be laid on top of the existing joists; however, floors may have to be thickened by attaching additional framing material to deepen the joist spaces so they can contain more insulation. If the floor is on a slab, it may be possible to dig around the foundation and insulate what is accessible.

Walls may be furred out (made thicker) for more insulation. These new furred-out walls will either rest inside the house on the floor adjacent to the existing exterior walls or rest on ledgers (thick framing members attached to framed or concrete walls) which are bolted to the rim joists on the outside of the house. Inside furred-out walls will take some of the floor space but may be cheaper to build than new outside furred walls. Thicker walls offer space at windows for movable insulation like window quilts and for pockets that can be used for sliding window covers.

Passive house retrofitting guidelines include eliminating air leaks, making the house air tight, installing a heat/air exchanger, thickening the envelope for more insulation together with the elimination of thermal bridges and installing super efficient windows and doors.

Furnaces

Once infiltration has been eliminated, the envelope has been thickened including additional insulation and better windows and doors installed, the furnace system should be modified. Moving the ductwork and furnace into the conditioned space can save up to 1/3 of the energy consumed for heating.[43] Tearing the old ductwork out of the walls and replacing it with insulation, repositioning the furnace and building new ducts is a complex retrofit. In some situations, unheated basements or crawl spaces may be made part of the conditioned space. The resulting tight, well insulated building will use only a fraction of the previous energy — and will improve comfort.

Attached Solar Spaces

Attaching solar spaces like greenhouses or sunrooms can provide a source of heat. Properly configured, small fans move heated air from the solar space into the living space in cold weather and ventilate the solar space in warm weather. Solar spaces typically incorporate heat storage mass, such as masonry or water. In cooler weather it is necessary to use insulated shutters or to close solar spaces off from the living area to limit nighttime heat loss. In warm weather, reflecting panels or window shades may be used to reject heat.

Appliances

Hot water heaters can be set on pilot light until hot water is required and then turned up. People use hot water in a relatively small time period. After the period of heavy use, the hot water setting could be returned to pilot. Electric hot water heaters can be modified with switches that turn the unit on and off at scheduled times. Moving the hot water heater closer to the points of use would reduce energy use, or one can install instant, so-called flash water heaters to replace standard units that keep water hot day and night.

Replacing old furnaces, air conditioners, refrigerators and freezers with new energy-efficient, high-end units would result in an energy use reduction. Another option would be to replace electric stoves, electric clothes dryers and refrigerators with natural gas units; this reduces total national consumption since the conversion of coal to electricity essentially wastes 2/3 of the energy.

Changing Practices

Changing habits is as important as changing infrastructure. Setting thermostats to 55° or 60° instead of 70° will be uncomfortable until one adjusts — but it's not dangerous. The world functioned without air conditioning for thousands of years, and it may be necessary to abandon it. Consider eliminating some appliances and doing the work by hand.

Keeping water hot day and night may not be viable in the future. Washing clothes in cold water should become the norm. Hanging laundry outside on sunny days or on an inside rack when it rains, as they do in Europe, makes good sense.

Cooking with pressure cookers saves more than half the cooking energy. Canning and drying of food can replace freezing. There are many other personal measures we can take to reduce energy use. They may be uncomfortable and inconvenient until we adjust, but they are necessary to reduce energy consumption to a sustainable level and stop global warming.

Retraining an Industry — Providers and Consumers

The construction industry requires a high degree of skill both for professionals, such as architects and general contractors, and tradespeople such as carpenters, electricians and plumbers. Most trades are licensed and require passing a comprehensive test and showing some years of experience in the relevant trade. Thus, the industry provides a pool of talented and experienced people who are capable of implementing changes rapidly. Framers could easily make walls from 2x6s, 2x8s, 2x10s, 2x12s, I-joists or SIP panels rather than today's standard of 2x4s. With a little practice they could become equally adept at building double exterior walls with sandwiched insulation, which are much more insulating compared to single walls.

In addition, we will need a major shift from new building to retrofitting; this will create new employment opportunities in construction. Retrofitting is labor-intensive and in the future someone who understands how to modify a house to use less energy will be in demand and paid well. Also, there is a large do-it-yourself movement in North America, and as people see the need they will begin to do their own retrofitting.

The problem, as always, is attitude. Government and the building industry tend to oppose legislation to alter building codes towards efficiency, so it will be up to individuals to make choices for an energy-constrained world and to limit CO_2. Architects and builders have historically focused on providing the maximum amount of floor space for the least amount of money. Thicker walls will reduce livable area and increase cost. To shift the emphasis from the largest possible size to energy frugal design is contrary to America's core belief that *Bigger is Better*. Building professionals and tradespeople have the skills to make this adjustment, but it will take a change in attitude and perspective from the general population. People in the building business are practical, and if consumer priorities shift, so will those of builders and designers.

It is said that necessity is the mother of invention and, as energy shortages appear and prices rise, more and more people will take responsibility for dealing with their homes in a personal and local manner. They will develop an understanding of building energy consumption along with the skills to upgrade their homes. The process will not be cheap in time or money. Maybe Web surfing and TV viewing will be replaced with caulking parties, window covering sewing bees and similar activities.

Americans must change their short-sighted habits and realize that their personal choices make a difference. Continuing to live and consume energy in a modern home is like continuing to drive a low-mpg car. America must change from a worldview of consumption to one of curtailment, choosing to share resources in space (across the world) and in time (with those yet to be born.)

Eleven

The Smart Jitney —
Rapid, Realistic Transport

T HE WORLD IS THREATENED with the combination of declining fossil fuel resources and a climate that is already severely damaged by the gases from fossil fuel burning, and automobiles play a significant role. The damage is already so bad that severe restrictions may have to be placed on the consumption of the remaining fossil fuels, making alternative transport systems vital. For many decades US transportation has been focused on the energy intensive private car. After World War II the US made transportation via the private car the top priority at the expense of public transportation. The private car, regardless of its convenience, can no longer serve as the principal mode of people transport. Its high cost, the depleting of fossil fuels and climate deterioration — along with high rates of deaths and injuries — make it unacceptable and unsustainable.

Since peak oil could arrive soon and the depletion rate could worsen, prudence requires a backup plan other than merely changing car technology. A Smart Jitney system could be developed rapidly and provide a very sizable (50-75%) reduction of both gasoline consumed and greenhouse gases generated by personal transportation in the US. It could also be the model for a new and more efficient approach to personal mobility. Ultimately, it could keep the US economy going by giving people a way to get to and from work if suddenly there was insufficient fuel for private cars.

The Private Car Paradigm

The US private car dominates our economy and our way of life. In spite of its numerous benefits, the many conveniences and the sense of freedom associated

Vehicle Type	Number	Median Life (years)	Cost to replace ½ the fleet (in 2003 $)
Automobiles	130 million	17	$1.3 trillion
Light trucks, SUVs, etc.	80 million	16	$1 trillion
Heavy Trucks, Buses	7 million	28	$1.5 trillion
Aircraft	8,500	22	$0.25 trillion

11.1: *US Transportation Fleet with Replacement Costs*
Robert L. Hirsch et al. *Peaking of World Oil Production: Impacts, Mitigation, & Risk Management.*

with the automobile, it is unlikely that the concept of the private car as known today is viable for the future. Traffic is worsening all over the world. We can't continue using a machine that has been so devastating for the planet. As energy resources deplete and pollution worsens even a 100 to 200 mpg automobile cannot be the main vehicle for billions of people.

On average, every American buys 13 cars in his/her lifetime.[1] Figure 11.1 shows the total US transportation fleet except for trains. Vehicles last a long time so that it would take many years to replace all of them with more efficient ones, assuming highly efficient vehicles were available. Heavy trucks are extremely important when considering the transportation of food and other materials. In addition, the 8,500 aircraft flying at 30,000 feet do more climate damage than their numbers suggest because the emissions from burning fuel are deposited at higher altitudes. The size of the transportation fleet is huge and the investment is in the trillions of dollars.

Performance Improvements and Growth Trends

In his testimony to a Senate Subcommittee, John German, Manager of Environmental and Energy Analysis for American Honda Motor Company, Inc. noted, "It is clear that technology has been used for vehicle attributes which consumers have demanded or value more highly than fuel economy .... If the current car fleet were still at 1981 performance, weight and transmission levels, the passenger car CAFE would be almost 38 mpg instead of the current level of 28.1 mpg. The trend is particularly pronounced since 1987. From 1987 to 2006, technology has gone into the fleet at a rate that could have improved fuel economy by almost 1.5% per year, if it had not gone to other attributes demanded by the marketplace."[2] His testimony points out that the problems of energy use are not technical but cultural. Americans want speed, acceleration and big cars.

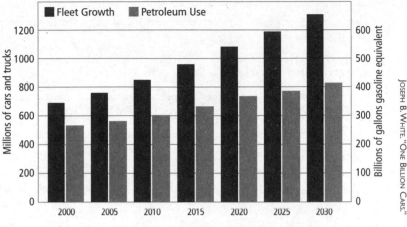

11.2: *Growth Projections — Number of Cars/Trucks and Petroleum Consumption*

Another reason our petroleum consumption (and accompanying CO_2 emissions) are steadily increasing is the rapidly growing number of cars and trucks not just in the US but worldwide.

Figure 11.2 shows world growth projections for automobiles and petroleum fuels. These projections are highly unlikely considering peak oil. Note that the rate of growth of petroleum (gasoline and diesel fuel) is less than that of cars, reflecting some improvement in efficiency. But the total fuel consumption is also increasing, once more making the case that better efficiency does not reduce total consumption.

When oil production peaks, there will be a steady annual decrease in the availability of diesel fuel and gasoline. Those who argue that basic changes to the transportation system are not needed because of improved car efficiency are not addressing the implications of going from about 800 million cars today to something like 1.3 billion cars in the next 23 years. Taking this a step further, today the average car in the world might get 35 miles per gallon with an average yearly mileage of 10,000 miles. In the future 1.3 billion cars getting 50-70 miles per gallon and being driven an average yearly mileage of 15,000 miles will be disastrous to the planet. The increase in the number of cars and the distances traveled far outweighs the mileage improvements from any new types of engines. And, even supposing there was sufficient oil to fuel this growth (highly unlikely), the amount of CO_2 generated would increase, worsening global climate change. Rapidly increasing use of cars, while improving performance relatively slowly, is neither sustainable nor survivable. We must increase the passengers per vehicle, along with increasing miles per gallon.

Car Deaths and Injuries

The current car paradigm encourages people to take as many car trips as possible. Such heavy use of cars requires building and maintaining an enormous number of roads, garages and parking areas. Advertising supports the cultural ideal of rugged individualism: people are encouraged to drive the largest possible cars while buses and trains become neglected alternatives. Walking and cycling are inconvenient and dangerous, and the priority is always, "don't delay the car."

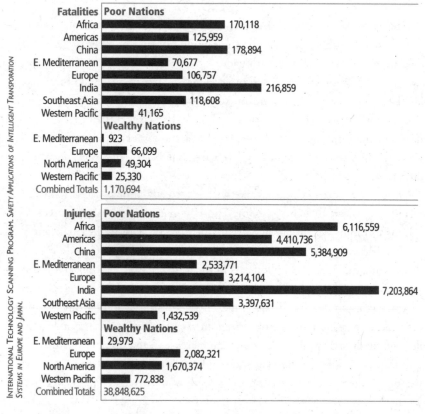

11.3: *Worldwide Traffic Fatalities and Injuries - 1998*

The cost of the private automobile goes beyond financial and climate considerations. Figure 11.3 illustrates annual auto deaths and injuries. The world total is about 1.2 million deaths and 40 million injuries yearly. In the US about 40,000 people die each year in auto-related accidents. There are hundreds of thousands of people injured in auto accidents who never fully recover, many disabled severely for the rest of their lives. Deaths and injuries are also high in the developing world where the infrastructure to support the car paradigm is not as well developed as in the US. As cars begin to penetrate societies such as China and India, pollution, injuries and deaths will increase there.

Results of the Private Auto Paradigm

Cars have played a major role in destroying community, by which I mean a feeling of home, family and neighborhood. With the private automobile, people are now footloose and free; we have gained speed and mobility but lost relationships with one another. We have chosen freedom for the individual over the integrity and support of community. Of our vaunted freedoms in the US none is more important than the freedom of the open road. Getting a license to drive is a rite of passage for our teenagers. The automobile allows a young person to leave their community, to experiment with high speed and, removed from family influence, with sex, alcohol and drugs. The automobile is constantly being marketed to them. We have accepted this so-called freedom for our children, ignoring potential damage and danger to their well-being. Parents' major fear is not teenage drugs or pregnancy but death or injury in a car accident. And no wonder parents are concerned: almost every beginning driver in the US has an accident. Parents don't want their children to be among the 40,000 yearly deaths or the 2 million injured — many with permanent disabilities.[3]

Because people crave what the car provides, they have accepted the destruction of communities, the negative impact on family life, the deaths and injuries. But now the private car is threatening to destroy life on the planet as peak oil and climate change challenge the current transport paradigm. Yet without these threats, it is inconceivable that Americans would consider that a good life is possible without a personal car.

The Limitations of Mass Transit

It is assumed that mass transit is a possible and obvious alternative to the private car. European cities are often praised for their superior transit systems.

Private Car	3,496
Light Truck (SUV)	4,329
Vanpool	1,294
Bus Transit	4,318
Airplane	3,959
Amtrak Train	2,760
Rail Commuter	2,569

11.4: *Mass transit Btu costs vs. other kinds of vehicles*

The New York City subway supposedly offers an alternative to the private car. But in all the cities with mass transit systems, the car population is still growing. Streets are becoming more crowded, and far more expenditures are made on roadways than subways and buses. Subways and other forms of mass transit today only supplement the car since high density is required for mass transit. In successful past implementations, residential developments were laid out in dense corridors, typically along a rail or streetcar line, with open spaces and farms between these corridors. The ideal configuration was analogous to a wheel, the hub being where people went to work and shopped, while the spokes represented where they lived. The space between was often used to grow food.

When the private car became popular, the areas between the spokes were more accessible and were eventually filled in. Food growing was transferred further and further away from where people lived. This led to suburbs and urban sprawl, making effective mass transit more difficult. After a time, there was no longer any attempt to build along mass transit lines which have mostly faded or disappeared.[4] Our North American urban sprawl has no precedent in history, so the feasibility of a contemporary mass transit system has yet to be proven. A true mass transit system for the US may, in fact, not be possible.

The potential energy savings of mass transit, in the context of implementing such a system in today's configuration of cities and urban sprawl may be highly overrated. Figure 11.4 depicts the Btus of energy per passenger mile (assuming average passenger densities) for each type of transportation. This demonstrates that existing mass transit systems in the US do not provide significant fuel savings. However, vanpool Btu per passenger mile is 1,294, hinting at the possibilities of a Jitney system.[5]

The Smart Jitney Option

A new transport paradigm would place the highest priority on minimizing the use of fossil fuels, a priority higher than convenience, speed or personal freedom. A new approach could solve some of the problems of the existing system. For example, it could be much safer. It could also give people precedence over vehicles. Walking, cycling and buses could be made more convenient and cars less convenient, reversing the trend of the last century. This differs from most of today's proposed solutions which involve combinations of mass transit and using coal generated electricity to fuel private electric automobiles.

The Smart Jitney proposal is an intermediate technology which increases service and reduces energy use by more efficiently utilizing existing vehicles. A jitney could be defined as a small vehicle that carries passengers over a regular route on a flexible schedule. Another definition of a jitney is an unlicensed taxicab. Basically, a jitney is a form of mass transit using cars and vans, not passenger buses. Jitneys typically are not required to travel specific routes on a specific schedule the way trains, buses and street cars do. Jitneys could provide anywhere, any time, and any place pick up and drop off service. They could also provide a very high level of security and safety. Jitneys are both ancient and contemporary.

A US jitney system could basically increase passenger occupancy from the current 1.6 persons per trip to 3-5 times that number. An increase of 3 times would use $1/3$ the number of vehicles to achieve the same number of passenger trips, removing most of the cars on the road and thus substantially reducing fuel consumption and CO_2 emissions.

The Smart Jitney's advantage is that it could be quickly implemented using the existing US vehicle fleet. A jitney system would make it possible for people to continue to travel fairly long distances to work, school and for necessities when gasoline shortages begin or when people realize that the deteriorating climate effects of CO_2 emissions can no longer be tolerated.

Smart Jitney Benefits

One key benefit of the Smart Jitney is faster transit time. Commuters sitting on freeways in any large American city experience stop-and-go traffic at rush hour, averaging only a few miles per hour for much of the journey. A Smart Jitney system eliminates most of the cars currently on the road, allowing much more rapid flow of traffic. Even time for stopping to pick up and drop off riders would be small relative to time spent in the current congestion.

A second benefit is that the Smart Jitney uses the existing car fleet instead of requiring all new vehicles. It is important to begin thinking about passenger miles per gallon, not car miles per gallon. An SUV getting 10 miles per gallon containing six passengers achieves the same passenger mpg as a Honda Insight with one passenger! The Smart Jitney changes the current car paradigm rather than waiting decades to replace the current fleet or improve car miles per gallon.

The third major benefit is drastically reducing consumption of fossil fuels. Increasing the number of passengers per vehicle would provide a large reduction in fuel use. This will help avoid economic disaster, lower the chances of worldwide wars over fossil fuel resources and, even more important, reduce CO_2 emissions substantially. This is a major step in eliminating the specter of global warming with its potential for massive disasters and loss of life.

The fourth benefit of the Smart Jitney is eliminating the tens of thousands of deaths and millions of injuries we currently accept as part of ordinary life. The technology proposed will include monitoring driving in real time and recording driver performance by Auto Event Recorders (AERs). Lives would be saved because of the associated decrease in traffic and because the best drivers would be at the wheel. In addition, lowering speed limits to save gasoline will lower the accident rate even more.

Smart Jitney Technology

The technology needed for Smart Jitney implementation is already available in the form of existing automobiles. Jitneys can be any vehicle, new or old, small or large, but with the minor addition of a special cell phone connected to the car. The cell phone would include GPS capability as well as an emergency call button for security. Whenever the rider or driver felt any sense of danger or threat, punching an emergency call button could automatically transmit information to the nearest law enforcement center for assistance.

Each passenger using the jitney system could use a personal cell phone, computer or regular phone to access the system. Initially there would be relatively small adjustments to the existing vehicle fleet and the ubiquitous cell phones currently dominating communication. Reservation tracking systems would need to be developed and installed. The reservation system would control both the ride management and bookkeeping of this new transportation modality. Rides would be planned and scheduled in a similar way to an airline reservation, except in a more timely, local and responsive manner.

Scientists have already developed many kinds of ride optimization algorithms to coordinate complex pickup and deliveries for both people and materials. Systems used by Fed Ex and UPS optimize pickup and delivery. An

Auto Event Recorder (AER) is analogous to the flight recorder on an airplane. AERs already exist on more recently manufactured automobiles; the National Transportation Safety Board (NTSB) estimates that 65 to 90% of all vehicles in the United States contain some type of AER.[6] These systems record driving activity that is taking place in real time including vehicle speed. This information would provide the basis for adding a new level of traffic safety and could be fully implemented nationally.

Smart Jitney Process

The Smart Jitney system will be accessed by the Internet or telephone. In either case, a request for service would be initiated by a passenger contacting the service and entering a pickup location and a destination location along with desired times for pick up and drop off. One could also specify the level of service desired (see Options for Levels of Service below).

The Smart Jitney control center would constantly be monitoring all cars that are part of the system, including the number of passengers, destinations and vacant seats available. Once the analysis was completed (requiring only a few seconds of computer calculation) the rider would be assigned to a participating vehicle. The driver of the vehicle would be notified and provided the pickup location and time, along with directions.

The rider would be picked up and dropped off as requested. After the trip, the rider would submit an evaluation by cell phone or via the Internet, similar to the evaluation used by the Internet based company E-Bay. By publishing customer satisfaction for all to see, E-Bay eliminates many complaints, because people simply stop buying from sellers with poor delivery performance. By having both a ride evaluation and AERs, driver records of long-term performance would be available.

Options for Levels of Service

The easiest and most efficient system would be one where all riders take whatever ride is available. It might be difficult for Americans to share in such a completely democratic jitney system. Therefore, different levels of service might be required. The first level of service could be more or less random. Only the pickup and destination locations would be entered along with the time of pickup and preferred time of drop off. The rider would input the data and the system would inform him or her of the car description, driver name and time of pickup. The rider would accept random assignment to the most available vehicle. This level would allow for the most possible rides and the quickest service.

A second level of service could allow a person to input preferences, requesting rides with certain groups of people. Possibly the most important would be for women to be able to request rides with other women. Men could also request non-coed trips. Another option would be to request certain age groups. Still others might want to put limits on the playing of radios or wish to ride with people who will be quiet. Any rider could be allowed to select the mode that best suits them. Of course, if a rider's preferences were too strict, availability of rides would decline.

A third level of service could allow scheduling future rides with a specific set of people. For example, a group of people with mutual interests who have a predictable schedule on a regular basis (such as work or school) could easily plan to travel together. This would mean that for family outings, all could ride together. Other levels of service would be added as experience dictates.

The Smart Jitney Driver

The Smart Jitney need not be implemented as a separate business like a taxi-cab service or a mass transit business. It is a form of ride-sharing using existing passenger vehicles and existing drivers. Overall, the number of people driving should decrease significantly. Although people could still drive and maintain an automobile, it is expected that eventually most people would accept the role of passenger. Anyone with a good driving record could serve as a jitney driver but certain limitations would be required. For example, inexperienced drivers could not be jitney drivers. Minimum age limits for drivers might correspond to age limits set by insurance and rental car companies, which reflect the higher accident rates of younger drivers.

More rigorous driving tests could be administered to grant qualification as a jitney driver. People with poor driving records, as measured by accidents and traffic citations, could also be barred from being Smart Jitney drivers. People with DWI convictions might not be permitted to be drivers until some time had elapsed or they had completed some type of re-qualification. People with child molestation records could be excluded. Similarly, existing Smart Jitney drivers could also lose driving privileges based on poor driving or the use of intoxicants. Finally, not everyone would want to be a jitney driver.

Drivers would be compensated for providing the transportation service, with the fee regulated similar to mass transportation fees. An additional benefit for drivers would be greater access to dwindling fossil fuels and more flexibility in transportation.

Addressing Concerns — Security, Safety and Privacy

Evaluators of this Smart Jitney proposal typically are concerned with issues of personal security, safety and privacy. In general, women are more concerned than men about security. Other issues deal with a feeling of loss, both of private time while driving and the loss of the self-esteem associated with ownership of a vehicle. Americans have been taught to believe vehicle ownership says something about who they are. The automobile has become far more than transportation — it represents the good life. It also represents a form of addiction.

The private automobile has also been responsible for the fears and concerns many of our Smart Jitney evaluators expressed. Cars certainly have made crime much easier — perpetrators can be miles away from the scene of the crime in minutes. Date rape becomes easier when two people are alone in a vehicle.

Moreover, the image of the private automobile, as presented in advertising, is typically one of power, speed and force. Cars are sold on that basis, with strong emphasis on the individual together with implied contempt for the community. The poor record of young male drivers is possibly based more on driving with a certain machismo image in mind than from a lack of driving skill. The Smart Jitney could serve as a vehicle for cultural change as well as a new transportation modality. But to do so, security, safety and privacy problems must be addressed.

Security

Security is a term that covers the risk and danger from other people who, for whatever reason, may intend some kind of harm to our persons or psyches. Concerns about personal security are not trivial. The US is a very dangerous culture, and its citizens are more violent than the majority of people in the rest of the world.[7] Women have good reason for concern. But most American men, although feeling more secure than women, must also take the necessary precautions for living in a violent society. "I wouldn't ride with a man," many female reviewers of the Smart Jitney have said, stating openly their fear of the violence in our culture. Initially, the ability to choose to ride only with other women must be part of the Smart Jitney system. Additionally, children and minors must also be protected from bullying or other anti-social behavior. Everyone — men, women and children — must be protected from the potential of violent or bullying passengers.

As noted earlier, at the completion of each ride, passengers could be asked to rate their Smart Jitney experience, covering such categories as the condition of the vehicle and the skill and suitability of the driver. With multiple passengers daily providing reviews, poor or unsuitable drivers could quickly be identified and their jitney license taken away. Eventually, selection of top-rated drivers could become an option when scheduling a ride. Obnoxious passengers could also be identified by the rating system.

Safety

Safety in relationship to automobiles refers to the accidents, deaths and injuries that come from a myriad of causes including auto and traffic equipment, roads, unintentional driver errors and reckless drivers. Initially, to insure vehicle safety there would have to be mandatory inspection of vehicles for Smart Jitney licensing. Annual inspections would also be required. Passenger reviews could include questions on the apparent suitability of the vehicle.

At first Smart Jitneys would be existing cars, but eventually, as much higher mpg vehicles became available, they would be replaced. Newer vehicles would be developed with a focus on safety rather than style. Instead of more car electronics for watching TV in the car, accessing the Internet or automatically parking the vehicle, collision avoidance electronics could be installed. Automobile companies have always given priority to speed, styling and image over safety. However, if the forty billion dollars spent annually on automobile R&D were redirected from styling changes, then major safety improvements could be realized quickly.[8] Furthermore, cars could be designed for longevity and ease of repair, which would contribute to reduced CO_2 emissions by minimizing the amount of embodied energy expended on the automobile fleet.

Traffic equipment and roads must be carefully evaluated, but they are not the main reason for accidents. Driver errors could be dramatically reduced by setting a lower speed limit; 45-55 miles per hour is the optimum speed for efficient performance of automobile internal-combustion engines.[9] Slower moving vehicles with higher passenger density would leave more of our streets available for bicycles and also reduce the risks involved in riding bikes in traffic. Through this shift to ride-sharing, the US could set a high priority on reducing highway carnage. Legislation and market demand for safe jitney vehicles could force automobile manufacturers to improve safety standards.

Privacy

Protecting privacy means respecting people's need to maintain the confidentiality of their personal identification including name, pictures, employer or place of residence. A breach in privacy occurs when people intrude in our life through inappropriate access to this personal data.

In modern times, real privacy is increasingly limited even though people have a sense of it in their private cars and homes. Internet access and phone records, along with other private information, can now be purchased by businesses, corporations and individuals. Government agencies such as the CIA, FBI and NSA maintain civilian databases. Marketing of people's personal information is now acceptable and viewed simply as a business opportunity. The 2006 Hewlett-Packard scandal on pretexting shows how easy it is for people's personal information to be obtained.[10]

With people sharing rides with strangers on a daily basis, protection of privacy will be a challenge. The Smart Jitney system could utilize the same methods of anonymity and protection as banks or any other institution promising confidentiality with the similar caveat that these institutions use. That is, they cannot absolutely guarantee that ride-sharing information will not one day be inadvertently revealed or stolen. Infractions of privacy could be traced back in the ride-sharing system by reviewing ride records, and appropriate responses to violations might include denial of ride service.

Implementation Strategies

Implementing a system of this complexity would not be difficult. Although the Smart Jitney is different than existing ride and car share systems, they serve as a model for how technology could be developed. One rental car company, Zipcar.com, has an Internet system with some of the scheduling features and GPS tracking proposed for the Smart Jitney. In the United Kingdom, liftshare.org administers a ride-sharing program which matches riders and loads to cars and trucks around the country, utilizing phone and Internet connections. Liftshare has more than 200,000 individuals and businesses as members.

Mitfahrzentrale.de, based in Germany, offers ride-sharing throughout Europe to 675,000 members.[11]

Creating a new video game for teenagers requires more technological effort than would be needed to develop the Smart Jitney system. An 18-month feasibility model could be done for less than one million dollars (developing a new car model can cost close to one billion dollars). Prototype systems could be made available a year after that with expenditures of a few more million dollars. This is a much lower-risk effort than building fuel cell cars or beefing up a national coal-based power grid for battery vehicles.

Changes in the legal system, the law enforcement system and many aspects of the existing transportation system are required. Because of resistance to such major changes, a grassroots effort to develop the Smart Jitney may be the best way to start. A cooperative public development, similar to what created the LINUX computer operating system, may be the best way to achieve early implementation. To date, all development of the Smart Jitney has been put into the public domain. This open source approach may attract programmers to begin rapid development. Hardware changes are minor and, should manufacturers with vested interests be reluctant to develop the ideal products, existing technology can be adapted. Once the system is underway, the market may find and develop lucrative options outside the purview and control of major auto manufacturers. An effort by a few hundred systems engineers and programmers could lead to this paradigm shift in an amazingly short time.

Transportation Lessons from Cuba

What Cuba calls the *Special Period in Peacetime* (still ongoing) began as an economic crisis caused by the disintegration of the Soviet Union in the early 1990s. As noted earlier this led to the cessation of Soviet oil shipments to Cuba. Economic agreements with other Soviet bloc countries disintegrated at the same time. This caused daily electricity blackouts and severe shortages of oil, fossil fuel products and food. There were no resources and not enough time or money to build a light rail or underground mass transit system or import efficient cars. So out of necessity, Cuba built an ad hoc surface mass transit system using whatever was available from hand-made bicycles to massive buses fabricated in machine shops. Cuban transportation today can only be described as fascinating, eclectic and difficult. Few Cubans have cars and it is unlikely that the percentage will grow. This may be one of the most remarkable things about Cuba — a whole nation giving up the worldwide vision of owning a private car.

Bicycles

Without imported oil from the Soviet Union, transportation in Cuba became totally paralyzed. There were no cars running, public transportation collapsed and the streets were empty. Cuba imported two million heavy Chinese bikes and manufactured half a million more. Everyone lost weight, partially caused by pedaling in the tropical heat. At the depth of the Special Period, the average Cuban lost 20 pounds.[12] By 1995 the worst of the economic crisis was over, and things slowly began to improve. Bicycles and yellow motorized two-passenger rickshaws are now prevalent in Havana and mix with cars and buses on Havana's streets.

Cuba did not have a culture of using bicycles, so it was very difficult for the people. Many had to bike long distances — up to 20 kilometers to and from work or 40 kilometers a day. When there were buses again, people stopped biking. Many now realize that to commit to using a bicycle requires more consciousness about energy. Most developed countries are focused on making the automobile more efficient, while driving longer and longer distances and buying more and more cars. Cubans say it is important to understand the energy required to produce and operate a car. Their challenge even now is to reduce the number of cars. They realize that the bicycle is not something that has to be used because there is no fuel, but understand that the bicycle never contaminates, is healthier to use and quite practical for short distances.

Buses and Ride Sharing

Most of Havana's buses are old, but they are always packed. One special Havana transport consists of a very large metal semi-trailer pulled by a standard ancient semi truck tractor. This vehicle can hold three hundred people and is called a Camel due to its odd shape. It is typically hot and crowded, but it is also very cheap. Dozens of old American cars from the 1950s, which would be valued collectors' items today in the US, are used as taxis all over Havana and elsewhere in the country. Cubans are master mechanics at being able to keep these cars running, particularly since the US trade blockade keeps the islanders from purchasing spare parts.

In outlying areas and small towns, donkey and horse carts, complete with a taxi license nailed to the frame, serve as public transportation. Many trucks have been converted to passenger transport vehicles by welding steps to the back so people can climb up and down easily. In some cases, two men, stationed at the back of a truck with a high bed, have the job of lifting passengers into and out of the truck. Many of these trucks have been equipped with canopies for shade. Ride sharing was basic to Cuba's transportation success during the Special Period. Hitchhiking is common, and government officials have the right to pull over government vehicles (indicated by the license plates) with empty seats and fill them with people needing a ride. It is not unusual to see an old Chevy with four people in front and four in the back. On the roads to and from Havana there are always hitchhikers soliciting rides. Few government officials have cars, but there are small buses to bring them to and from work or they share rides with someone who does have a car. The average Cuban consumes a fraction of the energy of the average American but is able with some inconvenience to get around the island by sharing vehicles.[13]

The Smart Jitney — Long Term Implications

The use of fossil fuels changed North America from a place of small local communities with limited mobility and resources to one of large urban concentrations with high mobility. Goods and food are shipped from thousands of miles away. This high mobility is based on the private car with its continuous use of significant quantities of gasoline. The advantages of this way of living, especially considering the effect on the climate, are becoming more and more questionable. Low-energy ways of living will need to include many changes, such as devolution from concentrated urban centers to smaller communities and local food supplies. Eventually a pattern of smaller neighborhoods and towns with a focus on walking and bicycling will be more the norm. This is not a return to some previous period in human history. Medical science and other advances will not be abandoned even if people drive less and share vehicles.

US culture has declined in many ways. Skills like politeness, good manners, courtesy and chivalry have atrophied. Misbehaving in public is cool. Conversing with strangers used to be an art form, and children were taught such social skills. One of the main cultural values of the developed world is competition; it is the key principle of our economic system. Cooperation, a key value in other cultures, is a sign of weakness in the US. Walking or getting in a car with a stranger or riding a bus may be just an inconvenience in other cultures. For

Americans, it is a threat to how we view ourselves. Peak oil and climate change will force us to be more cooperative.

As happened in Cuba, the Smart Jitney may start as a short-term emergency solution within the existing infrastructure, since it will allow us to keep similar patterns of living. Any inconvenience and discomfort experienced will be overshadowed by the possibility of stopping planetary degradation and its threat to basic survival. In the long run, the Smart Jitney could evolve into some mode of transportation not yet envisioned. It could help serve the larger physical community in the future as an intra-city mechanism for longer travel. It's possible that evolution of a jitney-based mass transit system, within the context of a decentralized local way of living, will naturally occur.

The world is at the end of the era of the private car, the ultimate example of American consumer values and the most destructive device ever made. The Smart Jitney can replace the private car and help restore community. Men may have to start behaving well to women. People may have to give up profane language in public for the same reasons smoking has been disallowed in public places. Just as people cannot drive when drunk, they may not be able to ride when drunk. Requiring respectful social behavior may appear to be counter to our so-called freedom, but to what extent has that freedom become nothing more than a license to be offensive? If all participants respected one another, a Smart Jitney ride could be a real pleasure as well as an energy-saving convenience.

Initially the Smart Jitney may be a traumatic change from using private cars. But the threat of energy shortages, loss of jobs and life threatening climate change provides motivation for trying out the system. The concept and design are such that long term benefits for the environment and society can accrue. Eventually, personal advantages in terms of time, safety and economics should become apparent, and this transport approach will not only help save us from climate disaster but prove to be superior to what we know now.

As this book was going to press, examples of implementations of the Smart Jitney concept appeared. Sean O'Sullivan, Executive Chairman of Mapflow, an Irish software company located in Kinsale, Ireland, demonstrated to the author a prototype Smart-Jitney-like system which is currently undergoing pilot trials.

Twelve

Food, Feed, Fuel and CO$_2$

WENDELL BERRY SAID there are really only two economic systems in the world, the agrarian and the industrial.[1] About 250 years ago, industrialism was born with the invention of a particular machine — the steam engine — and a particular philosophy — capitalism. And from that time on, the relationship between the old world and the new one has been one of conquest of the agrarian world by the industrial world. But because of peak oil (and future peaks for natural gas, coal and uranium) in combination with accelerating climate change, industrialism will be relatively short lived. I do not see this as a complete tragedy — the world we have created is violent, with extreme inequity and poverty. This industrial world is also destructive of what many agrarians hold dear — clean water, fertile soils, clear skies, wilderness and animals of all kinds.

Modern humans have become dependent on consuming increasing amounts of fossil fuels — resources that are dwindling even as their consumption generates more and more deadly greenhouse gases. The US has abandoned almost all sustainable practices of living and replaced them with practices that require fossil fuel energy. Hand tools and physical skills have been replaced with fossil fuel driven-machinery and fossil fuel-based chemicals. The unfortunate result is that, particularly in the developed world, much knowledge and many ordinary physical talents have been lost. If electricity were to suddenly disappear, not only would scientists and engineers not have slide rules to turn to but they might not know how to use them even if they could find a supply.

With food, this loss of traditional skills is particularly dangerous. Not only has much of the knowledge of how to grow food without fossil fuels been lost, but the understanding of good food and nutrition is also disappearing. Some of the most nutritious vegetables, such as kale, collard and Swiss chard, are no longer reported in the US government's agriculture statistics. Many people don't even know how to cook them.

Green Revolution = Fossil Fuel Revolution

In the mid 1940s, at the end of what I define as the agrarian period, the green revolution began in Mexico. Over the next 30 years, it spread throughout the world. In the popular view, the green revolution was based on miracle seeds — so called High Yielding Varieties (HYVs) which were designed to increase production. But HYVs significantly outperform traditional varieties only in the presence of adequate irrigation, agricultural petrochemicals and natural gas based fertilizers.[2] But in the absence of these fossil fuel inputs, traditional varieties may outperform HYVs. The production increases of the green revolution were actually due as much to refocusing WWII munitions technology on fertilizers and pesticides as HYV seed development. Thus the green revolution was a fossil fuel based agricultural revolution, not a biological one. The green revolution simply traded off a six fold increase in yields for the use of huge amounts of fossil fuels.[3] Before the green revolution it took no fossil fuels to produce a food Calorie. (It took one Calorie of energy (mostly muscular) for every five Calories of food produced).[4] Now it takes 10 fossil fuel Calories to deliver 1 food Calorie to a consumer in America (these 10 Calories include not just what is involved in growing crops but all the energy involved in getting food products to consumers — growing, processing, packaging, transportation and refrigeration).

The Loss of the Family Farm

In most of the rest of the world, food growing is still sustainable and a high percentage of the population still live on farms. But in the US, once the green revolution had proven itself, the government decided to change society. Monoculture crops require only ⅙ the labor. Farmers were driven from their homes and fields and into slums and factories under mottos like *Get Big or Get Out* (first formulated by US Secretary of Agriculture Ezra Taft Benson in the 1950s) and *Adapt or die* (US Secretary of Agriculture Earl Butz 20 years later).[5] Farmers were now free to find another line of work, but their vocation of farming and their love for the land was not considered. Similar to forced collectivization in the Soviet Union, it was a war on peasants. In the US this

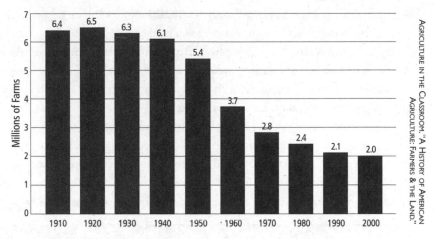

12.1: *Number of Farms in the US 1910 — 2000*

was highly successful with great suffering for family farmers and it continues still (Fig. 12.1).

As fossil fuel-intensive agribusinesses and petrochemicals replaced the skilled small farmer, much US food production became regionalized. Vegetables are grown in California, corn in the Midwest, potatoes in Idaho and wheat in eastern Washington. These foods are then shipped all over the country. Today, one bright spot in North America is an increasing appreciation of the need to grow food organically, without fossil fuel inputs. However, truly sustainable practices require that food be grown closer to the point of consumption in order to reduce the use of fossil fuels for shipping food long distances.

But making such changes will not be easy. Current farmers, who have become mere operators of machines and mixers of chemicals, may not have the skills to develop a local, sustainable agriculture. A new generation of farmers, numbering in the tens of millions, will need to be trained and relocated to rural communities. Other farmers (or more aptly gardeners) will be needed for suburban and urban agriculture. But to actually reduce greenhouse gases and save fuel, it will be necessary to change the American diet — and to do that we need to understand where our food comes from.

Manufacturing the American Diet

We can start to analyze the food habits of Americans by walking the aisles of a supermarket. There are 300,000 food and beverage products in the United

States, and an average supermarket carries 30,000 to 40,000. The popular view is that "the industry has brought Americans a food supply of astonishing variety, independent of season and geography."[6] But people don't eat 30,000 different foods. In fact, they eat a relatively small number of foods. The amazing choices are merely different recipes, or, in the parlance of the grocery manufacturing industry, different brands. Call it what you will — Wheaties, Wheat Thins, Yippee, Zoom, Real Crisp, Morning Delight or any other marketing name — breakfast cereals and snacks, like so many food products, are basically wheat or corn with sugar, salt and oil added. Factories combine white wheat flour, hydrogenated soybean oil and corn sweeteners with flavoring and coloring from chemicals in various ways to create much of the food Americans eat.

Crop (2004)	Harvested Acres	% of Acres	Yield/ Acre	Yield Unit
Grains				
Corn (grain)	73,631,000	25.2%	160.4	bu
Wheat	49,999,000	17.1%	43.2	bu
Sorghum	6,517,000	2.2%	69.6	bu
Barley	4,021,000	1.4%	69.6	bu
Rice	3,325,000	1.1%	69.9	cwt
Oats	1,787,000	0.6%	64.7	bu
Millet	595,000	0.2%	25.3	bu
Rye	300,000	0.1%	27.5	bu
Total	140,175,000	48.0%		
Hay				
Hay	61,966,000	21.2%	2.6	ton
Total	61,966,000	21.2%		
Oilseeds				
Soybeans	73,958,000	25.3%	42.2	bu
Sunflower	1,711,000	0.6%	12.0	cwt
Peanuts	1,394,000	0.5%	30.8	cwt
Canola	828,000	0.3%	16.2	cwt
Flaxseed	511,000	0.2%	20.3	bu
Safflower	159,000	0.1%	12.0	cwt
Mustard Seed	68,700	0.0%	8.2	cwt
Rape Seed	7,800	0.0%	13.9	cwt
Total	78,637,500	26.9%		

COMPILED FROM DATA IN AGRICULTURE STATISTICS 2006. UNITED STATES GOVERNMENT PRINTING OFFICE, 2006

Crop (2004) continued	Harvested Acres	% of Acres	Yield/ Acre	Yield Unit
Sugar				
Sugar Beets	1,306,900	0.4%	23.0	ton
Sugarcane	879,500	0.3%	31.0	ton
Total	2,186,400	0.7%		
Legumes				
Dry Beans	1,219,300	0.4%	14.6	cwt
Dry Peas	507,800	0.2%	7.9	cwt
Lentils	329,000	0.1%	12.0	cwt
Total	2,056,100	0.7%		
Fruits/Vegetables/Nuts				
Fruits	3,088,800	1.1%	1.0	ton
Vegetables	3,236,890	1.1%	1.0	ton
Nuts	926,200	0.3%	1.0	ton
Total	7,251,890	2.5%		
Grand Total	292,272,890	100.0%		

12.2: *Agricultural Land Area Harvested in US — 2004*

Even the flavor of processed foods is manufactured. America's flavor industry is located along the New Jersey turnpike, a small area that produces about ⅔ of the flavor additives sold in the US.[7] This $1.4 billion industry manufactures the additives that provide not just the flavor, but often the color, shape and texture for products as diverse as potato chips, corn chips, breads, crackers, breakfast cereals and pet foods, as well as ice creams, cookies, candies, toothpastes and mouthwashes. Once the core components have been mixed, flavored, shaped and dyed, they are placed in colorful, attractive packages — 300,000 products, yes, but in reality nothing more than variations of a few basic foods. Unfortunately, to transform these few basic food components into manufactured foods requires massive consumption of oil and other fossil fuels.

The Main Crops — Food and Feed

To determine what we actually eat — real foods and not the various recipes or branded products — we must figuratively walk the rows of crops in the fields rather than the aisles of supermarkets. Food comes from the soil, either as plants grown in fields or as meat and dairy products, which come from animals eating the plants grown in the fields. More than 99.7% of all US food comes from the land, while less than .3% comes from the ocean or other aquatic ecosystems.[8]

The United States Department of Agriculture (USDA) uses the word *food* to describe what humans eat and the word *feed* to describe what farm animals eat. The USDA also uses the term *crops* to describe the major food and feed plants. Most of the cultivated area in the US is devoted to four such crops — corn, hay, soybeans and wheat. Corn and hay are used principally to feed livestock, mostly beef cattle and dairy cows. Corn is also the major source of food sweeteners. Soybeans are a major feed crop for livestock, mostly for pigs and chickens, and are also a major source of food oil. Wheat is mostly used for human food, but a significant part is also used as animal feed. Figure 12.2 shows the distribution of these crops.

The total acreage harvested in 2004 for the four major crops (corn, hay, wheat, soybeans) was 265 million acres — about 85% of the land farmed in the US.[9] Other crops (as defined by the USDA) include the secondary grain crops of sorghum, barley, rice, oats, millet and rye. In addition to grain crops there are several plants that provide oils that are a key part of the American diet. These oil seed crops include soybeans, sunflowers, canola, flaxseed, safflower, mustard seed and rapeseed. Peanuts, cotton, sugar beets, sugar cane and tobacco are crops that require another 6 million acres (or 2% of the nation's fields) — rather insignificant when compared to the big four.

To give a more complete perspective of agricultural land use, we should consider fruits, vegetables and nuts as well. The USDA does not define these as crops, but places them in separate categories. These three food types use another nine million acres, about 3% of the agricultural area.

Measuring the Fields — Raw Materials for Manufactured Foods

As noted above, the industrial food system relies primarily on corn, white flour from wheat, soybeans and hay and has replaced more direct food production with a very complex manufacturing system heavily dependent on fossil fuels. The Grocery Manufacturers Association (GMA) represents the world's leading branded food, beverage and consumer product companies. GMA member companies employ more than 2.5 million workers across the US and account for more than $680 billion in annual sales.[10] The use of the word manufacturer in the organization's name is testimony to the industrial nature of the food products they make and sell, an industrial process that has led to soil depletion, air pollution, water pollution and unhealthy food. It's important to understand the food and feed crops that are the basis of this system.

Corn

The US is the largest producer of corn in the world, growing the grain on 400,000 farms. In the farming season of 2004/2005, the US produced 256 million metric tons of corn (about 12 billion bushels), 43% of total worldwide production (Fig. 12.3).[11]

Of the 11.8 billion bushels produced in 2004, 1.8 billion bushels were exported, leaving about 10 billion bushels for US domestic consumption. These 10 billion bushels convert to 560 billion pounds of corn, or about *1,900 pounds per person* (using a 2004 population number of 295 million).[12] That most of this corn is used in manufactured foods is clear since, on average, people in the US eat only 2,200 pounds of food per year.[13] USDA food consumption numbers show the average person directly consumes only about 11 pounds of

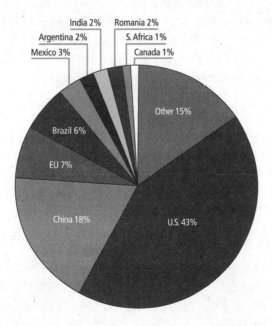

India 2% Romania 2%
Argentina 2% S. Africa 1%
Mexico 3% Canada 1%
Other 15%
Brazil 6%
EU 7%
China 18%
U.S. 43%

12.3: *World Corn Production 2004-2005*

NCGA.COM/WORLDOFCORN/2005/PRODUCTIONDATA3.HTM

NATIONAL CORN GROWERS ASSOCIATION.

corn and about 30 pounds of corn flour each year.[14] Little corn is consumed *directly*, but much is consumed *indirectly*, principally through meat and sweeteners. In 2004, 6.2 billion bushels were used as feed in Contained Animal Feeding Operations (CAFO).[15] So the US's largest crop is not used for direct human consumption but as feed for cattle and as sweeteners for manufactured food and drink.

Wheat

The second largest grain crop is wheat. Wheat is the fourth major crop in terms of acreage planted and harvested, following corn, soybeans and hay. It is the only grain crop used mostly for human food rather than animal feed. In 2004, 2,158 million bushels of wheat were harvested from 50 million acres, of which 1,063 million bushels were exported, or about 49% of the total. Domestic use was 1,172 million bushels, including 907 million bushels for human food and 79 million bushels for animal feed.[16] There are sixty pounds of wheat in each bushel so the 907 million bushels for food is about 184 pounds of unprocessed wheat per person.

Unfortunately for human health, most wheat in the US is turned into highly processed white flour. More than 98% of the 150 pounds of wheat flour consumed per capita in 1997 was refined, a process that removes fiber and many nutrients including vitamins, minerals and phytochemicals.[17] Most of these nutrients are not restored to refined flour, but instead fed to livestock.

Other grains

88% of grain acreage in the US is allocated to growing corn and wheat. The remaining grains (including sorghum, barley, oats, millet and rye) use only 12% of the farm land devoted to grain growing. These grains are also used primarily for feed with the exception of rice. Rice consumption in the US was 22.7 pounds per person in 2004.[18]

Soybeans and other Oil Seeds

The amount of arable land allocated to soybeans in the US is about the same as that allocated to corn, about 25%. The basic products of soybeans are oil, meal and hulls. According to the United Soybean Board, soybean oil, used in both food manufacturing and for frying and sautéing, represents approximately 80% of all edible oil consumed in the United States.[19] After the oil has been extracted from the soybean, the remaining materials (mostly complex carbohydrates) are fed to livestock (mainly pigs, chickens and turkeys) who consume over 30 million tons of soybean meal yearly. The hulls are used as a component of cattle feed even though corn is the main feed crop for beef cattle.

In the US, 94% of total oil seed acreage is allocated to growing soybeans. The remaining seven oil seed crops (sunflower, peanuts, canola, flax, safflower, mustard and rape seed) account for only 6% of the acreage.[20] Like corn, soybeans are not consumed directly but are used as raw materials for other kinds of foods and feeds. When consumed by people, soybeans are normally part of highly processed foods. Annually about 400 pounds of soybeans per person goes into feed for animals and manufactured foods.

Hay

Hay is the next largest planting in the US after corn and soybeans — 62 million acres for hay versus 148 million acres for the other two crops, with hay growing using 21% of arable land in the US.[21] Hay is the product of any of a variety of perennial crops, typically grasses or legumes, which are used as feed for ruminant animals, mostly dairy and beef cattle.

Sugar

Sugar cane and sugar beets used to provide most of our sweeteners. Acreage allocated for these crops is only about 7/10ths of 1% of farmed acreage in the US. Of the 141 pounds of sweeteners consumed by each person yearly, 61.5 pounds come from sugar cane and sugar beets, while 78.1 pounds comes from corn sweeteners, which dominate the manufactured foods market.[22]

Summarizing the raw materials

Hay, grains, oil seeds and plants grown for sugar cover 96% of cultivated land in the US.[23] Excluding wheat, which is mostly consumed as food rather than feed, the acreage devoted to the remaining food plants is 79% of the total acreage. The remaining land available (less than 4%) is used to grow nutritious foods such as legumes, nuts, fruits and vegetables. This shows that the US food system, which uses 10 Calories of fossil fuels to provide one Calorie of food energy, relies on a handful of plants (corn, hay, soybeans), mostly used to produce meat and manufactured foods.[24]

Measuring the Fields — Nutritious Foods

Dietary science suggests that we avoid manufactured foods and foods high in fats and sugar as well as modern meats which are high in fats. A healthier diet would avoid many of our common foods and focus on four main categories: beans (or legumes), vegetables, fruits and nuts.

Beans (Legumes)

The US consumes a disproportionately large amount of the world's grains and oil seeds but consumes far fewer beans than other nations. Only .7% of the harvested acreage in the US is allocated to beans, peas and lentils.[25] Historically beans have been a staple crop for protein in much of the world. Only in recent times has meat replaced them as the primary source of protein in many countries. Figure 12.4 below shows that the same weight of beans provides more protein but much less fat than meat.

Food		Kidney Beans	Beef Chuck
NDB No (USDA)		16027	13936
Nutrient	Units	Value/100 gr.	Value/100 gr.
Energy	kcal	333.0	129.0
Protein	gr.	23.6	19.5
Total lipid (fat)	gr.	0.8	5.1
Carbohydrate	gr.	60.0	0
Fiber	gr.	24.9	0

USDA.NAL.USDA.GOV/FNIC/FOODCOMP/SEARCH/

12.4: *Protein Comparison — Beans and Meat*

Vegetables

1.1% of US farmland is used to grow vegetables with the average American consuming 411.5 pounds of vegetables in a year.[26] Potatoes account for 134.5 pounds, about 1/3 of the weight of all vegetables eaten. There are 263 Calories in a pound of potatoes, significantly more than the other vegetables. Thus potatoes alone provide 47% of the vegetable Calories Americans consume each year.[27]

Fruits

The top five fruits (see list of all fruits in the next chapter) account for 70% of fruit production by weight and 69% by Calories. 1.1% of US farmland is devoted to fruit production. Americans consume about 272 pounds of fruit in a year with 113 of the 272 pounds consumed as fruit juices.[28] Many nutrients and most of the fiber are lost when fruit is juiced. On average, each pound of fruit contains about 240 Calories, almost twice that of vegetables.[29] Unfortunately much fruit is highly processed. Sweeteners and preservatives are also added to most commercial juice drinks, increasing Calories at the expense of nutrients.

Nuts

People in the US eat very few nuts. Of 10.9 pounds of nuts per person eaten each year, 6.7 pounds are peanuts, which is a tuber rather than a true nut from a tree. Peanuts, almonds and walnuts provide about 75% of the pounds and Calories in the nut category. Only .3% of farm land is used for nut growing.[30]

Harming Ourselves

What I have called nutritious foods are those that are minimally processed and which contain more vitamins, minerals and phytochemicals than manufactured products. They are also the foods that require more care and attention in growing and harvesting. These foods do not deplete the soil as much, require less fossil fuels and are not subsidized as heavily as US grain and oil crops. Essentially they contribute more to health both because they are more nutrient intense and also because they are lower in fats and refined carbohydrates.

Of all the industrialized rich nations, Americans are the unhealthiest. By way of example, the US now spends about $6,000 per person per year on health care and its citizens' life expectancy is 77 years, while Canada spends about $3,200 per person per year on health care and Canadians have a life expectancy of about 80 years.[31] US medical costs per capita are twice those of most Europeans.[32] In other parts of the world as people begin to eat more meat, they tend toward Western disease patterns, a trend so common that it has been named the *nutrition transition*.

The US is known for its cheap food (annual food expenses are about $3,600 per person),[33] and its citizens buy and consume more than they need. Two-thirds of Americans are overweight or obese.[34] The US economy is committed to growth, implying continuous increases in consumption for a wide range of products. Industrial food companies are no exception, increasing sales by changing the way people eat. Their advertising encourages people to eat animal products as well as numerous manufactured, highly processed foods made from combinations of plant products. The growth of industrial food companies has led to larger, fatter, unhealthy consumers. Thus, food companies have achieved growth at the cost of poor health for the consumer.

Meat Consumption

Historically, animals' grazing was on lands that were not easily cultivated, such as steep hillsides and other marginal land. Cows, goats and sheep can live on grass and turn this plant source, indigestible by humans, into meat and milk that humans *can* digest. For most of history people ate a diet with large amounts of vegetables and small amounts of meat and fish. The US diet changed dramatically from this norm after the rapid increase in the use of fossil fuels that began at the end of World War II. From World War II until now, world consumption of oil increased eightfold, from 11 million barrels per day to 84 million barrels per day.[35] During the same period global meat production increased five fold.[36] In 2005, total US meat consumption (red meat, poultry and fish) amounted to 203 pounds per person, 88 pounds more than the 115 pounds consumed in 1935. This is about half today's per capita consumption.[37] Fossil fuels made this increase possible.

In 1961 world per capita meat consumption was 51 pounds per person per year, divided into 21 pounds per person in the developing world and 116 pounds per person in the developed world. Today world meat consumption is 92 pounds per person, 68.2 pounds per person in developing countries and 187 pounds per person in developed countries.[38] World per capita meat consumption almost doubled in less than 50 years. North Americans eat over 100 pounds more meat per person than Europeans as shown in Figure 12.5.

North America	271 lbs.
South America	154 lbs.
Asia	62 lbs.
Sub Sahara Africa	29 lbs.
Europe	163 lbs.
Central America	103 lbs.
North Africa	57 lbs.

EARTHTRENDS.WRI.ORG

12.5: *World Regional Meat Per Capita Consumption — 2002*

Meat and Fossil Fuels

Of the ten Calories of fossil fuels necessary to provide one Calorie of food energy, about 40% is used for fertilizers, pesticides, fungicides and herbicides, about 23% for processing and packaging and about 32% in home refrigeration/freezing and cooking.[39] The US food system uses about 17% of the total fossil fuels consumed each year in the nation, about 10 boe/c (barrels of oil equivalent per person) per year for food alone.[40] Compare this to the *total average energy use* of the developing world (5.7 billion people) of 8.3 barrels of oil equivalent per person per year.[41] In other words, the amount of fossil fuel each American uses *for food alone* (about 10 boe/c yearly) exceeds the amount of fossil fuels used by citizens of the developing world *for all purposes* (8.3 boe/c). The approximate CO_2 generated from the fossil fuels used in the US food system is about 7,000 pounds per person per year.

Today, the average US citizen consumes 202 pounds per year of food grain and indirectly (through meat eating) 1,795 pounds of feed grains. The average Chinese person consumes directly 851 pounds per year of food grains and indirectly 154 pounds of feed grains. Essentially the Chinese are eating grain grown in the fields while Americans are passing the grain through animals, a highly inefficient process.[42]

The energy differential between generating protein from plants and generating protein from meat is profound. To produce one Calorie of plant protein requires 2.2 Calories of fossil fuel energy, while to produce one Calorie of factory raised animal protein requires 25 Calories of fossil fuel energy. Thus it takes 11 times as many fossil fuel Calories to get the same amount of protein from meat as from plants.[43] Meat produced by feeding corn and soybeans to animals provides much of America's diet. The increase in meat consumption is related to the increase in the production of corn and soybeans, the heart of the fossil fuel based green revolution.

Meat and Climate Change

The change from eating grains directly to eating animals fed by grains has and is causing great harm to the environment. Livestock are a major emitter of the greenhouse gases that contribute to climate change. As meat consumption increases around the world, changing our diets may prove to be as important and as difficult as changing our transportation vehicles. A 2006 report by the Food and Agricultural Organization of the United Nations found that the world's rapidly growing herds of cattle are a major threat to the climate, to forests and to wildlife. While the report also analyzes the damage done by sheep, chickens, pigs and goats, it is the world's 1.5 billion cattle that do the most damage.[44]

Raising livestock generates 9% of all CO_2 emissions, 37% of methane emissions, and 65% of nitrous oxide emissions on the planet.[45] Methane has 23 times the global warming potential of CO_2, and nitrous oxide has 296 times the potential. When methane and nitrous oxide are measured in CO_2 equivalent units, livestock are responsible for 18% of the total greenhouse gases that cause global warming worldwide — *more greenhouse gas emissions measured in CO_2 equivalents than that generated by transportation.*[46]

These emissions are not simply cattle flatulence and manure. Changing from pastures to feed crops as the basis for raising animals requires more use of fossil fuel energy to produce fertilizers, pesticides, herbicides and fungicides, along with electricity to pump water. Additionally, deforestation in developing countries removes one of the planet's *sinks* for greenhouse gases. Ranching is the major driver of deforestation worldwide, and overgrazing is turning grassland into desert.

Cows also drink vast amounts of water, requiring 990 liters to produce one liter of milk.[47] Pollution from this modern form of industrial meat and milk production also washes down to the sea, creating dead zones devoid of life. One such dead zone, in the Gulf of Mexico, is largely the result of chemicals associated with US beef production that is carried down the Mississippi River.[48]

Meat or the Planet?

Like many present day industrial practices, the process of providing meat for our tables has grown increasingly problematic. As climate change worsens, factory meat farming will become unsustainable. As fossil fuels become ever more limited and expensive, a return to humane practices — using sunlight to grow grasses rather than fossil fuels to grow grain — will most likely occur. Animals will again be raised on the same farm with crops so that their manure can be used as fertilizer. The Contained Animal Feeding Operations (CAFO) system is only 50 years old. Thus, more sustainable ways of producing meats should be neither hard to comprehend nor difficult to implement.

As with houses and cars, consumer food choices have a major influence on the environment. A recent study by researchers at the Union of Concerned Scientists named modern day food production as one of the most environmentally harmful consumer activities. According to this study, the second most effective environmental choice that a consumer can make is to eat less meat and poultry (second to driving less and/or driving an energy efficient car). The authors list buying organic produce as a very effective environmental choice after eating less meat.[49] They suggest that such food choices have a greater positive environmental impact than household changes such as installing efficient lighting and appliances, and certainly more impact than the much less significant options of *paper versus plastic* or throwing away a disposable cup.

The difference in the fossil fuel energy required to sustain a meat-based versus a vegetarian diet is surprising. David Pimentel calculates that providing a 3,600 daily Calorie diet with 1,000 Calories coming from animal products requires about 35,000 Calories of fossil fuel energy whereas a 3,600 Calorie vegetarian diet (with more than sufficient levels of protein) takes about 18,000 Calories of fossil fuel energy — about half that of the non-vegetarian diet. A lacto-ovo vegetarian diet (including milk and eggs) requires around 25,000 Calories of fossil fuel energy. From the standpoint of CO$_2$ generation, choosing a vegetarian diet, or at least one greatly reduced in animal products, significantly reduces the environmental impact.[50]

Other Meat Considerations

The previous sections deal with the energy costs of growing animal food and producing meat. There are several side effects that are also harmful.

Torturing Food Animals

The livestock revolution led to a system of meat production that also causes incredible suffering to animals. Animals, like people, have a natural way of living. Cows and sheep graze, pigs root and chickens scratch in the dirt — traditionally, animals ate foods readily available in the natural world around them. Today, animals are confined in buildings removed from the natural world. As an analogy, imagine a child born in a hospital who never leaves the building. Or, more aptly, imagine a child born who never leaves its crib — the crib being sized to allow a full growth to six feet or so. This large crib would be located so that the child would never see the outside world, all of which constitutes an appalling situation, but still not as bad as that which millions of animals actually face every day. Veal calves and pigs, for example, are imprisoned in cages so that they can never turn around. They spend their life facing one direction with a view of another animal in a cage in front of them. Chickens are placed six to a cage with a floor area about the size of a place mat. The animals live their lives constantly breathing fecal matter. Beef cattle are allowed to live in small pens and can move around, but they are always standing in fecal material and urine. Pig fecal material drops into vats beneath their cages from which a powerful odor constantly assail their nostrils.

Most of the antibiotics in the US are used to fight the bacteria rampant in these feeding enclosures. The antibiotics keep the animals alive but do nothing to alleviate their suffering. Their lives are agony from birth to death, and the mortality rate is high. The grain based diets are foreign to their natures and designed to produce as much meat as fast as possible. By the end of their short lives, their bodies are unhealthy with dangerous levels of fat embedded in the meat.[51]

Killing the Soil

A square foot of healthy soil contains millions of living creatures. In a natural cycle, food comes from the soil and is consumed by animals, including humans, who then give nutrients back to the soil in the form of feces, urine and corpses, enabling the soil to produce more food, which is consumed again by animals, etc. Humans have broken this cycle in dangerous ways, particularly with Confined Animal Feeding Operations (CAFO). Now, instead of the natural food-waste-food cycle, there are enormous amounts of animal sewage to contend with, along with declining soil fertility.

Failure to return decaying matter (both animal and plant) to the soil, combined with the aggressive use of machinery for tilling and harvesting, also leads to erosion, further undermining the natural cycle. Currently, the US is losing about an inch of topsoil from its croplands every 34 years.[52] Under an ideal agriculture situation, where soil is supplemented with large amounts of fertile organic matter, an inch of soil would be rejuvenated in perhaps 30 years. Unfortunately, left to heal itself present agricultural land may take 200-1000 years to form an inch of soil.[53] A significant danger to US food security is that our US agricultural land is so damaged that it will take several years of active rebuilding — using organic methods of soil restoration — to regain the fertility lost by unsustainable practices.

Rebuilding the soil is difficult but not impossible as shown in Cuba. Before the fall of the Soviet Union Cuban agriculture was the most automated in Latin America and used more tractors, pesticides, and fertilizers per acre. Cuba even exceeded the amount of fertilizer used per acre in the United States. All of this changed overnight. Suddenly there was no petroleum to run tractors, no fertilizers, no pesticides and no herbicides. Cubans found that their soil, recently farmed using petrochemicals, was so depleted and dead that their yields dropped drastically. Without a source of fertilizers and pesticides, Cuba chose to turn to organic farming. It took from three to five years to rebuild land fertility so that it could be productive again. Much of our agricultural land is in this predicament, so devoid of nutrients and life that yields would be extremely poor without fossil fuel inputs. We have a major job ahead of us in restoring our soils to natural fertility.

Exploiting Farmers and Farm Workers

Our food system is cruel to animals, damaging to other wildlife and destructive of the soil. It has also caused great harm and suffering to farmers. The suicide rate among farmers is three times that of the country as a whole.[54] People who love their farms, care about the farm animals and protect the soil for future generations have been replaced with large agribusiness farms and Contained Animal Feeding Operations (CAFO). The loss of the personal touch of the dedicated farmer at the expense of fossil fuel based methods of growing crops and animals has increased yields while damaging land, waterways and lives.

While the ranks of small farmers are being decimated, farm workers, most of them immigrants, take on the dangerous, arduous and toxic work of laboring in industrialized fields. The average US farm worker has a life expectancy of just 49 years. Farm laborers are generally paid piecework rates. Their average earnings are $7,500 a year, or $150 a week, the lowest wage of any occupation. Few receive overtime pay, medical insurance or sick leave and rarely are they permitted to organize. In many states, farm workers are excluded from workers' compensation and unemployment benefits.[55] Agricultural interests and government ignore the plight of the farm worker. The 1935 Wagner Act, allowing workers to organize unions without interference from employers and the 1938 Fair Labor Standards Act both excluded farm workers. Farming is one of the top ten most hazardous occupations after logging, fishing, commercial aviation, construction and refuse work.[56]

Since the 1970s, the public has demanded that Congress pass laws to protect the physical environment. Businesses in the United States are now forced to consider environmental factors as part of the cost of doing business. Environmentally abusive industrial methods might produce cheaper consumer products, but such an approach is no longer considered acceptable. Unfortunately human misery is not considered part of the environment. Consumers may criticize environmentally unsound growing practices but rarely speak up for exploited farm workers. Farmers are more at risk than any other group for cancer-caused mortality.[57]

Part of a sustainable world is to provide decent livings for both small farmers and farm workers, things sadly missing in the US. America's exploitation of illegal immigrants helps to obscure the poor working conditions of farm laborers. And the American disdain for manual work, plus people's insistence on cheap food, exploits and destroys family farmers.

The Bottom Line — Changing Diets

As we search for options to combat oil depletion and global warming, it is becoming clear that we must rethink all the patterns of living that consume fuel and generate CO_2. Many patterns can be changed with some discomfort. For example, without a car, a person can walk, hitchhike, ride a bus, ride a bike or share a ride. He or she can use a down sleeping bag at night and, if the situation is desperate, go without heat. But since people cannot live without food, we must reduce our consumption of energy by eating differently. Lobbying for government policy change is useful, and community food development can be important. But such actions will do little as long as Americans consume food in their habitual way. The most important step is for each person to begin changing their diet. No other option offers a way to dramatically cut energy consumption, stop the exploitation of farm workers and rebuild the soil.

Thirteen

Food, Health and Survival

PEOPLE OF A GENERATION or two ago had a better understanding of food and nutrition than a person with a graduate degree today. US citizens have been dumbed down by the advertising and public relations efforts of big growers, distributors, supermarket chains and the USDA. Americans have become target markets for the manufactured food industry, and the physical health of people today has been as severely compromised as if they had been gradually poisoned. As pointed out in the preceding chapter, the American diet has shifted dramatically to factory raised meat and manufactured foods high in fat and sugars. The application of fossil fuels to our food system has affected not only how we grow food but what we grow, with disastrous results for the planet. Our major grain and oil crops, along with hay, are transformed into foods high in fat and artificial sweeteners and low in nutrients. Fresh, diverse whole foods that were the basis of our pre-World War II diet are sparse in the US today. Transitioning to a low-energy diet could be the most important way for each of us to save the planet and ourselves.

Analyzing the American Diet

It is important to understand the negative effects of the American diet and to analyze the wide variety of food crops that are available as options to manufactured foods made from corn, white flour and soybeans. I discussed the relationship between the acreage of food and feed crops harvested and the food eaten in the last chapter. Now we will consider what we eat, who manufactures our food, the consequences to our health and the environment and what to do about it.

Calorie Intense Foods	Pounds	Nutrient Intense Foods	Pounds
Dairy Products	591.8	Vegetables	411.6
Caloric Sweeteners	141.5	Fruits	274.3
Red Meats	111.9	Flour and Cereal	192.3
Fats and Oils	93.7	Nuts	9.9
Poultry	72.6	Beans and Legumes	7.0
Eggs	33.0	Other	24.0
Fish	16.5	Subtotal	919.1
Subtotal	1,061.0		
		Total - Calorie & Nutrient	1,980.1

SEE NOTE 1, P. 299.

13.1: *US Annual Per Capita Consumption in Pounds — Calorie and Nutrient Intense Foods*

Calorie Intense	Nutrient Intense
Meat-Milk-Eggs	Vegetables
Fats-Oils	Fruits
Sweeteners	Grains
	Nuts
	Legumes

PAT MURPHY

13.2: *Calorie Intense and Nutrient Intense Food Classes*

To fully understand America's diet, we need to know what foods are consumed, measured in pounds (Fig. 13.1). Equally important are the number of Calories obtained from each of the foods (Calories per pound). This data is enumerated in subsequent tables.[1]

I have divided foods into two classes — Calorie intense foods and nutrient intense foods (Fig. 13.2). Calorie intense foods typically (but not in all cases) provide more Calories but proportionately fewer minerals, vitamins and phytochemicals. There are three categories in this class: *meat-milk-eggs* (animal products from soy and corn feeds), *fats and oils* (mostly from soybeans) and *sweeteners* (mostly from corn). Nutrient intense foods, organized in five categories, provide proportionally more vitamins, minerals, phytochemicals and fiber with fewer Calories and are typically associated with good health.

The tables which follow list the principle foods consumed in each of these eight categories by pounds and Calories. Most frequently eaten foods top the tables, and the least frequently eaten foods are at the bottom. Each entry also includes the percentage of total pounds and Calories each food item represents. These tables represent the natural foods that the average American eats each year.

The food system provides 3,600 Calories per day or 1,314,000 Calories per year per person for each American.[2] Some food is wasted, spoiled, partially eliminated in preparation or lost in other ways. The purpose of this chapter is to show on a gross basis how Calories are distributed from the major classes of food. It does not account for wastage and other factors. This is a gross approximation compiled from different sources and is indicative of distribution rather than a comprehensive analysis with exact numbers. Even so, the 1,314,000 Calories amount comes close to the 1,435,608 Calories I derive from individual foods (see Figures 13.6 and 13.14) later in this chapter.

Calorie Intense Foods

Calorie intense foods include meat, fish, milk and eggs produced primarily from some form of Containment Animal Feeding Operation (CAFO) which convert hay, corn and soybeans into animal products.

Meat, Milk and Eggs — Animal Products

The average American consumes 861 pounds of meat, fish, milk products (including cheese) and eggs each year (Fig. 13.3). These foods contain on average 434 Calories per pound and provide 26.9% of a person's yearly total Calories. The top four foods — milk products, beef, chicken and pork — provide 93% of the pounds consumed and 89% of the Calories consumed in this category.

	Annual lbs.	% lbs.	Cals. /lb.	Annual Cals.	% Cals.
Milk Products	596.5	69.3%	255	152,108	40.7%
Beef	65.3	7.6%	1,155	75,422	20.2%
Chicken	86.2	10.0%	782	67,408	18.0%
Pork	49.5	5.7%	768	38,016	10.2%
Eggs	32.7	3.8%	605	19,784	5.3%
Fish & shellfish	16.1	1.9%	655	10,546	2.8%
Turkey	13.1	1.5%	677	8,869	2.4%
Lamb	1.1	0.1%	1,041	1,145	0.3%
Veal	0.5	0.1%	945	473	0.1%
Total lbs.	861.0				
Total Cals.	373,769				
Weighted Av. Cals./lb.	434				
% Yearly Cals.	26.9%				

SEE NOTE 1, P. 299.

13.3: *Animal Products — US Annual Per Capita Consumption*

Fats and Oils

Americans consume 93.7 pounds of fats and oils per person every year (Fig. 13.4). These oils contain an average of 3,906 Calories per pound and provide 26% of our total annual caloric intake. The top two oils — salad oil (mostly from soybeans) and shortening (also from plants) — provide almost 80% of the Calories and weight. These manufactured oils are partially responsible for the increase in obesity mentioned in the previous chapter.[3]

	Annual lbs.	% lbs.	Cals. /lb.	Annual Cals.	% Cals.
Salad Oil	42.7	45.6%	4,018	171,569	46.9%
Shortening	29.1	31.1%	4,018	116,924	31.9%
Canola	6.8	7.3%	4,018	27,322	7.5%
Margarine	4.0	4.3%	3,268	13,072	3.6%
Butter	4.6	4.9%	2,314	10,644	2.9%
Tallow	3.2	3.4%	4,100	13,120	3.6%
Olive Oil	1.8	1.9%	4,018	7,232	2.0%
Lard	1.5	1.6%	4,100	6,150	1.7%
Totals lbs.	93.7				
Total Cals.	366,034				
Weighted Av. Cals./lb.	3,906				
% Yearly Cals.	26.4%				

13.4: *Fats and Oils — US Annual Per Capita Consumption*

Sweeteners

Each person in the US consumes 141.5 pounds of sweeteners each year directly or in manufactured foods (Fig. 13.5). There are 1,494 Calories in each pound of sweetener. Total yearly Calories obtained from sweeteners is 15.2%. The top three sources of sweeteners (High fructose corn syrup (HFCS), sugar cane and sugar beets) provide 88% of Calories and 86% of the pounds consumed in this category. With diabetes on the rise, it is obvious that the consumption of sweetened foods and drinks has become a serious national health problem.

Calorie Foods Summary

This food class provides over half the Calories in the average American diet which includes high amounts of saturated fats, few nutrients and very little fiber. Crops raised for these foods use most of the land and fossil fuels used in US agriculture (Fig. 13.6).

	Annual lbs.	% lbs.	Cals. /lb.	Annual Cals.	% Cals.
Cane and Beet Sugar	62.8	44.4%	1,759	110,465	52.3%
Corn – HFCS	59.0	41.7%	1,277	75,343	35.7%
Corn – Glucose	15.2	10.7%	1,286	19,547	9.2%
Corn – Dextrose	3.2	2.3%	1,300	4,160	2.0%
Honey	1.0	0.7%	1,382	1,382	0.7%
Edible Syrups	0.3	0.2%	1,450	435	0.2%
Total lbs.	141.5				
Total Cals.	211,332				
Weighted Av. Cals./lb.	1,494				
% Yearly Cals.	15.2%				

SEE NOTE 1, P. 299.

13.5: *Sweeteners — US Annual Per Capita Consumption*

Type	Weight In lbs.	Cals. per lbs	Total Calories
Meat-Milk-Eggs	861.0	434	373,769
Fats-Oils	93.7	3,906	366,034
Sweeteners	141.5	1,494	209,941
Total	1,096.2	866	949,744

SEE NOTE 1, P. 299.

13.6: *US Annual Per Capita Consumption of Calorie Intense Foods*

Nutrient Intense Foods

The words natural and nutritious describe foods that are considered healthy to eat. A piece of fruit is healthier and more nutritious than a piece of candy made from soybean oil and corn sweeteners. We say the candy contains *empty calories*, meaning that it has high caloric content but almost no nutrients. Calories provide the energy to move, digest food and other physical functions but do not contain the minerals, vitamins and phytochemicals which help our bodies function well and which also help resist diseases and illnesses — from colds to cancers to heart disease. Nutrient intense foods include vegetables, fruits, whole grains (for food — not feed), legumes and nuts.

The most important nutrient foods are vegetables. They contain more nutrients than other plant foods. A good diet will include a diversity of vegetables to obtain the most nutrients. Sufficient amounts must be consumed for the greatest health benefits. Americans have become less healthy, and part of this is based on the kinds and amounts of vegetables eaten, not just the excessive quantities of meat, fats and sugars.

Vegetables

Vegetables average 213 Calories per pound, and contribute 6.3% of the average American's daily caloric intake. Of the total daily Calories that vegetables provide, potatoes provide 3.4% and the remaining 34 vegetables provide 2.9%. Thus potatoes alone provide 54% of the vegetable Calories Americans consume. Potatoes are high in Calories compared to the other vegetables which average 146 Calories per pound. The top five vegetables listed in Figure 13.7—potatoes, tomatoes, corn, head lettuce and onions — dominate the US vegetable diet (72% by weight and 81% by Calories). Considered by weight, all 35 vegetables except potatoes weigh in at 277 pounds compared to potatoes alone at 134.6 pounds.

Vegetables are sub-divided into different categories with each category providing different nutrients. Starchy vegetables (potatoes, lima beans, green peas, winter squash, corn, yams and sweet potatoes) are one category. A second category is dark green vegetables (spinach, romaine lettuce, broccoli, collards, kale, mustard greens and turnip greens). Deep yellow vegetables (including carrots and sweet potatoes) form a third category. A balanced diet would include choices from each of these categories.

The variety of vegetables measured by government agencies is extensive. However, there are many nutritious vegetables (such as bok choi, eggplant, chicory greens, kohlrabi, leeks, rhubarb, shallots and turnips) which are not included. Unfortunately, Americans eat only a few of the many vegetables available, and those we do consume are not necessarily the most nutritious.

Fruits

On average, each pound of fruit contains 240 Calories. Fruits provide 4.8% of an American's daily Calories — oranges and apples provide about half the Calories and the remaining 27 fruits provide the other half. Five fruits — oranges, apples, bananas, grapes and watermelon account for 69% of the fruit by weight and 72% by Calories (Fig. 13.8).

Fruits and Vegetables Nutritional Comparison

US vegetable and fruit consumption is not as diverse as might be expected when considering varieties available. The tables show that Americans eat only a few kinds of vegetables and fruit in volume. Figure 13.9 shows that the high volume vegetables and fruits are not necessarily the most nutritious. The more

	Annual lbs.	% lbs.	Cals. /lb.	Annual Cals.	% Cals.
Potatoes	134.6	32.7%	350	47,110	53.8%
Tomatoes	94.1	22.9%	82	7,716	8.8%
Sweet corn	26.2	6.4%	391	10,244	11.7%
Onions	22.7	5.5%	182	4,131	4.7%
Head lettuce	20.3	4.9%	64	1,299	1.5%
Romaine & leaf lettuce	12.1	2.9%	77	932	1.1%
Carrots	11.8	2.9%	186	2,195	2.5%
Cucumbers	10.3	2.5%	68	700	0.8%
Cabbage	9.3	2.3%	114	1,060	1.2%
Broccoli	8.3	2.0%	155	1,287	1.5%
Snap beans	7.6	1.8%	141	1,072	1.2%
Bell peppers	6.6	1.6%	91	601	0.7%
Chili peppers	6	1.5%	182	1,092	1.2%
Celery	6.1	1.5%	73	445	0.5%
Pumpkin	5	1.2%	118	590	0.7%
Sweet potatoes	4.5	1.1%	391	1,760	2.0%
Squash	4.7	1.1%	114	536	0.6%
Mushrooms	3.9	0.9%	123	480	0.5%
Spinach	3	0.7%	105	315	0.4%
Green peas	2.7	0.7%	368	994	1.1%
Garlic	2.4	0.6%	677	1,625	1.9%
Cauliflower	1.9	0.5%	114	217	0.2%
Asparagus	1.5	0.4%	91	137	0.2%
Eggplant	0.9	0.2%	109	98	0.1%
Beets	0.7	0.2%	195	137	0.2%
Artichokes	0.6	0.1%	214	128	0.1%
Collard greens	0.6	0.1%	136	82	0.1%
Radishes	0.5	0.1%	73	37	0.0%
Mustard greens	0.4	0.1%	118	47	0.1%
Turnip greens	0.4	0.1%	145	58	0.1%
Lima beans	0.4	0.1%	514	206	0.2%
Okra	0.5	0.1%	141	71	0.1%
Kale	0.4	0.1%	227	91	0.1%
Escarole	0.3	0.1%	105	32	0.0%
Brussels sprouts	0.3	0.1%	195	59	0.1%
Total lbs.	411.6				
Total Cals.	87,579				
Weighted Av. Cals./lb.	213				
% Yearly Cals.	6.3%				

SEE NOTE I, P. 299.

13.7: *Vegetables — US Annual Per Capita Consumption*

	Annual lbs.	% lbs.	Cals. /lb.	Annual Cals.	% Cals.
Oranges and temples	80.4	29.3%	214	17,206	26.1%
Apples	48.0	17.5%	236	11,328	17.2%
Bananas	25.1	9.2%	405	10,166	15.4%
Grapes	21.9	8.0%	314	6,877	10.4%
Watermelon	13.8	5.0%	136	1,877	2.8%
Pineapple	13.5	4.9%	227	3,065	4.6%
Cantaloupe	10.1	3.7%	155	1,566	2.4%
Peaches and nectarines	8.9	3.2%	177	1,575	2.4%
Grapefruit	7.4	2.7%	191	1,413	2.1%
Strawberries	7.7	2.8%	145	1,117	1.7%
Lemons	7.2	2.6%	91	655	1.0%
Pears	5.2	1.9%	264	1,373	2.1%
Tangerines and tangelos	3.6	1.3%	241	868	1.3%
Avocados	3.3	1.2%	727	2,399	3.6%
Limes	2.7	1.0%	136	367	0.6%
Plums	2.4	0.9%	209	502	0.8%
Honeydew	1.9	0.7%	164	312	0.5%
Mangoes	1.9	0.7%	295	561	0.8%
Cranberries	2.0	0.7%	209	418	0.6%
Cherries	1.8	0.7%	286	515	0.8%
Olives	1.4	0.5%	523	732	1.1%
Papayas	0.9	0.3%	177	159	0.2%
Apricots	1.1	0.4%	218	240	0.4%
Blueberries	0.8	0.3%	259	207	0.3%
Kiwifruit	0.5	0.2%	277	139	0.2%
Figs	0.3	0.1%	336	101	0.2%
Raspberries	0.3	0.1%	236	71	0.1%
Dates	0.1	0.0%	1,259	126	0.2%
Blackberries	0.1	0.0%	195	20	0.0%
Total lbs.	274.3				
Total Cals.	65,950				
Weighted Av. Cals./lb.	240				
% Yearly Cals.	4.8%				

See Note 1, p. 299.

13.8: *Fruits — US Annual Per Capita Consumption*

nutritious foods are at the top of the left side of the table. The most eaten foods are listed in the right hand column, the lower number representing the most frequently eaten. Not only are Americans eating far less diversity than is healthy, but the most popular vegetables are towards the low end of nutritional benefits.

Nutrional Density: What People Should Eat Most (highest to lowest)	Rank	Popularity: What People Actually Eat Most (highest to lowest)
Broccoli	1	Tomatoes
Spinach	2	Oranges
Brussels sprouts	3	Potatoes
Lima beans	4	Lettuce
Peas	5	Sweet corn
Asparagus	6	Bananas
Artichokes	7	Carrots
Cauliflower	8	Cabbage
Sweet potatoes	9	Onions
Carrots	10	Sweet potatoes
Sweet Corn	11	Peas
Potatoes	12	Spinach
Cabbage	13	Broccoli
Tomatoes	14	Lima Beans
Bananas	15	Asparagus
Lettuce	16	Cauliflower
Onions	17	Brussels Sprouts
Oranges	18	Artichokes

13.9: *Nutrition Order and Popularity Order of Vegetables and Fruits*

CHARLES R. ATTWOOD, DR. ATTWOOD'S LOW-FAT PRESCRIPTION FOR KIDS

Grains

As noted in the previous chapter, wheat is the major grain Americans eat directly, followed by corn. Wheat, corn and rice provide 97% of both the weight of grains eaten and the Calories consumed in this category. Americans consume 192.3 pounds of grain annually per person. Grains average 1,655 Calories per pound and provide 22.9% of the Calories in the American diet. The top grain (wheat) accounts for 70% of the pounds and Calories consumed while oats, barley and rye provide only a little more than 3% of food pounds and Calories. Grains are listed in Figure 13.10.

Today, 95% of the flour used in the United States is highly processed white wheat flour, which has many valuable components removed during processing. These nutritionally valuable components are used to feed chickens and other animals.[4] Some portions of the nutrient materials refined out of the whole wheat are reintroduced into the white flour. But this artificial method does not return all the important nutritional components. This highly processed white flour is used in a multitude of manufactured products, which are flavored and colored for consumer appeal. Removing key nutrients, along with the over coating of bran, creates a product that will have a long shelf life, one that will not spoil or go rancid and one that food insects will not eat (Fig. 13.11).

	Annual lbs.	% lbs.	Cals. /lb.	Annual Cals.	% Cals.
Wheat	134.1	69.7%	1,655	221,936	69.7%
Corn	31.4	16.3%	1,659	52,093	16.4%
Rice	21	10.9%	1,627	34,167	10.7%
Oats	4.6	2.4%	1,768	8,133	2.6%
Barley	0.7	0.4%	1,568	1,098	0.3%
Rye	0.5	0.3%	1,609	805	0.3%
Total lbs.	192.3				
Total Cals.	318,230				
Weighted Av. Cals./lb.	1,655				
% Yearly Cals.	22.9%				

SEE NOTE 1, P. 299.

13.10: *Grains — US Annual Per Capita Consumption*

	Whole Wheat	White Unenriched
Calories	400	455
Protein (g.)	16	13.1
Fat (g.)	2.4	1.3
Carbohydrates (g.)	85.2	95.1
Calcium (mg.)	49	20
Phosphorus (mg.)	446	109
Iron (mg.)	4	1
Potassium (mg.)	444	119
Thiamin (mg.)	0.66	0.08
Riboflavin (mg.)	0.14	0.06
Niacin (mg.)	5.2	1.1

USDA RELEASE 20 NUTRITION DATA BASE

13.11: *Whole Wheat Flour vs. White Flour — Energy and Nutrients*

Nuts

Of the 9.9 pounds of nuts eaten per person each year, 6.7 pounds are peanuts. Nuts have a high Calorie content, averaging 2,595 Calories per pound. The top three nuts consumed — peanuts, almonds and walnuts — provide about 77% of the pounds and Calories consumed in this category (Fig. 13.12).

	Annual lbs.	% lbs.	Cals. /lb.	Annual Cals.	% Cals.
Peanuts	6.7	67.4%	2,577	17,266	66.9%
Almonds	0.5	5.3%	2,614	1,385	5.4%
Walnuts	0.4	4.2%	2,973	1,249	4.8%
Coconuts	0.6	5.7%	1,609	917	3.6%
Pecans	0.5	5.2%	3,141	1,633	6.3%
Pistachios	0.2	1.9%	2,532	481	1.9%
Macadamia	0.1	0.9%	3,264	294	1.1%
Filberts	0.0	0.3%	2,855	86	0.3%
Others	0.9	9.0%	2,795	2,488	9.6%
Total lbs.	9.9				
Total Cals.	25,798				
Weighted Av. Cals./lb.	2,595				
% Yearly Cals.	1.9%				

13.12: *Nuts — US Annual Per Capita Consumption*

Legumes (Dried beans and peas)

Beans average 1,561 Calories per pound. However, beans provide only .8% of the daily Calories in the US. Legumes are a minuscule part of the nation's diet since

	Annual lbs.	% lbs.	Cals. /lb.	Annual Cals.	% Cals.
Pinto	2.6	37.1%	1,577	4,100	37.5%
Navy	0.7	10.0%	1,532	1,072	9.8%
Black	0.5	7.1%	1,550	775	7.1%
Red Kidney	0.6	8.6%	1,532	919	8.4%
Lima	0.1	1.4%	1,536	154	1.4%
Dry Peas/Lentils	0.7	10.0%	1,605	1,124	10.3%
Others	1.8	25.7%	1,545	2,781	25.5%
Total lbs.	7.0				
Total Cals.	10,925				
Weighted Av. Cals./lb.	1,561				
% Yearly Cals.	0.8%				

13.13: *Legumes — US Annual Per Capita Consumption*

SEE NOTE 1, P. 299.

Americans consume meat for protein. This is far different than in the rest of the world where legumes provide much of the protein. The top four beans listed provide over 60% of weight and Calories consumed in this category (Fig. 13.13).

Nutrient Intense Foods Summary

The most nutritious foods are natural and high in nutrients. They come from plants and have not been heavily processed, so they have fewer Calories and more nutrients per pound than manufactured food. They are more subject to decay and loss of nutrient value with time, so freshness is important. Most (except for dried beans and grains) must be refrigerated, frozen, dried, canned or stored in a root cellar to have *shelf life*, unlike nutrient poor manufactured foods that keep stable at regular temperatures. Because there are fewer market-ing opportunities to add value to these natural foods, manufacturers are less interested in them (Fig. 13.14).

Type	Weight In lbs.	Cals. per lb.	Total Calories
Vegetables	411.6	213	85,759
Fruits	274.3	240	45,152
Grains	192.3	1,655	318,230
Nuts	9.9	2,595	25,798
Legumes	7.0	1,561	10,925
Total	895.1	537	485,864

See Note 1, p. 299.

13.14: *US Annual Per Capita Consumption of Nutrient Intense Foods*

Challenging Diversity

The 30,000 products in the average supermarket can be broken down into combinations of 7 kinds of meat, 8 kinds of grains, 45 vegetables, 34 fruits, 20 legumes, for an actual total of about 120 foods. There are many different vari-eties of each food, such as the different potatoes — red, russet, Idaho, etc. Still the numbers are not impressive. If we assume ten variations of 120 foods then we would have about 1,200 foods, a very small number compared to the 300,000 created by manufacturers over the years.

The previous tables show the wide variety of plant foods that are available. But consumers do not eat that variety. In each of the categories the actual vol-umes Americans eat are from the top few foods on the lists. For example, of the 35 vegetables listed in Figure 13.7, about six provide the bulk of the food.

Although there are over 5,000 varieties of potatoes in the world, there are only a few sold in the US.[5]

The varieties of other vegetables offered in the marketplace today is quite limited. For example, 80.6% of the varieties of tomatoes have been lost since 1903. The main food tomato in the US is the beefsteak. A list of lost or rarely grown tomatoes include momotoro, nova, lemon boy, better boy, black krim, early girl, celebrity, yellow roma, charlie chaplin, cherokee purple, milano plum, great white, striped german, san marzano, el paka, stupice, yellow brandywine, mister stripey, brandywine, Dixie golden giant, san remo, yellow ruffles, orange queen, carrot paste, reif red, persimmon, marble white, black crimson, sabarocca, chadwick cherry, sunsweet, black plum, sungold, cascade, green vine, rose quartz crystal, sweet 100, yellow pear, red pear, german stripe, Italian gold, golden Pandora, green zebra, red brandywine, chioggia, marvel stripe, caro rich, ropreco, tappy's finest, pale perfect purple, florida pink, peace yellow roma. mountain gold, anna Russian, mountain and orange mandarin.

92.8% of the varieties of lettuces have been lost since 1903. Twenty seven are no longer seen. Forty-six varieties of corn are no longer grown. 86.2% of apples (over 50 varieties) have been lost to consumers since 1903. Of the 30 US varieties of potatoes that were commonly eaten in the past, most are no longer available.[6] The American diet does not provide variety or freshness. Foods that are healthier to eat are basically secondary while the fattening foods (potatoes, meat and manufactured foods high in fats and sugars) top the consumption list.

Corporations and the Food Supply — 300,000 Products

Food manufacturers generate a wide variety of brands from a narrow range of food raw materials. A good example is Phillip Morris, a major producer of cigarettes and manufactured food. The company was renamed Altria to disconnect it from the familiar cigarette name. The list on the next page represents only a few brand name foods marketed by Altria/Phillip Morris. Brands are added and removed and also may be sold or purchased from other companies; this list represents only a fraction of the corporation's products at a particular point in time.

Altria/Philip Morris is only one of the many giant food corporations that determine what Americans eat and thus how healthy we are. Such corporations must continually *add value to* basic foods, inserting themselves between farmers and consumers in order to control the lucrative food market. By adding numerous layers of processing and long distance transportation, corporations take most of the profit on food sales. The farmer makes only a

Beverages, Desserts and Cereals

Beverages — Capri Sun, Country Time, Crystal Light, Kool-Aid , Tang

Coffee — Gevalia , Maxim, Maxwell House, Sanka, Starbucks

Desserts — Baker's, Balance Bar, Calumet, Certo, Cool Whip

Cereals — Alpha-Bits, Fruit & Fibre, Golden Crisp, Oreo O's, Pebbles

Biscuits, Snacks and Confectionery

Cookies/Crackers — Better Cheddars, Oreo, Premium, Ritz, Cheese Nips

Confectionery — Altoids, Tobler, Creme Savers, Farley's, Gummi Savers

Cheese, Meals and Enhancers

Cheese — Athenos, Cheez Whiz, Churny, Cracker Barrel, Kraft

Dairy Products — cottage cheese, Breyers yogurt, Kraft dips, sour cream, , yogurt Meals — Kraft macaroni & cheese, Minute, Stove Top, Taco Bell, Velveeta

Oscar Mayer and Pizza

Meats — Louis Rich, Louis Rich Carving Board , Lunchables, Oscar Mayer

Pizza — California Pizza Kitchen, Di Giorno, Jack's, Tombstone

Selected International Brands

Coffee — Blendy, Carte Noire, Gevalia, Grand'Mère, Kaffee HAG

Powdered Soft Drinks — Clight, Fresh, Frisco, Kool-Aid, Mañanita

Cheese — Dairylea, Eden, El Caserío, Invernizzi, Kraft Cracker Barrel

Snacks/Confectionery — Aladdin, Artic, Cerealitas, Chips Ahoy!, Club Social

Convenient Meals — Dairylea Lunchables, Fleischmann's, Magic Moments

Beer

Miller Lite, Miller Genuine Draft, Miller Genuine, Draft Light, Miller High Life.[7]

marginal amount, and it is difficult for the consumer to easily obtain local, natural, healthy foods.

Government's Role — Spreading Ignorance

Americans are confused about food. Food labeling is a mystery; the language used does not provide clarity. Probably the ultimate confusing concept is the Food Pyramid, a construct invented by the United States Department of Agriculture (USDA) to communicate nutritional information and good dietary practices to consumers. The Pyramid actually does the opposite. The geometric form (a pyramid) used to denote proportions is graphically misrepresentative, and the areas of the pyramid do not correspond to the serving numbers suggested. The definition of servings is ambiguous, contradictory and misleading. It is doubtful if one American out of a hundred could clearly explain the concept.

The USDA's calculation of recommended minimum servings is based on a 185 lb. middle class Caucasian male office worker and is not adjusted for height, weight, age, activity, sex or state of health. No consideration is given to whether foods are fresh, frozen, canned or manufactured. Nor is there any consideration given to conventional versus organic farming. The method of preparing food — fried, broiled, grilled, roasted — is ignored. The Food Pyramid assumes

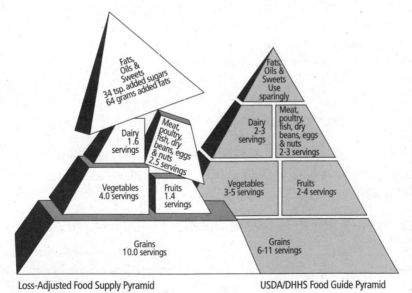

Loss-Adjusted Food Supply Pyramid   USDA/DHHS Food Guide Pyramid

PUTNAM, SCOTT, KANTOR AND ALLSHOUSE, "PER CAPITA FOOD SUPPLY TRENDS: PROGRESS TOWARD DIETARY GUIDELINES."

13.15: *The Unbalanced American Diet (Servings Per Person, Per Day)*

that the length or type of storage does not affect the food. There is no direction or consideration given regarding the importance of integrating healthy eating with the modern lifestyle where fully 50-60% of meals are eaten outside of the home. There is no additional value assigned to eating fresh vegetables, fruits and grains. Calculating quantities using the serving concept is next to impossible since the USDA allows manufacturers to set serving sizes that are not in concert with the USDA serving sizes. The food pyramid does not communicate the known dangers of eating fatty meats. Figure 13.15 shows graphically the degree to which the diet of Americans is seriously out of balance.

The USDA does not protect the health of Americans. That organization's priority seems to be protecting the sales and profits of grocery manufacturers. It subsidizes growing Calorie crops like corn and soybeans that are the basis of manufactured food. The USDA's relationship and support of the food industry at the expense of the citizenry and small farmers is well known.[8] In practice, all food labeling information for consumers must be approved by food manufacturers before it can be released to the public.

Michael Pollan, author of The Omnivore's Dilemma, makes the astonishing recommendation that "if you're concerned about your health, you should probably avoid food products that make health claims." He points out that a health claim on a food product is a good indication that it's not really food, and food is what humans should eat. Pollan's food advice is threefold — first eat food, not manufactured "food like" products, don't eat too much and eat mostly plants. He suggests that this short advice is the preferred option to the complicated and confusing question of what humans should eat to achieve maximal health.[9] Marion Nestle, author of Food Politics and What to Eat, has similar advice that bypasses the complexity of the Food Pyramid and other confusing advice from the USDA. Her short summary is eat less, move more, eat lots of fruits and vegetables. She adds a clarifier "go easy on junk foods."[10] In the broadest sense junk food is the popular term for manufactured food, often those with extravagant health claims on the label.

Government's Role — Subsidizing Manufactured Food

Michael Pollan noted that Adam Drewnowski, an obesity researcher at the University of Washington, wondered why the people who spend the least on food are most likely to be overweight. Drewnoski discovered that processed foods and soft drinks offered more Calories per dollar. For example, one dollar bought

1,200 Calories of cookies or potato chips, 875 Calories of soda, 250 Calories of carrots or 170 Calories of orange juice. In general, processed foods are more Calorie intense and nutrient poor than fresh foods, particularly since they include added fats (soybeans), white flour (wheat) and sweeteners (corn). Calories from these kinds of products may be cheap but they are also the least healthful to eat. Thus people with the smallest budgets consume poorer quality, fattening foods.

Periodically the US Congress passes *farm bills* that set agriculture policy and subsidies. These bills have been passed since the 1930s, the most recent being passed in 1985, 1990, 1996, 2002 and 2007.[11] US farm bills once supported prices and limited production but now they support volume production of a few crops. The result of the policy is that the price of fruits and vegetables between 1985 and 2000 increased by approximately 40% while the price of soft drinks (based on corn sweeteners) declined by approximately 23%. The reason the least healthful Calories in the supermarket are the cheapest is that those are the ones manufactured from crops the farm bill encourages farmers to grow. Small farmers and organic farms do not receive government aid. Michael Pollan further observed that US farm bills help determine the kind of food in school lunch programs. In addition, the bills affect the landscape and environment of the country, either setting the priorities for land preservation and recovery or setting them for maximum production with maximum use of fossil fuel chemicals. The bills affect the health of soil, the purity of water and biodiversity.[12]

Some of us recognize the real cost of artificially cheap food measured in poor health, degraded land, tormented animals and the loss of family farms. Government policies are needed that make the most healthful Calories price competitive with the least healthful ones. Policies are also needed that encourage schools to provide children with fresh food from local farms. New policies that focus on long term land preservation and the health of soil and water supplies are needed to replace those that support industrial agriculture based on commodities. A farm bill that focuses on health and food quality and support of family farmers is desperately needed.

Evaluating the Results

Possibly the most succinct comment on the broader context of the US food system is one by David Pimentel who points out that the world population is over 6 billion people and 3 billion of those are undernourished.[13] Since globalization is the rule of the day and agriculture is one of its key industries, this statement is a damning one. Inequity in food availability has grown during the decades of the industrialization of agriculture. Pimentel notes that the average person in the US consumes 2,200 pounds of food in a year and consumes 3,600 Calories per day. However, humans only need 2,500 Calories per day so US food consumption could be reduced by up to ⅓, which would improve health.[14] As previously noted, ⅔ of the US population is overweight or obese.[15] Making foods artificially cheap has encouraged gluttony in the country.

Steps to Take

As fossil fuel resources decline and the climate changes, food shortages will occur if we don't develop new options. There are many changes needed and an important first step is *modifying food purchasing, cooking and eating habits*. Choosing to change one's diet offers a way to reduce CO_2, develop better food security and be healthier. It is necessary to begin with personal change — national change will follow.

With any new activity, there is theory and practice — study and action. The first big step is to allocate time for studying. This is vital for surviving the coming energy crisis, but it can also be both educational and enjoyable. In past times, people enjoyed gardening and food processing, often sharing the work and the food. Below are some options for you to consider when determining your own strategy for change.

Gardening

Replace some part of your lawn with a vegetable garden or find a garden plot to use or share. One can start small, developing a single bed and begin composting kitchen scraps. In Cuba, urban gardens held off starvation during the early years of the Cuban Special Period. Between 1994 and 2001 production of vegetables more than doubled every year. Cuba's urban gardens now produce 60% of all fruits and vegetables consumed in Cuba and 50% of the vegetables eaten in Havana. In smaller cities and towns, urban agriculture supplies 80-100% of the fruits and vegetables eaten. Many such farms also produce an excess of food that can be transported to other locations. Cuba now protects agricultural land around each city and town from development, maintaining it for growing food close to where it is needed.[16]

Garden stores and nurseries are a major business segment in the US, showing that many people still enjoy a natural affinity for soil and plants. This affinity with the land is important since people will need to learn how to garden without using petrochemicals. Out of necessity Cuba began organic gardening, crop rotation and the development of bio-pesticides from plants. Now Cuba uses 21 times fewer pesticides because of its large-scale production of these materials and bio-fertilizers. All food and animal waste products are collected, composted and returned to the soil. Healthy soil means fewer pesticides are needed. Today 80% of Cuba's agricultural production is organic, and production has risen to be equal to and in some cases greater than what was produced previously using petrochemicals.[17]

The objective is not only to provide food but to reestablish and cultivate a natural connection to the land. The actual experience of providing some food is essential. Through this effort, you will learn about the richness and complexity of gardening and the exquisite taste of fresh produce.

Learn about food production

Its only through understanding the US food production system — including the energy used, CO_2 generated, soil destroyed, farm workers exploited, health compromised — that we can begin to see the changes to be made and the initial steps to be taken. The information in this and the previous chapters provides a unique overview of the food system. Without understanding the roles that government, corporations, media and the medical industry (including dieticians) have played in developing the current wasteful and unhealthy way of obtaining food, systemic change will be more difficult.

Study nutrition

It is important to understand the components of food and which vitamins, minerals and phytochemicals are essential to health. It is also necessary to understand which foods provide what nutrients. This information cannot be obtained from a government mandated food label or from food corporations. Furthermore, the diet industry is committed to the existing food system and can be obstructive to understanding. Knowledge about nutrition was ubiquitous in earlier times when people took responsibility for their own health.

Eat Differently

The most straightforward way to reduce climate change and save energy is to eat less and eat differently. Cubans made fundamental changes to their diet when fossil fuels and imported foods were cut off in the early 1990s. Importing food from Europe had meant that most foods were processed, canned or bottled and shipped thousands of miles. Cubans learned to eat more fresh fruits and vegetables, avoiding the energy costs of processing and refrigeration. Cubans had been large consumers of meat, but meat required fossil fuel inputs to which they no longer had access. The amount of meat eaten was reduced significantly, and their focus turned to growing basic nutritious foods.[18] The result has been a much healthier diet (with reduced rates of heart disease and diabetes), improved soil fertility, and reduced fossil fuel consumption. Healthy low energy foods typically imply more fresh vegetables and fruits while giving up high fat and sweetened manufactured foods.

Eat seasonally

Eating foods out of the season in which they can be grown locally, means they must be refrigerated or processed in some way and then transported — usually — long distances. For this reason, a person should know what foods are available and in what season and eat accordingly. As fossil fuels become scarcer, learning how to do this will become an enjoyable challenge. Books like Eliot Coleman's *Four-Season Harvest* show us that we can still have incredible variety in fresh food during winter.[19]

Don't eat grain-fed animals

Factory meat is the most fossil fuel intensive food we can eat. As it is raised today, it is also unhealthy for the consumer. Excessive consumption of industrial meats leads to heart disease, cancer and other illnesses. Containment feeding operations are inhumane and are an important contributor to global warming and water pollution. Meat requires grains which could be used to feed people if eaten directly. The eating of fish contributes to the dangerous decline of ocean fish populations.

Don't eat manufactured groceries

Giving up manufactured groceries means abandoning corn sweeteners, excessive salt, hydrogenated soybean oil and white flour. Manufactured foods are very expensive when health effects are included. Their processing and packaging also make them more destructive to the environment. Fresh natural foods require little processing and do not require the same level of packaging. As our societal crisis deepens, maintaining physical health will become more critical. In times of crisis, medical care may be too expensive or not easily available. Eating organic food that comes from your own garden or a local farm will help.

Don't imbibe refreshments

Avoid eating or drinking refrigerated beverages such as soda pops and anything else with sugar added. Canned and bottled drink factories need enormous amounts of water for their products. The beverages they manufacture are sugar intensive (up to 14 teaspoons of sugar per soft drink) and harmful to our health; also the crops from which sweeteners are made require natural gas-based fertilizers for growing and processing. Making cans and bottles for soft drinks and juices consumes energy. Drinks also require constant energy for cooling in retail stores and homes. "A 12-ounce can of diet soda requires a total of 2,200 kcal to produce (over 70% of which goes toward the aluminum can) and may provide only 1 kcal in food energy."[20]

Prepare your own food

Avoid *convenience food* — that is, prepackaged and highly processed food — both solid and liquid. This means frozen food, snacks, fast food and precooked meals. It is a way to avoid the additives, fats and sugars in most prepared foods. When we cook using natural fresh ingredients we eat closer to the sources of our food and the food is more nutritious. And there is far less CO_2 generated.

Use pressure cookers

Pressure cookers, double boilers and insulated cookers are some of the ways to reduce the energy used in preparing foods. Much of the energy used in cooking food (over 50%) can be saved by using a pressure cooker. Dried beans that would take two to three hours to cook in a pot boiling on a stove can be cooked in a pressure cooker in 20 to 30 minutes.

Start canning and eat less frozen foods

Part of learning about food is to learn about storing it. Gaining experience in canning and bottling is well worth doing. This is especially important as refrigerators may no longer be used as they are today. In the future, communities will be able to process and can large amounts of food from local sources during the farming season. This will eliminate much of the need for keeping food frozen for months.

Eat locally grown food

Food should be produced as close as possible to the place where it will be eaten. The benefits are manifold, the two main ones being that local food production reduces fossil fuel use in transportation and the more quickly food gets to the consumer the more nutrients it retains, providing more health benefits when eaten. Reduction in transportation is particularly true for vegetables and fruits, which have a high weight per Calorie ratio. They also need to be eaten fresher than staples such as beans and grains. If food is transported, it should be dense food such as grains and beans that require less energy for transportation per Calories contained and none for cooling. As we begin supplying our food needs from local farms and businesses, we will stop being so dependant on agribusiness and manufacturing corporations.

Buy organically grown food

Organic agriculture is the only way to raise food in a sustainable manner. It is becoming increasingly clear that the ongoing use of petrochemicals cannot continue. Either we will run out of the hydrocarbons or fossil fuel-based food will become too expensive. Organic agriculture will rebuild our depleted soils and buying organic foods means the farm workers will not be exposed to health endangering chemicals. Organic agriculture is also a way to develop food security for today and for generations to come.

Feeding Change

Global warming and the foreseeable shortages of fossil fuels call for revolutionary changes in all areas of living, including food. This change will require new knowledge and new practices. The average American considers food growing beneath him or her; and this contempt shows up in our willingness to pay non-livable wages to those who work the fields. This has led to a new kind of wage slavery in the US based on the exploitation of Latin American immigrants. Americans must stop assuming food growers are inferior humans and that food growing is beneath our dignity. Everyone should become involved at some level of the food process. It must become a valued part of the culture. Those who love growing, storing and preparing fresh foods should become models for the community instead of anachronisms. Diets must change, and methods of food production must change. Farmers and farm workers must be paid a living wage.

The ideas presented here suggest a new way of being relative to food. They are not a set of rules. The problems with manufactured food, industrial agriculture and farm labor exploitation are not new. What is new is that peak oil and climate change mean we can no longer avoid dealing with long standing food issues. Shortages or global climate degradation will be driving forces for making the needed changes. But each person can choose now to change how and what they eat, rather than waiting for an emergency to occur.

PART III

Fourteen

Changing Practices

THE UNITED STATES WAS THE FIRST COUNTRY to develop an industrial economic system based on oil. This has given us the unenviable record of having generated 1/3 of the world's historical CO_2 emissions while having only 1/20 of the world's population.[1] And we continue to generate a disproportionate amount of such emissions (about 25%) with less than 5% of the world's population.[2] This means that each American generates the same amount of CO_2 as seven non-Americans.

Our national story is that Americans are good and kind and that our prosperity comes from hard work, innovation and the blessing of God who recognizes our innate goodness. Our nation's problems are being viewed as a combination of betrayal or aggression by evil nations or evil peoples (for example Islamic nations) or the abandonment of God's beneficence for supposed immoralities. This naïve view makes it extremely difficult to create a new world (one being forced on us by peak oil and climate change) based on different principles and values. As energy supplies shrink, failing to develop different values could lead to a level of violence far greater than any that the country has known before, including first use of nuclear bombs. Declining energy resources and increasing CO_2 levels from burning fossil fuels are challenging the past and present values and attitudes of the nation.

Curtailment and Personal Action

Curtailment and community define Community Solution's Plan C — a vision of a new way of living which rejects consumption as its core principle. Community replaces consumerism. Values of novelty, comfort, convenience, ease, fashion, indulgence, luxury and competition along with other indolent values associated with declining empires must give way to different values, such as cooperation, temperance, prudence, moderation, conviviality and charity.

As noted in Chapter 8, curtailing differs from conserving. We *conserve* natural resources by making minor adjustments to our lifestyle. Curtailing implies a much more severe reduction in consumption (80-90%). It is too late to merely conserve. Curtailment must become the main driving force of Western civilization for the next century, just as consuming drove the last century. The need to curtail is so urgent that we must begin to husband fossil fuel resources now so that we will have some energy left to ease the transition into a future with much less energy.

I began this book from the perspective of peak oil, but global warming is potentially an even more serious problem that may require a deeper level of curtailment. We may not be able to burn fossil fuel resources in the future, not because the supplies are limited, but because the CO_2 burden on the atmosphere (generated by burning oil, natural gas and coal) may be too great to allow their continued consumption. Curtailment pressure comes both from depleting fossil fuel sources and from the inability of the lands and oceans to absorb the CO_2 we are generating.

Nobody wants to begin curtailing. It is human nature to wait until another person takes the first difficult step. Those who delay may think they have an advantage, continuing to enjoy the current fossil fuel-based pseudo prosperity until the last possible moment. But they may find themselves far less prepared to live in a low energy world than those who begin the practice of curtailing now. Americans are very competitive, and there is little reason to suspect this basic value will disappear in a time of depleting resources. So it is unlikely that the transition to a low energy lifestyle will be without great suffering. Those who desire to make the transition successfully with minimal risk must start now to toughen and strengthen themselves physically and psychologically for difficult times to come. Such people will be more prepared to live in a future that is poorer in material goods but richer in spiritual, psychological and community benefits. Those who delay may not have the physical and emotional stamina to survive in a more physically difficult environment.

Curtailment is both a goal and a methodology to reach the goal. It will require the development of new skills and disciplines that are not easy to acquire. Groups and communities will need to make fundamental changes to survive the coming world crisis, but unless individuals can make steps to change the current way of living that has brought on the crisis, group actions will have little effect. It will not be sufficient to focus only on local community organization without addressing personal responsibility. Forming a local community of people who are committed to maintaining the energy status quo is quite different than forming a local community of dedicated curtailers. The first group will attempt to organize, make local surveys and develop local businesses. The second group may do the same but their priority will be on reducing each member's energy use.

Curtailment and Energy Measurement

Curtailment implies sacrifice, a word that is anathema to most Americans. It will be neither easy nor convenient. It goes beyond the familiar lists of 51 ways to save the environment including trivial suggestions such as "Wear green eye shadow" and "Remove the tie."[3] Lists like this create complacency, generating thoughts like, "I can do that," "that doesn't look so hard" and "when and if change requires it, I can take those steps." A recommendation to "turn the thermostat down at night" is very different than a recommendation to "turn the thermostat down to 45 degrees at night and no higher than 55 degrees during the day." The first suggestion is comforting while the second demands we sacrifice some comfort. Committed people have already made difficult sacrifices while having no idea exactly how much energy has been saved — they just know reductions must be made.

Media feel-good proposals lack measurements. The saying "if you can't measure it, you can't manage it" is very relevant to making the changes our future requires. For any curtailing action, we must be able to articulate the percentage reduction in fossil fuel consumption and CO_2 emissions. If the total savings of a set of recommendations is only a few percent of total energy used, then the steps have been ineffective. Proponents of a happy green philosophy rarely calculate actual net reductions. An example of such complacency is the Energy Star promotion of programmable thermostats that began in 1995. The original estimate was a 10%-30% savings on heating and cooling bills. 25 million such thermostats were installed in homes. In 2007 Energy Star stated that such thermostats would no longer be certified as contributing to savings, since research demonstrated that they were ineffective.[4]

Accurate measurements show that such supposedly easy fixes are less effective than popularly assumed. If the media endlessly tell us to use Compact

Fluorescent Lights (CFL) but never articulate the actual savings, then they encourage complacency and discourage initiatives to curtail. After 30 years only 2% of household incandescent lighting in the US has been replaced with CFLs. A national commitment to CFL use in homes would save about 5% of US total electrical consumption and, based on success to date, might take many decades to reach. But the challenge facing us is to reduce total energy use by 5% each year in order to meet limits required by climate scientists![5] After we make the simple changes like CFLs, we must then deal with much bigger changes — the heating, air conditioning, hot water and refrigeration systems that constantly run day and night and which consume most of the energy in homes.

Curtailment and Machine Efficiency

Many energy and environmental experts claim that massive energy savings will come from future efficiency improvements.[6] But the efficiency of machines that consume energy — from power plants to car engines to food processors — has been constantly improving for decades. Efficiency improvements for the internal-combustion engine have been ongoing for over a century. Unfortunately in America's consumer society, improved efficiency, which could have reduced the energy cost of operation, has led to increased consumption. As miles per gallons improve, we just drive further. Curtailing energy consumption and CO_2 generation essentially means curtailing machine use — not just improving machine efficiency.

There are only a few basic machine types that form the core of our industrial society. They include the automobile internal-combustion engine (both gasoline and diesel), the turbine engine (jet engines for airplanes and gas turbines for electricity generation), steam engines (for locomotion and for power generation) and nuclear reactors (for electricity generation and submarine propulsion). These key machine types have been and currently are under constant improvement by car companies, airplane engine manufacturers and companies that make generators for the production of electricity. These represent the giants of world industrial manufacturers, including GM, Ford, Daimler Chrysler, Toyota, Honda, GE, Westinghouse and Rolls Royce. For large equipment such as cars, airplanes and power plants, these companies spend tens of billions of dollars annually on R & D.[7] Over many decades, these machines have shown a steady 1-2% efficiency improvement per year. However, this rate of improvement is not sufficient to deal with the rate of population growth and increases in per capita energy use. Thus curtailing the use of machines — rather than waiting for them to become even more efficient — is necessary in the short term.

Our Machines

As fossil fuels are burned in hundreds of millions of mechanical devices, CO_2 comes from their exhaust. A committed curtailer will eliminate all unnecessary machine equipment, accepting that the discomfort that comes from doing so is the first step in developing a new set of values. The average person is familiar with the 100s of millions of automobiles as a major source of CO_2 since they are being used daily. But other polluting machines are less obvious. To know where and how to curtail energy use requires developing a new awareness of the dozens of machines that are basic to today's lifestyle and replacing them with changed practices and hand tools.

Power Plants

Many small machines and appliances are operated by electric motors, not necessarily inefficient themselves, but they obtain their power from relatively inefficient power plants. The electrical power generating plant is the largest machine made that consumes fossil fuel. The thousands of power plants in the US consume more fossil fuels and produce more CO_2 than the 217 million cars in the US auto fleet.[8] The consumer rarely sees a power plant. Instead he or she experiences the power plant by using a wide variety of electrically powered machines. Since Thomas Edison set up the first power system in New York City in 1882, power plants have steadily improved their efficiency. The original principle is simple and remains the same — heat water until it

| | Natural Gas | | | Hard Coal | | |
	1974	1990	2003	1974	1990	2003
United States	37%	37%	43%	34%	37%	37%
Western Europe	39%	40%	49%	32%	38%	39%
Japan	40%	42%	44%	25%	39%	42%
World	36%	35%	42%	30%	34%	35%

14.1: *Efficiency of World Power Plants — Percent Efficiency of Fossil Fuel to Electricity Conversion*

ENERGY TECHNOLOGY PERSPECTIVES, SCENARIOS AND STRATEGIES TO 2050, IEA.

becomes steam which is then directed to the blades of a generator whose rotation in a magnetic field creates electricity.

Figure 14.1 shows the relatively small rate of improvement of worldwide power plant efficiency in recent decades. The efficiency improvement has been much less than 1% per year, far lower than the internal-combustion engine. This supports my thesis that machine efficiency improvements are not going to be the main methodology to deal with the coming energy and climate change crisis.

Small Appliances

There are a surprising number of small home appliances, mostly in the kitchen, that when combined with those from a hundred million homes represent machinery that requires hundreds of giant power plants. Many of these electric appliances — electric tooth brushes, carving knives, can openers, hair dryers, garbage disposals, clothes dryers, vacuum cleaners, toasters, blenders, food processors and clocks for example — could be replaced with hand tools and changed practices. Lawn care machines such as electric hedge trimmers, lawn mowers and leaf blowers may need to be eliminated or replaced with manual versions. Manual tools — toothbrushes, carpet sweepers, hand can openers, towels, knives, hand egg beaters, manual garden equipment — are examples of replacements.

A second set of machines that generate CO_2 indirectly via power plants include our home entertainment machines. TVs, DVD players, VCRs, printers, computers, monitors and other electronic gear are large users of electricity. Some consume electricity even when not turned on by using electric power to keep the device warm so that the start up delay is eliminated. The always on lights of power strips also use energy. Any equipment with a clock or active display, answering machines that are *always on* and background music CDs, TVs and radios could be replaced or eliminated.

Smaller TVs and black and white TVs consume much less electricity and can replace large color TVs. Slower computers with laptop low energy chips may become popular. Internet connections may not be on constantly but accessed as infrequently as possible. Instant communication could be replaced by other slower technologies that require low power. For example, simple faxes may replace e-mail, depending on the results of an energy consumption analysis. Lower power computers and more frugal bandwidth are needed. Using energy to download movies and other high graphic content via the Internet may no longer be energy affordable.

On the other hand, new work patterns may alleviate some of these changes. A high speed computer at home may justify its electricity use if it saves a 20 mile commute to work. Also personal choice and priorities must be considered. Some will give up many machines and do more hand work in order to have Internet access. Others may save their energy for vacations.

Food Machines

There are many energy consuming machines associated with food storage and cooking: refrigerators, freezers, cooking stoves and microwave ovens. Refrigerators will need to be replaced or upgraded to much smaller ones with much thicker walls.[9] Automatic defrosting will go the way of other energy expensive conveniences. We could use innovative, non electrical devices such as double walled pots that use water evaporation to keep foods cool.[10] During cooler parts of the year, food could be stored outside to save refrigeration energy. Freezers are an energy drain that will need to be greatly reduced, since they constantly use electricity to store food for months. Food could be canned, dried or smoked. We can cook with pressurized pots and pans, reducing energy use considerably.[11] Microwaves may be more efficient for certain cooking tasks. Future research will be needed to provide specific and detailed information on energy consumption of food machines.

Heating and Cooling Machines

We will need to get used to a wider range of house temperatures — cooler in winter and warmer in summer. It is unlikely that we'll continue to use air conditioning as it consumes so much electricity; we will need to retrofit houses to stay cooler during hot days. Room or area units might replace centralized furnaces. Ducts and registers could be modified to allow selective area or room heating or be relocated into the conditioned space in renovations and new construction. Safer and more efficient natural gas space heaters could support decentralized heating of the house. Coal could return as a room or area heating source. Temperatures will vary throughout the house based on proximity to heating units. Central climate control will become a thing of the past.

Hot Water and Clothes Dryers/Washers

Flash water heaters which use fuel only when the water is running have long been used in Europe and are beginning to be used in the US. In some areas of the country, solar water heaters may provide hot water at an energy cost lower than flash heaters. Clothes lines and indoor clothes racks eliminate energy intensive clothes dryers. We may even see a resurgence of hand operated washing machines.

Transport Machines

We will have to dramatically alter transportation. The cars that remain will be smaller, simpler and designed to use much less fuel. Manual transmissions will return, eking out a few more miles per gallon. Speed limits will need to be set at a maximum of 50 mph — and probably lower. Even if cars are built that get 200 mpg, we will still have to drive less. Hitchhiking will become common. Jitneys will become the basis for intra-city transportation along with enhanced bus and trolley service. Bicycles will be everywhere. The long distance bus systems of the North American past may be reborn, providing cheap intercity transportation. Train passenger transportation may also become popular again, replacing energy intensive air travel. The trains of the future will not be bullet trains but will operate at a relatively low speed to optimize fuel use. Air travel will be limited to the very rich.

Curtailment Practices

The list of machines to be abandoned and replaced with manual tools or with much lower energy consuming versions is long. Machines are the core of our current culture. The average American may use an automobile, cell phone, iPOD, TV and computer during a large part of her or his waking hours. Having a TV in every room of the house is common in the US, and often they are running as background noise even when no one is present. To abandon such familiar machines is to abandon the American way of life. But whatever machines have provided for us cannot offset the threat to planetary survival from their use nor the coming fuel shortages which shows their long term use is not sustainable.

On a more hopeful note, with fewer machines there will be less time and money spent buying, maintaining, repairing and disposing of them. Living costs may go down. We will need less living space and fewer hours working to earn money for machines; our air and water will be cleaner and our communities stronger.

Reducing our present standard of living and present level of fossil fuel consumption will have major effects on the American lifestyle. What will those changes look like? As machine use declines, past practices will be revived and new practices will be developed.

Diet

The practice of raising farm animals in containment facilities can be replaced by practices from the past and from other nations in the contemporary world. Animals will be raised in natural ways. *Free range* will apply to all animals, with cattle, sheep, goats, pigs and chickens grazing on grasses. Our diets will change. Less meat will be eaten and dairy products will be less available. People will begin to eat a more plant based diet. They will eat more foods in season and import fewer exotic foods. Many people will add growing and preserving foods to their daily activities. Manufactured frozen fruits, meats and dairy products will be a small part of the new diet. Keeping soft drinks cold for days will be a luxury that cannot be continued — which may provide a net health benefit. People will drink tap (not bottled) water when thirsty.

Food Shopping

Eating will be both seasonable and local, and we will shop more frequently for food. When in season, growers will bring food to local markets several times a week, as is done now in the developing world and in a growing number of farmer's markets across the US. Local markets will be closer, sometimes even in neighborhoods — a common practice in the past. We will generate fewer leftovers that need refrigeration. Food will no longer be shipped by air under any circumstances. Locally grown foods will increase while those from international markets will disappear.

Water Consumption

Providing drinking quality water for homes and industry is very energy intensive. Sometimes water is transported long distances at high energy cost. For example, Los Angeles now uses water from the Colorado River. Once water is transported, it is purified, another energy intensive process. More energy is needed to heat water for bathing, clothes washing and dish washing. Washing clothes and dishes in hot water may be a thing of the past. People may wear their clothes longer between washings. We will bath using very little water and less often. Soaking in large tubs filled with hot water or taking a hot leisurely shower may become rare occurrences, and people will take more sponge baths.

Today water is transported and purified and then this clean drinking water is used for watering lawns, an extremely energy wasteful practice. Plants that need minimal watering and gardens will replace lawns. Water catchments practices will be used for watering plants and gardens. Grey water (household waste water other than waste from toilets) will also be used in gardening. Cisterns will return. Neighborhoods may dig wells and install hand pumps to protect against municipal water system outages.

Mobility

Excessive mobility in the US came with cheap oil and is now an addiction. Mobility will need to be severely limited as the world attempts to control global warming. We can begin to spend much more time at home, taking walks, riding bikes and visiting with neighbors instead of driving to movies, rock concerts or similar long distance social activities. We could reduce mobility by working both at home or in our local community, providing local goods and services. Mega malls could become a thing of the past while local entertainment returns. Singing, music of all sorts and local theatrical productions could become commonplace. Conversation, telling stories and playing non-mechanical games could be reborn as watching energy wasting TVs and Internet monitors becomes more and more costly.

Energy Budgeting

To curtail, people must learn to measure their energy consumption in detail and know the energy cost of each action they take. In the past, people have known how to budget and manage their expenses to stay within their incomes. Unfortunately, in recent years Americans have lost many money management skills, relying on cheap credit and hoped-for appreciation in the value of their homes. To measure and manage energy is more difficult than measuring and managing money partially due to the variety of different measuring units used, e.g. barrels of oil, therms of natural gas, tons of coal and kilowatt hours of electricity. Further analysis is needed to determine the different levels of CO_2 generated from different fossil fuel mixes. Although not difficult, the work is tedious, and many Americans may not have the fortitude to develop this kind of energy budgeting practice. Various government agencies monitor this data, and they should provide it in an easy to understand format.

Curtailment vs. Sustainability

Since the peak of US oil production in 1970 and the crisis that followed, the world has been in denial about the ultimate effects of diminishing fossil fuels. In the ensuing decades, the threat of declining supplies has become more apparent, along with the climate effects of burning such fuels. World per capita energy consumption, which has been rising since the 1950s, has flattened. The term *sustainability*, together with the terms efficiency, green and conservation, have so far been used as rationales to avoid facing the need for curtailment actions.

The Bruntland Commission's 1987 report defined sustainable development as development that meets *"the needs of the present without compromising the ability of future generations to meet their own needs."*[12] The terms sustainability and sustainable development were then adopted by corporations, environmental groups and governments as slogans. The term *development* always refers to economic development which in the modern world always means more industrialization. And this means more fossil fuel consumption. In others words, all development is fossil fuel based and therefore not sustainable. The only truly sustainable development is non-industrial.

Countries, companies, universities and other institutions continue to consume just as they have done in the past but have now formed sustainability departments. Sustainability students commute to classes, live in air conditioned dormitories and eat food grown a thousand miles away and transported by diesel truck. New corporate accounting systems include *triple bottom lines* which supposedly expand the traditional company reporting framework to take into account environmental and social performance in addition to financial performance. But if earnings begin to decline, only financial performance matters.

Sustainability is far too vague a word to have any practical meaning. It lacks firm measurements. To avoid "compromising the ability of future generations to meet their own needs" (definition of sustainability) while development uses all the finite resources of the planet is both ludicrous and hypocritical.

Curtailment and Economic Contraction — Depression and Recession

The US economic system, which at its core is the summation of the livelihoods of over 300 million people, operates by consuming fossil fuels and generating CO_2. The main product of the present economy and the main product of people's individual jobs and possibly the main product of modern civilization is CO_2. To dramatically reduce energy use and CO_2 generation is to dramatically reduce economic activity. Euphemisms such as "the more oil you burn, the more GDP you deliver" proclaim this underlying truism. The US refused to approve the Kyoto protocol because it would harm the US economy by causing a reduction in oil consumption because, as just noted, reduction in oil consumed or CO_2 generated will hurt the economy of any country that decides to do so. If a county's economy is harmed enough — that is, if a country reduces fossil fuel consumption enough — then it contracts first to recession and then to depression. This is a desperate time in history, since to save the living environment including people, it will be necessary to take steps that will seriously damage the economy. This will be disastrous if not planned for and carefully managed.

This is rarely stated explicitly. It is the infamous *elephant in the room* about which no one can speak. But slowly reality is beginning to penetrate the deep sleep of denial. The 2006 movie *An Inconvenient Truth* indicated the magnitude of coming changes. Without stating it in words, the term die-off was implied, a term with frightening implications. Die-off means death in large numbers from starvation when a species population grows beyond its food supply. America's options narrow each passing day as our government refuses to recommend reduced consumption and the general population increases its energy use. Unfortunately as fossil fuels begin their decline, population continues to grow.

Figure 14.2 shows how fossil fuels consumption correlates with a massive increase in human population. One obvious conclusion is that world population will have to decrease. This can be accomplished by starvation and war. Alternately, it can be accomplished by voluntary population control. As the crisis deepens, a one child family should become a key value for Americans and all other nations. The earth cannot support the present number of people.

More and more people are becoming aware that they must prepare for drastically reduced lifestyles. Curtailment begins that preparation. But this does not mean that people need be depressed psychologically. It could be argued that in this time of unparalleled prosperity (which is unfortunately totally dependent on fossil fuels) people are no happier than they were before this relatively recent period of rapid industrial growth. The coming crisis is as much an opportunity as a problem. The American lifestyle has been positive for

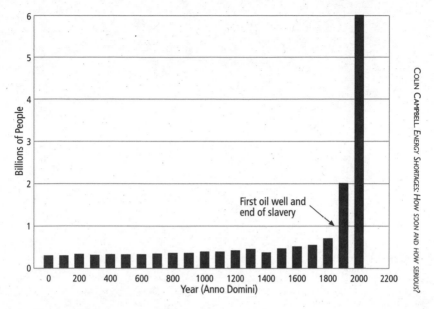

14.2: *World Population Growth — 2000 years*

some but very limited for most. Americans must take responsibility for our current problems and accept that we are responsible for what could be the destruction of creation. The country must search its soul for a vision without arrogance and abandon its feelings of racial and national superiority. We must establish a new society where the values of wealth and power are secondary to values that have yet to be imagined. New outlooks and a new way of life are needed. This is the great challenge for the nation.

Fifteen

Kicking the Media Habit

IT IS OBVIOUS THAT I view the future well-being of people as having been compromised by our market driven corporate structure. I am proposing that we need to eliminate many habits that support this structure. Specifically we must stop our blind consumption of fossil fuel based products. This consuming lifestyle is promoted by corporate owned and controlled mass media, especially TV, but also corporate owned newspapers and magazines as well as radio. If your world view is formed by *USA Today* for instance, your view is created by the editors according to dictates from its corporate owners. If you are of a more liberal persuasion and listen to NPR (National Public Radio) news or watch PBS (US public television), you are exposed to more liberal news and programming. But it too is paid for by corporate and government contributions; thus there are certain limits to programming content. To gain the wisdom to survive the dual crisis of peak oil and climate change, we may have to abandon our media habit — not just TV but also electronic games and entertainment. All teach consumption, competition and violence and tend to make us think along lines that support a corporate consumer agenda.

Finding a New Model

One way to find an alternative to corporate media is to consider what people do in parts of the world where media is not a national pastime. What would one see in those countries? Oddly enough, the same activities one sees on TV but with a different emphasis and a different number of occurrences in a given time period. Naturally people everywhere experience everything, including sex and violence. But those not addicted to media have personal experiences rather than fantasy ones. Thus they do not experience violence vicariously, many times a day, but rather by direct experience on a far less frequent basis. Their minds are concerned with what is actually happening to them, not involved with a fantasy from watching screens. If such people have sex once a week and a fight once a year, then they experience that — not many times in a single day as a media addict does. People who imbibe less media *have time to actually be out living*, while media users are *merely observing life* — unfortunately a fantasy life.

Sports are played everywhere in the world and have been around at least since the Greek Olympics of 8th century B.C. The first rubber ball was used in the 15th century to play the basketball-like Aztec game *tlachtli* in ancient Mexico.[1] In countries with little TV watching, sports are played extensively while in advanced industrial societies people watch other people play sports on TV. Thus less industrialized cultures experience life directly rather than vicariously by looking at flickering screens. At some level, it may be difficult for Americans to make the distinction between living life and watching it being lived in TV stories. But most of the world does not live life via media as we do.

Regaining and Reusing Time

We humans spend most of our time and attention on work, marriage or dating, children, friends and recreation. Events in far away places in the world are not our primary concern. This is how it should be. Our focus should be on giving concern and attention to one's home, extending that concern out to the neighborhood and community, and from there to the region, to the nation and to the world. But because of mass media, most people know more about the slums of Baghdad than the slums of their nearest large city. This is not worldly sophistication but rather a form of ignorance. Relationships, children and the community (including strategizing on alternative ways of living) and helping those in need around us (in our town and region) should be our focus. An awareness of world events is of some use but minimal time should be expended since we have little effect on the larger world. And we should remember that the further away an event is, the less reliable the reporting.

A healthy, outgoing, active child goes out into the world each day, interacts with nature and deals with social relationships whether it be a romantic crush or responding to the schoolyard bully. Such a child is far different than one who moves from class to bus to TV and video games. One child is living in the real world. The other is living a good part of life vicariously, experiencing life through imaginative participation in the world. However, it is the role of parents to help their children deal with the real world and that takes time. From time surveys, parents spend about two hours per day with their children compared to the six hours per day their children spend with media.[2] Obviously parents could spend more time with their children, but they would have to stop spending time watching TV or sitting at their computers.

Parents often find it difficult to find such time for their families or even for each other. Their quality time may be sharing a media experience, which is really not a human interaction. By reducing time spent on media, parents can discuss topics such as resource limitations and climate change. Exploring and defining new lifestyles can be done together as a family and with friends and neighbors, possibly the most important subjects today for a child's future. If we avoid this task, we will continue to teach children the main lessons of the culture today — how to consume and pollute. Children, as well as adults, need to learn conserver ways. Good parents typically transmit values like cooperation, frugality and mutual aid to their children. Paradoxically, we are living in a society where even though parents can interact with their children to establish such core values, a few minutes later the child is observing a presentation on TV of an opposing set of values.

Defending against Disinformation

It is important to know that media affects us strongly just by its form, not solely by its content. Mass media, principally in the service of corporations, obscures the reality that the world is rapidly moving toward a series of crises — peak oil, global warming, record inequity and global militarism. In fact, mass media is to some extent responsible for the crises, having successfully *"dumbed us down."*

If media is a negative force which provides propaganda rather than information or education, then it is a threat to society and must be resisted. Instead of seeing it as a source of information it should be viewed as a source of disinformation, no matter if a few useful tidbits appear amongst the constant barrage of spin. To protect ourselves from the media, it is necessary that we find some form of defense. One way of doing this is to become informed about the sources and content of media itself. Find out what is left out, what the mass media isn't showing on the evening news or what isn't written up in news in our papers. Project Censored is an organization in California that reviews mass media for important stories that are not covered and publishes them.[3] Pacifica Broadcasting also airs stories the major networks pass over. By such efforts, stories that are not acceptable to corporate media are exposed. To develop a defense against media propaganda one starts by becoming aware of and working against its hypnotic effect, especially that of TV, mostly by reducing time spent on it.

Reports vs. Reporting

Reporting in the mass media usually has the *spin* of a corporation behind it. Fortunately there are some examples of a different approach to informing the public. One is *Consumer Reports*, a product testing institute and magazine that provides product information only — without advertising. It uses a standard format for presenting product information, making it easy to use. The organization uses information gathered from many organizations. A person choosing their products from *Consumer Reports* is basically selecting impartial analysis as a basis for purchases rather than misleading advertising. Annual revenues for *Consumer Reports* are about $200 million. By comparison annual revenues of the *Washington Post* are about $3,900 million and the *New York Times* about $3,447 million.[4]

Another example is Worldwatch Institute, an organization with about 40 people who provide detailed statistical information and trends on the environment. Their publications are excellent and comprehensive and provide a unique perspective on world situations. They publish a variety of short and long position papers, avoiding reporting on details of the day. Their yearly budget is about $3,000,000, which they spend on independent research for an environmentally sustainable and socially just society.[5] A third example is *The State of Working America*, a biennial report published since 1988 by the Economic Policy Institute. It includes a wide variety of data on family incomes, wages, taxes, unemployment, wealth and poverty — data that enable the authors to closely examine the effect of the economy on the living standards of the American people. Their yearly expenditures are about $5,000,000 and they have a staff of about 40.[6] The budgets of such small groups represent a tiny fraction of the expenditures of the media industry. Yet the data they report is highly accurate and extremely relevant to the important problems of the world. A person might locate a handful of such organizations and become involved in their work. Such a person would be able to contribute a much higher level of quality information to his or her community. In this case, the quality of the work provides accurate information versus the misleading hype of more popular publications.

A Different Approach to Media

US media such as Z *magazine,* Pacifica and *The Nation* are alternatives to corporate or mass media. They represent a very small part of the total volume of media produced each year. Alternative media typically reflect the form of mainstream media by offering an opposing outlook on some topic. Recent alternatives have appeared using Internet technology, making it possible to have millions of blogs (news and commentary websites) which follow mainstream trends. But there is something missing in the current world of communications, and both mainstream and alternative media are limited by this missing something. Both are extolling and trying to convince their audience of one point of view. But people still remain ignorant of very important and essential issues. Possibly we need new ways of sharing real information. A different news media could dispel the types of ignorance described in this book. Some attributes of a different approach to communication could be described as follows.

> Limited quantity — The volume or bandwidth of media requires too much of our time. Probably people should spend no more than $1/10^{th}$ of the time they currently do — maybe 30 minutes per day — on high quality content. The only way this could happen would be to rigorously weed out all forms and sources of propaganda.
>
> Topical — There should be relatively small numbers (a few dozen or so) of topics, so that people can focus on core information.
>
> Trend oriented — Topical media information should focus towards trends. So called *breaking* news would be of less interest, as the major focus would be on trends and updating trends. Understanding key trends makes it easier to see through propaganda.
>
> Media Components — Any tool of the existing media which manipulates people should not be used. Advertorials, infotainment and puffery should be avoided. If this cannot be done within our society, then one's own involvement should be

limited as much as possible. People should pay for what they watch directly, rather than paying higher product prices to subsidize misleading media.

Media Staff — Reporters and others could be paid for performance based on completeness and accuracy. Possibly they should be licensed like civil engineers, teachers and home builders.

Media and Elections — All people running for office should have a limit on spending and equal air time and print space to cover trends and topics, not personality digs. Furthermore, tracking and reporting political voting records could defend against manipulation of the citizenry.

Corporate Media vs. Community Conversations

Americans get something (entertainment, data, information, motivations, truths, falsehoods) from conventional media which is global (focused on far away events), corporate (run by extremely large companies) and elite (controlled by wealthy individuals). Mass media must constantly manipulate and deceive us in order to sell products. Readers and viewers are referred to as *target markets* and *consumers*, which define the relationships between humans and the corporations. The most fundamental deception perpetrated on the public is that consumption of material goods is the source of human happiness. A secondary deception is hiding the fact that such consumption leads to major *collateral damage* — the possible end of human life on the planet. Other deceptions include these:

- America's military superiority is a source of pride (massive expenditure on our military).
- Our suffering is most important (almost exclusive focus on Americans killed in Iraq).
- Patriots are willing to fight (portray a sense of shame on any who disagree).
- Might makes right (if we can take it, it's ours).

Many people acknowledge the negative aspects of media, but few want to give up *knowing* what *is going on*. Without breaking news or *scoops*, people feel they are not up to date. We tend to believe that to not know the latest news is somehow to be inadequate. Presumably mass media provides us a core set of information that is vital for day-to-day functioning. But even high priority news is only important for a brief moment.

An alternative to corporate mass media is community conversation. Put another way, knowledge, insight and inspiration that is gained within one's community can replace corporate media propaganda. We can meet one another frequently and talk face-to-face. This is two-way, person-to-person communication rather than the one-way, machine-to-human (even if the machine simulates the appearance of a human speaker in dialogue with its talking heads). The information that serves as a basis for effective conversations is better provided by books, which are less susceptible to corporate manipulation and control. Books have better quality control and a long life. They have a much higher density of information than magazines or electronic communication. Well designed book visuals typically contains useful graphical statistical data, possibly boring in appearance when compared to the flashing images of the video screen, but pertinent to the subject.

But there are many other ways of learning within community that do not depend on books or electronic media. Workshops, conferences, classes and other forms of meeting add an additional dimension to the basic information provided by books. Book discussion groups, such as provided by Northwest Earth Institute and Just Living/Just Faith, are invaluable in reaching a deeper understanding of the world. There is an interactive component in learning this way that must not be overlooked. Contact and dialogue increase learning and makes it more enjoyable. This quality is missing in any kind of interactive machine communication, even the Internet. Distance learning does not provide the same experience as human contact. In all its forms, modern media tends to support alienation and separation and destroy community and open inquiry.

In the final analysis, humans want and need to communicate with each other. Mass media purport to provide this communication, but they can never be a substitute for one person communicating with another. Mass media, being unable to provide real communication, offer a poor substitute by telling its stories in a competitive manner (known as *balanced reporting*) with watchers and readers judging the success or failure of media's presentation. People are mere observers, celebrating when their side picks up a point or feeling discouraged when a point or two is lost. But judging is not participation, and people want to be participants more than critics. When people return to a way of living where communication is in conversations with people in a community, mass media as they exist today will fade into the background.

Suggesting that media is in general harmful and should be eliminated (or a dramatic reduction in the time spent imbibing it) at first seems absurd. But it is no more absurd than suggesting the age of oil and other fossil fuels is over. Media, energy and corporate control have evolved together. We need different concepts and new world views to transition away from fossil fuels and its infra-structure of corporations (including those of the media).

It is clear that human communication needs rethinking and redesign. But while that is in process, we can still free our minds from media domination by experimenting with reducing our use of all forms of media. Start by counting the hours you use media in your daily life — activities like reading novels, watching TV, videos or surfing the Internet. Then take a day, a week or a month off and observe your reactions. List your options; see what else is in your community to be a part of. Find some friends who will join you in this experiment. Listen to local bands, make music, talk with friends. It's vital to regain control of our lives by removing ourselves from the domination of mass media, for each of us to find and develop other sources of information and entertainment.

Localization

CURTAILMENT INCLUDES a very large number of personal actions. There are hundreds of ways energy is consumed and CO_2 generated, and there will be hundreds of changes — some major and some minor — to be made. But in some cases necessary actions cannot be taken in the existing social and economic environment. Long commutes required by living in large urban areas may no longer be possible if curtailing gasoline consumption is necessary. The structure and the logistics of society itself will have to change. Cheap energy brought centralization, urbanization and globalization. Expensive energy will bring decentralization, de-urbanization and localization. These terms imply that people may need to do more than change their consumption habits. Many of us may have to change our place of residence and type of work.

Localization, Re-localization and Decentralization

The peak oil and climate change movements have generated new models of low energy and low pollution ways of living. One key concept that is increasing in importance and interest is living locally. The term was first used in conjunction with new economic principles before peak oil or climate change came into popular consciousness. The anti-globalization movement uses the word local in contrast to the word global. For example, in his book *Localization, A Global Manifesto* Colin Hines suggested localization as a counter to globalization.[1] *Going Local: Creating Self-Reliant Communities in a Global Age* by Michael Shuman addresses alternatives to the economic dominance of large corporations.[2] Yet neither of these books paid much attention to the rapidly increasing CO_2 levels or discussed peak oil. These new factors reinforce their basic premises.

Localization describes the desired direction. Re-localization reflects the idea that at one time people were living locally but at some point ceased to do so. In the US, a major move from towns to cities took place during and immediately after World War II. Re-localization recalls the dominant, more rural lifestyle of the 1940s. A good post-fossil fuel life, in a world experiencing climate crisis, may depend on reversing the long term population move from country to city that is now common in most countries of the world. The term *decentralize* refers to cities and economies. Like re-localize, it implies there was another time when they were not centralized.

The term local has different interpretations. We sometimes use the word as an adjective to precede the nouns that describe goods and services, for example local transportation, local energy supplies, local food production, local industries and local economies. But local and localize, like the words sustainability and green, are not well defined. The words can imply important considerations such as reducing energy to transport goods, maintaining money circulation within the community rather than sending it to the far away headquarters of large corporations, tending toward more equitable income distributions and not externalizing costs to other communities. But they can mean other things as well.

Although there are many benefits to local economies, some economic activities are unlikely to be done locally. Very low power computers using a low-power Internet will probably be developed in the future. PC chip factories are huge projects, sometimes requiring billions of dollars to build. Building small chip fabrication units in towns and neighborhoods is unlikely. So, we need to rethink all economic activity, deciding which is to be scrapped (possibly the personal car), which is to be changed or developed (the Smart Jitney to replace the personal car), which will be developed locally using local material (food, carpentry, masonry) and which will be manufactured regionally or globally and installed locally (solar panels, computers).

The context of localization as a response to the damage done by globalization may differ from the context of localization as a response to depleting energy resources and problems created by climate change. In the first case, the localization might involve the return of jobs that have been sent offshore. In the second case, localization may refer to different kinds of jobs that use much less energy and more manual labor. Thus understanding and applying localization or relocalization requires detailed analysis of particular problems in differing parts of the world.

Localization and Migration

Throughout history, people have migrated from one area or country to another to escape difficult or emergency situations. Often these migrations have occurred after events in nature like droughts, floods or earthquakes. Wars — both civil and between nations — have also led to migration. Economic migrants, like the millions of Latin Americans who have come to the US, move from poorer countries to richer ones. Climate change and peak oil will lead to population migration on a world wide basis.[3]

After World War II migration occurred in the US from the agrarian south to the industrial north largely due to the automation of agriculture. Inventions like the cotton picker eliminated many jobs.[4] Fossil fuel driven farm machinery rapidly reduced the numbers of small farms. Workers in agriculture became workers in industry. Rapid industrial growth brought about a rapid increase in per capita energy consumption.[5] Just as the increase in fossil fuel consumption changed farm workers into industrial workers, so a coming decrease in fossil fuel availability may change today's industrial and service workers into agricultural workers. We should expect that tens of millions of people will migrate from city to country.

Localizing Cities — From Suburb to Neighborhood

Los Angeles, California and Phoenix, Arizona are examples of desert cities dependent on imported foods and water transported long distances. Minneapolis, Minnesota and Chicago, Illinois, on the other hand, are surrounded by rich farm lands. A low energy society will affect each city differently. The size of cities will likely decline if buildings and homes that have aged to a point where they are no longer useful are neither replaced nor repaired. As these structures disappear, the resulting open areas could be used as urban gardens. People may slowly leave such cities, settling in areas close to the cities, in smaller towns and villages which can be more self-sustaining.[6]

It would be difficult to relocate all the people in Los Angeles. But ways of living can change within physical boundaries. Allocating one house in every block as a convenience store could bring back neighborhood stores. Office workers may be able to work at home. Suburban garages may be turned into small manufacturing facilities or repair shops. The End of Suburbia could become the End of the Commute rather than the death of a neighborhood. Restructuring cities in these ways will require rethinking the ways we use the built environment.

For example, localizing a centralized school system would require reallocating existing building space in the community for local school use. Cities will not be totally abandoned — there is far too much embedded energy in metropolitan areas to just throw away. But they will change dramatically and become a set of more self-sufficient neighborhoods.

Localizing Food

During the second half of the 20th century, agricultural land practices like organic, biodynamic and permaculture forms of farming were revived or newly developed. These techniques do not rely on fossil fuel derivatives like herbicides, pesticides, fungicides or fertilizers; instead they focus on the health of the soil. Cuba is the best example of a country using these techniques today. In the 1990s Cuba began a forced change to organic methods on a nationwide basis, caused by the rapid decline in energy supplies. Initially crop yields decreased, but over time the land recovered and yields increased.

US government subsidies for large monocultures place these alternative agricultural methods at a disadvantage. But as fossil fuel supplies decrease and prices increase, there should be a resurgence of the small family farm providing a diversity of foods to local consumers. Land will no longer be treated with chemicals. Soil fertility will be achieved by crop rotation of nitrogen fixing crops such as alfalfa and other legumes. Animals that provide meat, eggs and milk will be raised on the family farm so that their manure can be composted and used to fertilize the fields. Land cannot be used continuously as is done with fossil fuel based farming. Some fields will have to be left fallow in order to recover soil fertility. We will need higher yields from the land in use, and diverse labor intensive forms of gardening will obtain more Calories per acre.

Many current localization activities wisely focus on local food production. This is an obvious area to pursue since it eliminates the transportation of food thousands of miles. Local organic food sources are critical to food availability in a post peak oil world. Entrepreneurs are beginning to establish gardens in or near large urban areas, either foreseeing the coming change or simply meeting the needs of people looking for a healthier supply of food. Since food transported long distances is no longer fresh, it is less nutritious. Food should be produced as close as possible to the consumer not only to diminish fossil fuel energy used for transport but to maximize nutrient recycling.

Nature recycles by using manure from animals to replenish nutrients removed from soil when plants are harvested. Current US farming practices disrupt this cycle, creating two problems. First, animal and human manures are treated as waste and typically discarded into rivers or, mixed with toxins, placed on marginal land, removing needed nutrients from the agriculture cycle. Secondly, the nutrients that are no longer available are replaced by fossil fuel fertilizers or from mined minerals such as phosphorus. Repugnant though it may seem to some, eventually human waste must be returned to the soil as well, using techniques followed by subsistence farmers in the developing world for many centuries.

Today, children and many adults have no understanding of the food system. They do not know where their food comes from, how it is processed and who is providing it. Many children cannot relate the food they eat to land or animals. Such ignorance makes it easy to develop policies such as the current ones that are so destructive. With local food production, people will be able to connect their health and well being with how land is used. This should make Americans less willing to accept practices which damage the land or exploit others.

In the post oil era, many more farmers will be needed. The Green Revolution replaced farmers with machinery and fossil fuels. As fossil fuel resources decline, farmers will be needed to replace machines and chemicals. A low energy society will require farmers to be located in the areas containing the most fertile land. The last century's migration from the US heartland to the coasts and from farms to cities will need to reverse as fertile land in the center of the country and around cities and towns is used for labor intensive methods of farming.

Localizing Power Generation

Power generation is currently centralized in a few thousand large power plants distributed more or less uniformly around population centers. The fuels for power plants typically do not come from the area where the power plants are located. For example, much of the coal consumed in the US northeast is transported from Wyoming. Wood and biofuels are often proposed as local energy sources. However, wood is in short supply, and using farm land to grow biofuels is morally questionable and may not actually lower CO_2 levels. In addition, biofuels grown in the traditional way use fossil fuels, particularly natural gas and oil. Biofuels are not a viable long time strategy. They might be imported from poorer countries, but this too has moral implications since doing so will degrade their fertile land, convert their food sources to exports and damage their local economies.

Building a large number of smaller power plants that are more local offers no obvious advantages, considering that fuels may still need to be transported long distances and will still be generating CO_2. However, local power plants, even if no more efficient in operation or in access to fuels, do offer potential for saving energy. Electrical power plants generate an enormous amount of heat. Denmark decided to reduce its energy consumption after the energy crisis of the 1970s. The country developed a combined heat-and-power system which transports surplus heat produced as a byproduct of electricity generation in insulated pipes to heat homes and offices. This cogeneration or district heating technology was not new and has been used in close-knit communities such as university campuses. But Denmark built district-heating systems throughout much of the country. Now heat for buildings is transported from hundreds of small power plants near cities. Prior to this effort 15 big power plants had supplied electricity nationwide in the mid-1980s.[7]

In the US, cogeneration for individual homes is being offered by Honda in partnership with Climate Energy, LLC. The two companies have begun retail sales of *freewatt*, their collaborative Micro-sized Combined Heat and Power (Micro-CHP) cogeneration system for homes. The freewatt Micro-CHP system consists of an MCHP cogeneration unit developed by Honda paired with a furnace or boiler produced by Climate Energy. The ultra-quiet MCHP unit — based on Honda's GE160EV natural gas engine — produces 3.26 kW of heat and 1.2 kW of electric power. In relation to energy costs, Climate Energy test data has shown that when the freewatt Micro-CHP system replaces a typical 80% efficient furnace, homeowners can realize an average of 30% savings in energy costs. The system produces 30% less carbon dioxide emissions than a conventional heating system with electricity provided from the grid, according to Honda. A similar version of an MCHP system is retailed in Japan, with more than 45,000 units sold to date since its introduction in 2003.[8]

The viability of local power generation, either in a small community or in individual homes, is uncertain. Cogeneration added to existing infrastructures of buildings and roads will be expensive. Yet cogeneration does have potential. Each local area will need to assess its electricity needs and sources of fuel. But to make any form of local power viable, electricity use must be curtailed significantly (more than 50%).

Localizing Retail

Building a globalized economy based on growth and cheap fossil fuel consumption severely damaged small shop owners — the owners of hardware stores, lumber yards, shoe stores, repair businesses, butcher shops and the like. Just as giant agribusiness destroyed the livelihood of the family farmer so giant retailing destroyed the livelihood of the local shop keeper. More and more giant corporations began to provide basic goods and services for communities in huge megamalls. Unfortunately, these corporations, such as Cargill and Wal-Mart, have destroyed the economic life of local communities both in the US and many developing nations.

Cheap labor and cheap oil have made these changes possible. Cheap labor is provided in factories in the developing world and provided to North America or Europe by importing low paid workers. Cheap oil keeps the costs for shipping goods low. Wal-Mart is the chief example of a US corporation which has destroyed small businesses in local communities. It has taken advantage of local workers and obtains its products from around the world.[9] This process will be reversed as fossil fuel use declines.

Localizing Manufacturing

Products manufactured locally will have much less embodied energy. The kinds of products created in and for such a low energy world will need to be made so they are reparable as was done in the past. Reparability will be a key factor of product design and products will have to last much longer. But we need not simply return to a pre-industrial economy; there are too many useful scientific and engineering advances to ignore. We can start by defining life cycle costs of everything made, including embodied and operating energy requirements. Part of the new economy will include a resurgence of repair shops; people will simply not buy products that are not built to last.

Localizing Investment and Banking

It's not too soon to begin analyzing where and how capital is obtained and invested. In a globalized world, investments are almost always made outside the local community. However, in past times, wealthy people in a community felt a responsibility toward their fellow citizens and acted accordingly. This is less true today. Banks need to have local roots so they have knowledge and concern for the financial health of their community. Consolidated savings from low wealth individuals provides another source of possible local investment.

Most investment today, other than the equity in homes, is in stock markets. This kind of investing directly supports the current economic system with powerful corporations controlling the economy. To invest locally would mean to invest in small businesses rather than in globalized corporations. This is difficult as our current financial system makes it easy to invest in stocks and hard to invest in individual businesses. Local communities should address this problem as the basis of revitalizing local businesses.

The Great Migration

Most of these ideas have been discussed before — the localizing literature is extensive. But there are few real life examples — localization still remains more theoretical than actual. The changes I have proposed are difficult and are contrary to the ideas and implementations of our modern culture which are based on cheap fossil fuel. As it was in Cuba, change is likely to be forced upon us by circumstances rather than a comprehensive plan. Out of necessity, Cuba found ways to encourage people to stay in their towns or leave Havana and move to the countryside. They saw the need to decentralize, so brought amenities and culture of the City to the outlying areas of the country and offered land to those who wanted to farm and garden. Just as people in the US were forced by circumstances to leave their homes after World War II and move from their farms in the south to the industrial cities of the north, people may be forced by difficult circumstances to decentralize and relocate. Industrial fossil fuel based growth caused the first migration — fossil fuel depletion will drive the next one.

The changes are not simply changes of location but will involve changes of occupation and changes in standards of living. The key parameter for all future plans and decisions will be the amount and kind of fossil fuel consumed. Localization may require both a move and a career change. If moving is the proper course, understanding the energy cost for every product and action will give us an indication of when to move, where to move and what to do. At the core of a successful transition is going to be voluntary life style changes that dramatically reduce the energy cost of living.

Seventeen

Reviving and Renewing Community

Curtailment covers personal actions individuals can take. Localization describes coming structural changes in society. Both curtailment and localization require a new social context: community. Community is the essence of a different America. The word community resonates with people as do the words home or family. There is a yearning in people for the times before rampant economic growth, materialism and consumerism challenged the values of home, neighborhood and community; the fundamental vision of the former is competition while the vision of the latter is cooperation. Looking to community for support and solutions is an alternative to relying on public policy from national governments and powerful corporations. Most of the solutions to the coming crises must evolve at much smaller levels than the national one. I believe that solutions will be developed in local communities of small towns and neighborhoods based in particular places. So far, US leadership looks only for massive solutions found in advanced technology provided by large corporations whereas local people can start applying low tech local solutions in their communities where they live.

Community — A Core Value

We each need to revive and renew our community. Revive means to restore from a depressed, inactive or unused state. Renew means to make new, to restore to freshness, vigor or perfection.[1] Reviving or renewing differs from creating or building community. Community has existed in the US in the past, although not in perfect form when we consider historical racial and sexual inequities. But the core value of caring was strong for many generations, and over time inequities and prejudices have decreased. It is important to review the values and beliefs that informed US culture in the not too distant past and reinvigorate them in forms appropriate to life today. More than anything else, the core values of community revolve around cooperation rather than competition. Equally important, community cares for its place on the earth and the health of that place both for its own members and for their progeny.

In contrast to the familiar slogan *think globally and act locally*, community thinks locally and acts locally. It does not ignore the global — for to do so would be to ignore the source of danger to itself. It is the global that has threatened and harmed the local both in the US and abroad. It is globalization that argues for infinite growth and infinite resources always found in other places far away. It is the global that may use your community as a dump and the global that praises increasing inequity, cynically arguing that a smaller piece of a larger pie for the vast majority of humans creates well being. Global thinking has damaged both the physical places and the spirit of those groupings of people known as communities.

Defining Community

The term community can have many meanings.

+ A group of people who are socially interdependent, who participate together in discussion and decision making, and who share certain practices that both define the community and are nurtured by it. *Robert Bellah.*[2]

+ A group of two or more people who have been able to accept and transcend their differences regardless of the diversity of their backgrounds (social, spiritual, educational, ethnic, economic, political, etc.) enabling them to communicate effectively and openly and to work together toward goals identified as being for their common good. *Foundation for Community Encouragement.*[3]

+ A relatively self-sufficient population, residing in a limited geographic area, bound together by feelings of unity and interdependency. *Bryon Munson.*[4]

+ By community, I mean the commonwealth and common interests, commonly understood, of people living together in a place and wishing to continue to do so. To put it another way, community is a locally understood interdependence of local people, local culture, local economy and local nature. *Wendell Berry.*[5]

+ A "community" is a group of people attached to a particular place with common interests concerning the issues of their shared place (and here, obviously, I omit the new artificial "communities-of-interest" that we hear so much about, such as the "black community" or the "arts community," et cetera). "Civic amenity" refers to goods and benefits that the inhabitants of a community enjoy — for instance, well-designed public space, parks, squares, and the like; or good sewer and water service; or good public transit; or architectural beauty available for all to enjoy; or museums and other such cultural institutions; or good schools. *James Kunstler.*[6]

+ A community is an association of individuals and families that plan and act in concert as an organized unit in meeting their common needs. Always some action is reserved for individual or family initiative. The extent to which action is unified and in common, and the extent to which it is individual or family action, varies endlessly, and therefore the term "community" cannot be closely defined. To whatever extent the general and varied needs and interests of groups of persons and families are dealt with by unified planning and action which grows out of a spirit of common acquaintance, interest, loyalty, and fellowship, and a sense of common responsibility, to that extent a community exists. *Arthur Morgan.*[7]

Selecting the word community to describe the preferred post fossil fuel way of living has its dangers. As Kunstler points out, the word can describe ways of being that differ from the understanding of community I am proposing. My core definition of community includes a group of people attached to a particular place with common interests concerning the issues of their shared place. In other words, communities are people with common interests *living in a particular area*, an interdependent population of various kinds of individuals in a *common location*. Often communities are defined as place based, a useful phrase. Such communities of place have been the norm for all of human history.

The Destruction of Community

The opposite of community is individuality and isolation. Individuality implies separate or distinct existence. Isolation describes a feeling of being separate.

Obviously every human person is an individual. But in modern times, the ideal individual has become one who answers to no less an authority than the nation. In the US today, there are only private individuals living within the public population. Some people find this isolating and lonely. Others revel in the implied competition. But this is a recent development in the history of humanity. Before this focus on the individual as supreme, people lived in communities where there was a balance between the individual and the needs of the whole. Each person was a member of a community first and a member of the nation second. A tribe or nation was a set of communities within which people lived. Isolation rarely existed.

The individualistic world view, often associated with Adam Smith, came into existence in the 18th-century as people became less self-reliant members of a community and more dependent employees of corporations. British enclosure laws were designed to destroy the commons (land held for a community's use within a locale) forcing people to leave their communities and seek work in urban factories. Neoconservative economic and political thinkers are modern representatives of this early point of view, one that disregards the needs of the whole if there is economic benefit for themselves. At the same time as the US military was destroying peasant societies in Vietnam in the 1970s, US Secretary of Agriculture Earl Butz began destroying small farms in America. In both cases, a small community farmer was denigrated. The myth still perpetuated by government agencies and corporate interests is that backward rural people all over the world need to be dragged into modern times and should be grateful to their transnational corporate employers. But in reality, the fossil fuel-based, non-sustainable industrial paradigm needs to destroy its competition, the agrarian sustainable way of living. This destruction continues as more and more rural people around the world are driven from their farms and local communities into the sweatshops of globalized factory systems.

Major propaganda campaigns have aided this destruction. Media and literature stereotypes buttress this harmful effort. A wide range of terms have been used to create separation. Urban people are worldly-wise, cool, hip, sophisticated, blasé, trendy, upscale, tony, chic, urbane, suave and smooth. Rural people are provincial, unsophisticated, hayseeds, bumpkins, yokels, hicks, peasants, hillbillies, natives, indigenous types, rubes, country-cousins, rustics and rednecks. The same arrogance that Stalin showed to the Kulak farming class in Russia was the basis for the destruction of the family farmer in America. Until very recent times, cities obtained their fresh vegetables and dairy products from truck farms in the countryside surrounding them. Close proximity showed city dwellers the source of what they ate. But since such farms are located fairly near metropolitan areas, they have been converted to valuable building sites. Because of this, most people in the affluent world do not and cannot experience the source of their food, living in ignorance of the soil and its products.

Funded by cheap energy, the 20th century witnessed rapid urbanization of world population, as the global proportion of urban population rose dramatically from 13% (220 million) in 1900, to 29% (732 million) in 1950, to 49% (3.2 billion) in 2005. The increase from 1900 to 1950 was 16% while the increase from 1950 to 2005 was 20%. A 2005 report projected that the figure is likely to rise to 60% (4.9 billion) by 2030.[8] Without well-developed neighborhoods, community is impossible in such places simply due to size. Community is at its strongest within groups of a few thousand. In populations of millions, it is difficult for community as I have defined it to survive for more than a generation or two.

The Activities of Community

When community is defined and measured by the interrelationships people have with each other on a day to day basis in a particular place, then community is the most important element in a satisfactory quality of life. This means that people's relationships — not material goods, wealth or status — are the fundamental source of happiness in life.[9] We can explain many social problems in affluent countries by the lack of this kind of community. Increasing mobility combined with the increasing inequity throughout the world has badly damaged community. The resurrection of community will require changes in values and new world views. We can observe these attitudes and activities in a vibrant community.

- *Living with Many Familiar Personal Relationships* — This means having relationships and contact with many people who know each other well. It assumes friendliness. Each relationship will have a different intensity, from casual acquaintance to intimate friend, but no matter the level, many people know one another.

- *Identifying with a Particular Place* — Such identification includes attachment to a particular place, like a small town or a neighborhood. The identification is often articulated in phrases like "sense of place," "liking the place," "belonging to the place / belonging here" or "feeling at home in this place / feeling at home here."

- *Practicing Unity and Cohesion* — This involves cooperation with and support from other people, who are described as acquaintances and friends. A bond is felt with others in the community. Community members are concerned with the welfare of the place (town, village or neighborhood) and its people. People assume they will be cared for if they are in need of help. People trust and rely on other people. The rugged individualist is hard to find in such a community.

- *Assuming Mutual Concern and Mutual Assistance* — Fundamentally, people care about each other. People do things for each other voluntarily and with joy. People give and receive, incur obligations to each other and feel gratitude toward each other, experience concern and give assistance. There is a sense of interdependence. Contributions to each other are voluntary. Reciprocity is assumed and both happily provided and gratefully received.

- *Focusing on Common Collective Concerns* — People have a sense of civic responsibility. There is a philosophy of joint ownership and joint responsibility, including a feeling of our town, our people and our facilities. People take responsibility for the activities and facilities of the community.

- *Including Celebrations, Traditions and Rituals* — People develop a sense of local history. They know the events and dates that are significant in the history of the place. These events and dates are celebrated together. The history of the community is known, remembered and discussed.[10]

Communities described in this way can be weak, mediocre or strong. All people live in community in the sense that they may have a residence with neighbors in some municipality of some size. But when one doesn't know one's neighbors, the bonds of relationship may be quite weak. Even surrounded by other people individuals may feel lonely, isolated or alienated. Building community means to increase relating and socializing with other people so that levels of intimacy increase while feelings of alienation decrease.

Community and Consumer Capitalism

The current US economic system requires the consumption of more and more fossil fuel based products and services. Consuming is so pervasive in modern times that even what could be consumption's nemesis — community — is often described in the language of money and investment. Robert Putnam uses a money term, *social capital*, to describe the relationships and practices that enhance the factors of friendship, security, cooperation, civil conversation and pleasant social interactions.[11] Pre-industrial societies and current societies in other parts of the world where consumption-based industrialism has had limited influence devote much of their time and energy to maintaining these social relations and draw support and satisfaction from them.

Community is very weak in conglomerations of people living urbanized, industrialized lives. In those places the following characteristics hold sway.

+ *Living in Isolation* — Many people live either as isolated individuals or in isolated nuclear families. People have little to do with their immediate neighbors. People live very privately, with only limited sharing and cooperation; they often distrust each other.

+ *Constantly Competing* — People believe that life in modern society is a competitive struggle between individuals for money and possessions in an environment where one person can only advance at the expense of another. This attitude is not limited to poor countries; the struggle is as intense in rich countries, as evidenced by poverty and unemployment in wealthy nations. The poor and downtrodden are given little assistance or sympathy since they are simply viewed as being noncompetitive. Modern society is organized to provide excess wealth to a minority.

+ *Being Excessively Mobile* — People in industrial urban societies move frequently, eliminating the possibility of identifying with a place. Most people commute long distances, limiting the time for interaction with family, neighbors and friends. One of the consequences of this mobility is a loss of continuity within a community. History (connection to the past) and other connections of value are vital; they take time to develop and frequent moves make this difficult.

One tragic consequence of this mobility is the poor care of older people. Care of the old is best done by all the members of a community rather than within a single family. In an established community with a long history many of those who are now old would have at one time cared for those who were young. As the young matured, they would in turn attend to those who were aging. Mobility eliminates building up and paying off of these types of natural obligations. Other relationships that can develop between young and old in vital communities include work (employer and employee), commerce (business and customer) and education (teacher and pupil).

+ *Having only a small number of impersonal relationships* — Many people do not know personally the people with whom they trade or work. In an urban environment there are more people but fewer close relationships. Interactions are based more on the buying of goods and services from strangers rather than social interactions with friends and acquaintances.

+ *Missing emotional support* — Intimate and caring relationships are absent. Many people who are lonely and depressed begin using alcohol and drugs. Many self-destruct or become socially destructive. A large number of people may become impoverished or homeless.

+ *Teaching lust, violence and competition* — Through corporate media giants, young people are taught violence and sexually inappropriate behavior. Most American TV shows, including cartoons for small children, are about little more than aggression, violence and sexual desire in some form or the other. The mass media also teach people to be fiercely competitive in sports, school, social life and work. Americans are taught that material possessions are the primary determiner of happiness.

+ *Having no time* — Many people think they have too little time to become involved in local affairs. Working, commuting and spending hours viewing video screens in one form or another provides no time for strengthening relationships and community. In recent times, family members have had to work longer hours. Since mass transit is not readily available in urban areas and children today rarely ride bicycles parents must transport children from one activity to another by car. Children are discouraged from walking due to fears for their safety.

+ *Accepting a class system* — Consumer society idealizes celebrities, sports heroes, the wealthy and corporate executives: models of competitive individualism. Those who have most of the wealth and power and status are admired while those who are poor and lonely are considered losers and completely responsible for their inadequacies. We come to believe that ordinary people lack the ability and skills to manage their local social and economic systems. American democracy is not participatory but controlled by power and wealth via advertising, kickbacks and public relations.

+ *Having no sense of place* — There is little identification with one's geographical area and thus any feelings of belonging or being at home are missing. Few people devote time to working for the good of their local places. Suburbs are more dormitories than close neighborhoods, and houses are commodities where people separate themselves from others — often even other family members!

+ *Having few common tasks and responsibilities* — There is little citizenship. Modern people spend very little time working cooperatively in their neighborhoods and towns to improve them or to perform useful functions. There is little public work in communities — everything is put out to bid. Insurance companies restrict volunteer labor in a municipality. However, working together on a common task is an important way to strengthen community.

+ *Privatizing the public sphere* — The domains of activity that were public in the past are now being privatized. Shopping malls, museums, railways, schools, prisons, hospitals, care of the aged and leisure spaces are increasingly being taken over and controlled by profit driven corporations. We are less able to think of these as our public institutions, our services and spaces which serve the people. Rather, what was once public property have become assets for corporate stockholders. We have been convinced that corporations can produce consumer goods and services more efficiently than ordinary people or elected governments.

+ *Missing meaningful festivals, rituals and traditions* — Local, community based socializing, recreation and entertainment have been replaced by corporate entertainment sold for money. Locally owned movie theaters and concert spaces have disappeared, replaced by mega malls, huge amusement parks and arcades for electronic games.

The lack of strong community most seriously affects people with disadvantages, such as single parents, the disabled, poor people and elders. The affluent can, to some extent, find or buy alternative satisfactions. But without community many with limited financial means (the majority of the population) are condemned to a frenetic life of working at low wage jobs, isolation and boredom.

Community, Socialization and Education

For centuries, the community has been the crucial agent of socialization. As people interact with others in a strong community, good social values are constantly reinforced. People experience the benefits of helping and cooperation. Children hear their parents and their parents' friends talking about important local issues, expressing concern for the welfare of the area. People work together toward high standards and develop useful traditions. Everyone sees the satisfaction that comes from participating in festivals and civic duties.

Children who live in distant suburbs and whose parents shop as isolated individuals in supermarkets and malls lack key role models precisely at the time when they are forming an identity and beginning to see themselves as useful and valued citizens. In the modern world, they are solely students who receive a purely theoretical education. In a community environment, theoretical education is supported by the practical experience of living in a caring place.

We pay a very high price for our competitive way of living. Increasing numbers of discontented people are causing harm to themselves and to others. If people experienced stronger community, fewer people would become depressed or turn to drugs or crime. Friends could foresee problems such as domestic violence and child abuse before they became serious. The cost of break-ins and muggings along with the cost of police, courts, prisons and social workers could be reduced. Far more important, the emotional cost associated with violence, drug abuse and suicide could be eliminated or reduced. In communities of place and relationships, social bonds are strong and individuals participate without the need for a large government with great powers, vast budgets and large numbers of bureaucrats and experts.

Community Harm and Economic Development

Economic development is the principal interest and activity of affluent modern societies. The world is divided into developed nations and developing nations, with a view that the developed nations are the models for the rest of the world. However, there are good reasons for concluding that if economic development is put before the good of a country's people, it tends to weaken or destroy community. If a society's top priority is to constantly increase the amount of available goods and services, then community, as I define it here, will tend to atrophy.

An alternative to global economic development based on large transnational corporations is economic development of local businesses and local farms. The basic theory of economics of scale — big is always better — is countered by the advantages of living in a community of place and a community of relationship. Contrary to Adam Smith's view of humans, money and position are not the top priorities of most people. Keeping economic development, especially capital, within the community supports a different more equitable way of life.

It is in the interests of corporations that people remain isolated; individuals who do less for themselves purchase more. Corporations spend vast advertising budgets persuading people to buy products. When people become bored or lonely or depressed they buy entertainment, go shopping or pay for professional counseling.

Most US capital and development resources flow only into ventures that produce products for sale and therefore more passive, private consuming. Few resources are offered to projects that might stimulate community self-sufficiency and involvement. For example it is difficult to get funding for neighborhood workshops, drama clubs or leisure environments. Such projects not only contribute nothing to *getting the economy going*, they actually reduce GNP by enabling people to live better while purchasing less.

Market Relationships Drive Out Social Relationships

The values of the free market system and consumption damage community and social cohesion more than any other factor in the US. When selling to consumers becomes the main mechanism whereby people acquire the things they need, desirable social values, attitudes, bonds and relationships are lost.

In a competitive market situation solely focused on buying or selling, people must maximize their advantage and minimize that of others. This situation does not stimulate thought about what would be good for other people or society as a whole. But the quality and health of society depends on social and moral values other than merely self-interest. Shared social values like being honest, doing the right thing, seeing justice done, high standards, the public good and supporting what is good for others are crucial. This is the most disturbing effect of the recent rise of neo-liberalism which has all but eliminated concern for the common good. Everyone becomes an individual entrepreneur who must focus on self-interest and survival in a difficult and hostile marketplace, knowing that not everyone can get a good job, prosper or be secure. This competitive individualism makes altruism, cooperation and concern about social issues irrelevant, or makes them even liabilities that hold us back from success. By contrast, the basic outlook of a healthy society is collective. People are concerned about what is good for others, for their society and the least fortunate. Neo-liberalism is not just generating a more selfish, mean, unequal and brutal society; it thrives by destroying the fundamental social bonds without which you cannot have a good society.

The transition to predominantly market driven economics with emphasis on consumerism began just a few centuries ago. No previous societies allowed commercial markets to dominate daily living. In earlier societies markets were under social control. The main factors that determined what goods should be produced and how things should be distributed were considerations of morality, justice, community history and what was good and healthy for people. Corporations (as legal but not actual people) have no societal conscience as their purpose is only to make a profit. So markets under corporate control damage society and the living world. In the last few decades, the pressures towards economic globalization have moved more and more human activities into corporate market control. Governments have been forced to deregulate, turning many areas of social support over to corporations. As I have noted before, the result is increasing inequity, the destruction of community and desirable social relationships. The state's role in human affairs has declined as rich and powerful corporations obtain more and more power and control. Today the fate of nations as well as communities depends more and more on corporate whims.

Fossil fuel shortages and the growing threat of climate change will eventually undermine our consumption based economy. As the situation deteriorates, we can only hope more and more people will turn their back on the corporate consumptive lifestyles and regain control of their communities and their lives.

Community Values and Beliefs

Values are principles or qualities that determine the way one views and lives in the world. Values are the basis of belief systems; they are fundamental statements about what we experience and perceive. Community values do exist which in many cases oppose the existing values of global consumer capitalism.

Figure 17.1 contrasts community with consumer values. Combined with the explanations in this chapter, these terms can help describe a post oil world more fully.

Community	Consumer	Community	Consumer
Physical			
Durable	Temporary	Renewable	Extractive
Organic	Mechanistic	Shared rides	Individual mobility
Intermediate tech	High tech	Tools	Machines
Simple homes	Showcase homes	Organic food	Manufactured food
Social			
Community	Individualism	Participation	Domination
Neighborliness	Competition	Social diversity	Homogeneity
Mental Moral			
Spiritual			
Selfless	Selfish	Players	Winners/losers
Cooperation	Competition	People/animals equity	Machines inequity
Simplicity	Prosperity	Elegance	Ostentation
Economic			
Frugality	"Conspicuous consumption"	Fair trade	Free trade
Quality	Quantity	Service	Profit
Health	Wealth	Steady state	Economic growth
Care	Convenience	Sustainability	Comfort
World			
Sustain the world	Subdue the world	Sustainability	Progress
Local prosperity	Central power	World cooperation	World competition
Diversity	Uniformity	Physical world	Virtual world
Local community	Mass society	Agrarian community	Industrial society
Miscellaneous			
Serves community	Serves markets	Generational driven	Self driven
Place based	Global based	Relationship value	Money value
Buy longevity	Buy innovation	People driven democratic	Technology driven hierarchies
Prefers public	Prefers private	Corporate focus	Government focus

17.1: *Conserver and Consumer Values*

PAT MURPHY

Envisioning Strong Communities

There can be no solution to the problems of community within a corporate controlled consumer society. Our problems are caused by the pursuit of affluence and the over consumption of economic goods and services. Through advertising and the mass media, corporations continue to gain increased control of ordinary life. Only by shifting to a non-consumer orientation can community values and relationships be restored.

This shift to a non-consumer oriented lifestyle will be easier in small, local, self-sufficient communities and neighborhoods where many economic exchanges do not involve cash sales but take the form of giving and receiving. In such communities, mutual aid and surplus goods are given to others in need. People directly govern their community of place. Such communities are very supportive, and people know that they are making a valuable contribution. Everyone has a strong incentive to contribute, to help each other and do what is best for the community. These acts and experiences of mutual aid generate strong feelings of familiarity and support. Members clearly understand that their own welfare depends on how well the local society functions. Living in community requires and rewards behavior that benefits others and the community. For example it can be enjoyable to help paint the community windmill or work in the gardens. Such productive tasks are important and bring people together into cooperative, shared activity.

As our fossil-fueled economy wanes, more economic activity will be transferred into a large non-cash sector where giving, cooperation, mutual aid, and working together will build social bonds. Such community cohesion is not likely to be restored by simply calling for voluntary cooperation in the present affluent and individualistic society. They are most likely to emerge once conditions cause people to come together locally, to cooperatively organize their own economic affairs and together deal with issues of survival.

Conclusion

Community and Survival

The popular discourse concerning peak oil and climate change includes concerns about the *collapse of civilization as we know it today, imploding economies* and the longevity of the *American Way of Life*. These euphemisms obscure the reality that survival is not an abstraction about societies, economies and cultures but rather about life and death for billions of people. Thus a change to a different way of living — a low energy way — is not negotiable. We need to reduce our use of fossil fuels or we will die. Skills of low energy living, proven over thousands of years, have atrophied in our culture and must be relearned. This will not be an easy process; hundreds of community practices must be rediscovered.

Plan C addresses the issue of survival by offering ideas and techniques for living with less. The strategies and tactics described are tools for a life long effort towards becoming a different kind of human being. My wish is that you, readers of this book, will find the creative seed within yourselves to transform your lives with your whole heart, soul and strength, and, with a joyful spirit, do this with your neighbors in your communities for the future of humankind and for all life on earth.

Ralph Waldo Emerson said, "I grasp the hands of those next [to] me, and take my place in the ring to suffer and to work." It will not be easy. But what generation has ever been given such a chance and a challenge to transform its world?

Endnotes

T HROUGHOUT THIS BOOK, the term Calories is capitalized in keeping with the convention to use a capital C to designate kilocalories.

Preface

1. "Toward a healthy community: an interview with Wendell Berry — essayist, author, and poet." *Christian Century*, October 15, 1997. [cited March 10, 2008]. findarticles.com/p/articles/mi_m1058/is_n28_v114/ai_19930370/pg_4.

Chapter I

1. *An Inconvenient Truth.* Davis Guggenheim, Director, 96 min. Paramount, 2006. [DVD].
2. Intergovernmental Panel on Climate Change. These multivolume reports are outlined at the website ipcc.ch/ipccreports/index.htm.
3. United Nations Framework Convention on Climate Change. *United Nations Climate Change Conference — Bali, 3 - 14 December 2007.* [cited January 3, 2008]. unfccc.int/2860.php.
4. The Community Solution. *About Us.* [cited January 3, 2008]. communitysolution.org/.
5. M. King Hubbert. *Nuclear Energy and the Fossil Fuels.* Publication 95, Shell Development Company, June, 1956. [cited November 6, 2007]. hubbertpeak.com/hubbert/1956/1956.pdf. This paper was presented at the spring meeting of the Southern District Division of Production, American Petroleum Institute, March 7-9, 1956.

6. M. King Hubbert. "Energy from Fossil Fuels." *Science Magazine*, Vol. 109 (February 4, 1949), p. 108. [cited January 3, 2008]. hubbertpeak.com/hubbert/science1949/.

7. Gerald O. Barney. *Volume 1: The Summary Report — Global 2000 Report to the President of the United States: Entering the 21st Century.* Pergamon Press, 1980.

8. Ibid, page 328.

9. John Gever, Robert Kaufmann, David Skole and Charles Vorosmarty. *Beyond Oil: The Threat to Food and Fuel in the Coming Decades.* Ballinger, 1986.

10. C.J. Campbell. *The Coming Oil Crisis.* Multi-Science Publishing Company and Petroconsultants S.A., 1997.

11. Association for the Study of Peak Oil and Gas . "The General Depletion Picture." ASPO Newsletter #85 (January 2008), p. 2. [cited January 3, 2008]. aspo-ireland.org/contentFiles/newsletterPDFs/newsletter85_200801.pdf.

12. Joseph J. Romm. *The Hype About Hydrogen: Fact and Fiction in the Race to Save the Climate.* Island, 2005, p. 16

13. Martin Flanagan. "Shell seeks to end reserves saga." *The Scotsman*, April 12, 2007. cited January 3, 2008]. thescotsman.scotsman.com/energyutilities/Shell-seeks-to-end-reserves.3275702.jp.

14. Ann Davis et al. "BP Settles Charges, Submits to Watchdog." *Wall Street Journal*, October 26, 2007, p. A3. [cited January 3, 2008]. online.wsj.com/article/SB119332810057671536.html?mod=googlenews_wsj.

15. Greg Geyer. "ASPO-USA Response to ExxonMobil Peak Oil Advertising." March 3, 2006. [cited January 3, 2008]. aspo-usa.com/index.php?option=com_content&task=view&id=21&Itemid=91.

16. *Wall Street Journal*, October 24, 2007.

17. Guy Chazan. "Chevron Pitch: Climate Change Is Its Concern, Too." *Wall Street Journal*, October 18, 2007, p. B7. [cited January 8, 2007]. online.wsj.com/public/article/SB119266020194662604.html.

18. Colin Campbell. "Comment: Just how much oil does the Middle East really have, and does it matter?" *Oil & Gas Journal*, April 4, 2005 [cited February 13, 2008]. peakoil.net/CC4April2005OilGas.html.

19. US Government Accountability Office. *Crude Oil: Uncertainty about Future Oil Supply Makes It Important to Develop a Strategy for Addressing a Peak and Decline in Oil Production.* Publication GAO-07-283, February 2007. [cited November 6, 1007]. bartlett.house.gov/uploadedfiles/GAOCrudeOil.pdf.

20. US Energy Information Administration. *Annual Energy Review 2008.* Early Release, page 12. [cited January 4, 2008]. eia.doe.gov/oiaf/aeo/.

21. Julian Darley. *High Noon for Natural Gas: The New Energy Crisis.* Chelsea Green 2004, p. 183.

22. C.J. Campbell. *Oil Crisis.* Multi Science Publishing Company, 2005, p. 245.

23. Congressman Roscoe Bartlett. GAO *Report on Peak Oil.* Congressional Record, US House of Representatives, March 29, 2007, p. H3353. [cited January 4, 2008]. bartlett.house.gov/UploadedFiles/GAOspecialorder032907.pdf.

24. Energy Watch Group. *Coal: Resources and Future Production.* Document EWG-Paper 1/07, Final Version 28032007. [cited November 6, 2007].energywatchgroup.org/ fileadmin/global/pdf/EWG-Coalreport_10_07_2007.pdf.

25. B. Kavalov and S.D. Peteves. *The Future of Coal.* Document EUR 22744 EN, European Commission, Directorate General, Joint Research Centre, Institute for Energy, February 2007, pp. 4-5. [cited November 6, 2007]. ie.jrc.cec.eu.int/publications/scientific_publications/2007/EUR22744EN.pdf.

26. Richard Heinburg. *Burning the Furniture.* Museletter #179, March 2007. [cited November 6, 2007]. richardheinberg.com/museletter/179; Richard Heinberg. *Peak Moment: Peak Oil, Peak Coal and Beyond.* Global Public Media, June 9, 2007. [cited November 6, 2007]. globalpublicmedia.com/peak_moment_peak_oil_peak_ coal_and_beyond; Richard Heinberg. *Coal's Future in Doubt.* MuseLetter Special Update, May 2007. [cited November 6, 2007]. richardheinberg.com/museletter/ may102007update.

27. Tom Stevenson. "Uranium price jumps to record 40-year high." *Telegraph* newspaper, April 11, 2007. [cited November 6, 2007]. telegraph.co.uk/money/ main.jhtml?xml=/money/2007/04/11/cnuranium11.xml.

28. International Atomic Energy Agency. "Reactors under Construction" and "Number of Reactors in Operation Worldwide." Nuclear Power Plant Information webpage. [cited January 4, 2008]. iaea.org/cgi-bin/db.page.pl/pris.charts.htm.

29. Energy Watch Group. *Uranium Resources and Nuclear Energy.* Document EWG-Series No 1/2006, December 2006. [cited November 6, 2007]. lbst.de/publications/studies e/2006/EWG-paper_1-06_Uranium-Resources-Nuclear-Energy_ 03DEC2006.pdf .

30. Intergovernmental Panel on Climate Change. *About IPCC — Membership and Mandate of the IPCC.* [cited November 6, 2007]. ipcc.ch/about/index.htm.31. Intergovernmental Panel on Climate Change. *IPCC Reports.* [cited January 4, 2008]. ipcc.ch/ipccreports/assessments-reports.htm.

31. Union of Concerned Scientists. *The IPCC: Who Are They and Why Do Their Climate Reports Matter?* [cited February 14, 2008]. ucsusa.org/global_warming/science/ the-ipcc.html.

32. Geoffrey Lean. "Global warming 'is three times faster than worst predictions.'" *Independent* newspaper, June 6, 2007. [cited November 6, 2007]. environment.independent.co.uk/climate_change/article2609305.ece.

33. Robert Lee Hotz. "Geochemists Chart Carbon Dioxide Levels at 650,000-Year High." *Wall Street Journal*, December 14, 2007, p. B1. [cited January 4, 2008]. online.wsj.com/public/article/SB119749713077524669.html.

34. George Monbiot. "This crisis demands a reappraisal of who we are and what progress means." *The Guardian*, December 4, 2007. [cited January 4, 2008]. guardian.co.uk/Columnists/Column/0,,2221497,00.html.

Chapter 2

1. Colin Campbell. *The Dawn of the Second Half of the Age of Oil.* ASPO Newsletter No. 50 (February 2005), p. 7. [online] [cited November 7, 2007]. aspo-germany.org/e/aspo_news/aspo/newsletter050.pdf.

2. Ivan Illich. *Energy and Equity.* First published in *Le Monde*, 1973. [cited January 7, 2008]. reactor-core.org/energy-and-equity.html.

3. Jeffrey D. Sachs. *The End of Poverty: Economic Possibilities for Our Time.* , Penguin, 2005, p. 29.

4. US Census Bureau. *Income Limits for Each Fifth and Top 5 Percent of Households — All Races: 1967 to 2006.* Historical Income Tables — Households, Table H-1. [cited January 7, 2008]. census.gov/hhes/www/income/histinc/h01ar.html.

5. US Census Bureau. *Share of Aggregate Income Received by Each Fifth and Top 5 Percent of Households, All Races: 1967 to 2006.* Historical Income Tables — Households, Table H-2. [cited February 14, 2008]. census.gov/hhes/www/income/histinc/h02ar.html.

6. Full OECD membership includes the US and most members of the second level of industrialized nations. The subset used here (designated OECD-L) places the US in a category by itself. It also transfers Mexico and Turkey from the OECD to the category Rest of the World (ROW) since their economies are closer to those of the poor nations of the developing world.

7. M. King Hubbard. *Exponential Growth as a Transient Phenomenon in Human History.* World Wildlife Fund Conference, 1976, pp. 83-84. [cited November 8, 2007]. hubbertpeak.com/hubbert/wwf1976/.

8. Society of Danish Engineers. *Oil-based Technology and Economy, Prospects for the Future.* April 2004, p.24. [cited January 7, 2008]. tekno.dk/pdf/projekter/p04_Oil-based_Technology_and_Economy.pdf.

9. The Community Solution. *Cuba: Life after Oil.* New Solutions #2, May 2004. [cited November 8, 2007]. communitysolution.org/pdfs/NS2.pdf; *The Power of*

Community: How Cuba Survived Peak Oil. Faith Morgan, 53 min. The Community Solution, 2006 [DVD]

10. See John Cobb and Herman E. Daly. *For the Common Good.* Beacon, 1997; Richard Douthwaite. *The Growth Illusion.* Lilliput, 1992; Richard Douthwaite. *Short Circuit: Strengthening Local Economics for Security in an Unstable World.* Green Books, 1998; Michael Perelman. *The Perverse Economy: The Impact of Markets on People and the Environment.* Palgrave Macmillan, 2003; Michael Albert and Robin Hahnel. *Looking Forward: Participatory Economics for the Twenty First Century.* South End, 1991; John E. Ikerd. *Sustainable Capitalism: A Matter of Common Sense.* Kumarian Press, 2005; Michael H. Shuman, *Going Local: Creating Self-Reliant Communities in A Global Age.* Routledge, 2000.

11. Michael Perelman. *The Perverse Economy: The Impact of Markets on People and the Environment.* Palgrave Macmillan, 2003, p. 183.

Chapter 3

1. George W. Bush. *Address to a Joint Session of Congress and the American People.* United States Capitol, Washington, D.C., September 20, 2001. [cited January 7, 2008]. whitehouse.gov/news/releases/2001/09/20010920-8.html.

2. Adam Hochschild. *King Leopold's Ghost: A Story of Greed, Terror, and Heroism in Colonial Africa.* Houghton Mifflin, 1998.

3. James A. Frieden and Deborah Elliott. British India: "Just Rule" or "Divide and Rule"? Learning Guide to A Passage to India. [cited January 7, 2008]. coat.ncf.ca/our_magazine/links/issue47/articles/a03.htm.

4. Margaret MacMillan. *Paris 1919: six months thast changed the world.* Random House, 2001, p. 317.

5. Winston Churchill. *The River War: An Historical Account of The Reconquest of the Soudan,* 2 Vols., ed. Col. F. Rhodes. Longmans, Green, 1899, scanned and modernized by Jerome S. Arkenberg for the Internet Modern History Sourcebook. [cited November 13, 2007]. fordham.edu/halsall/mod/1898churchill-omdurman.html.

6. John Malkin. "Hidden Power: Noam Chomsky On Resurrecting the Revolutionary Spirit of America." *The Sun,* Issue 352 (April 2005), p. 8.

7. Cora Agatucci. *African Timelines Part III: African Slave Trade & European Imperialism.* [cited November 13, 2007]. eb.cocc.edu/cagatucci/classes/hum211/timelines/htimeline3.htm#THE%20HOLOCAUST.

8. Roger A. Lee and History Guy Media. *Philippine American War.* [cited November 13, 2007]. historyguy.com/PhilipineAmericanwar.html.

9. "Table on The 1895 Partition of Africa" from Yosef A.A. ben-Jochannan. *We, The Sons And Daughters Of "AFRICA's" Great Sperms And Ovum, Let Us This Day Of 6086 N.Y./*

1986 C.E. Speak As One Voice Academically. [cited November 13, 2007]. nbufront.org/ html/MastersMuseums/DocBen/ASCACAddress/ AddressTable1.html.

10. "Table 3.1 - Japan's Democide in China and World War II: Estimates, Sources and Calculations" in R.J. Rummel. *Statistics of Democide: Genocide and Mass Murder Since 1900.* [cited January 7, 2008]. hawaii.edu/powerkills/SOD.TAB3.1.GIF.

11. Iris Chang. *The Rape of Nanking: The Forgotten Holocaust of World War II.* Penguin, 1998, p.4.

12. Matthew White. *Losses in the Second World War.* [cited February 15, 2008]. users.erols.com/mwhite28/ww2-loss.htm.

13. Noam Chomsky. *The Dýyarbakir Speech.* March 25, 2002. [cited November 14, 2007]. zmag.org/content/ForeignPolicy/chomsky_march26.cfm.

14. "Casualties" in NationMaster Encyclopedia. *Mau Mau.* [cited November 14, 2007]. nationmaster.com/encyclopedia/Mau-Mau.

15. Agence France Press news release (April 4, 1995) quoted by Ray Smith. *Casualties — US vs NVA/VC.* [cited January 9, 2008]. rjsmith.com/kia_tbl.html#press.

16. Larry Rohter. "Panama and U.S. Strive To Settle on Death Toll" *New York Times,* April 1, 1990. query.nytimes.com/gst/fullpage.html?res= 9C0CE0D8123AF932A35757C0A966958260.

17. Peter Bahouth and Willian Arkin. *San Francisco Chronicle,* May 30, 1991.

18. Edward S. Herman. *The price is worth it.* [cited January 10, 2008]. zmag.org/hermanworthit.htm.

19. Neil King Jr. "Iraqi Death Toll Exceeds 600,000, Study Estimates." *Wall Street Journal,* October 11, 2006. [cited January 10, 2008] /online.wsj.com/public/article/ SB116052896787288831815AMVpCdg07M3w6XdmTXoPuzno_ 20061109.html?mod=tff_main_tff_top.

20. Opinion Research Business Newsroom. *September 2007 — More than 1,000,000 Iraqis murdered.* [cited January 10, 2008]. opinion.co.uk/Newsroom_ details.aspx?NewsId=78.

21. See Mark Weisbrot. "Holocaust Denial, American Style." *AlterNet,* November 22, 2007. [cited January 10, 2008]. zmag.org/content/showarticle.cfm?SectionID= 15&ItemID=14346; Gilbert Burnham et al. *The Human Cost of the War in Iraq: A Mortality Study, 2002-2006.* [cited November 15, 2007]. web.mit.edu/cis/human-cost-war-101106.pdf.

22. Asociated Press. *US Military Deaths in Iraq at 3,875.* November 25, 2007. [cited January 10, 2008]. apnews.myway.com/article/20071126/D8T5112G0.html.

23. Calculated by the author from multiple sources.

24. Naomi Klein. "Torture's Part of the Territory." *Los Angeles Times*, June 7, 2005.

25. Vandana Shiva. "The Polarized World Of Globalization." *Z magazine*, May 27, 2005.

26. Noam Chomsky. *Year 501: The Conquest Continues.* South End, 1992.

27. Noam Chomsky. *Hegemony or Survival: America's Quest for Global Dominance.* Metropolitan, 2003.

28. John Perkins. *Confessions of an Economic Hit Man.* Berrett-Koehler, 2004.

29. Matthew R. Simmons. "Energy: A Global Overview." Deloitte & Touche's 2004 Oil & Gas Conference, November 17, 2004, slide 11. [cited November 16, 2007]. simmonsco-intl.com/files/Deloitte%20&%20Touche.pdf.

30. Paul Erdman. *The Crash of '79.* Secker, 1977.

31. Gerald Posner. *Secrets of the Kingdom: The Inside Story of the Saudi-U.S. Connection.* Random, 2005, p. 124.

Chapter 4

1. Gabriel Kolko. *Wealth and Power in America: An Analysis of Social Class and Income Distribution.* Frederick A. Praeger, 1962; US Census Bureau. *Table H-2: Share of Aggregate Income Received by Each Fifth and Top 5 Percent of Households, All Races: 1967 to 2006.* Historical Income Tables — Households. [cited December 16, 2007]. census.gov/hhes/www/income/histinc/h02ar.html.

2. Liu Binyan and Perry Link. "A Great Leap Backward?" *New York Review of Books*, Vol 45, #15 (October 8, 1998), note 11. [cited November 19, 2007]. nybooks.com/articles/717.

3. US Central Intelligence Agency. "Field Listing — Distribution of family income — Gini index" *World Factbook 2007.* [cited January 10, 2008]. cia.gov/library/publications/the-world-factbook/fields/2172.html.

4. Anup Shah. *World Military Spending.* Global issues — Artms trade website. [cited January 10, 2008]. globalissues.org/Geopolitics/ArmsTrade/Spending.asp#USMilitarySpending.

5. GlobalSecurity.org. *World Wide Military Expenditures.* [cited February 15, 2008]. globalsecurity.org/military/world/spending.htm.

6. Matthew 16:26 Geneva Study Bible.

7. Michael S. James. "Is Greed Ever Good?" *ABC News*, August 22, 2002. [cited January 11, 2008]. clubs.anu.edu.au/clubs/Navigators/Material/Is%20Greed%20Ever%20Good.pdf

8. David Teather. "'Architect' of WorldCom collapse is jailed." *Guardian*, August 12, 2005. [cited January 11. 2008]. guardian.co.uk/business/2005/aug/12/corporatefraud.usnews.

9. Jimmy Carter. *Public Papers of the Presidents of the United States: Jimmy Carter. Book 1.* US Federal Reserve, 1977, p: 656. [cited November 19, 2007]. bartleby.com/73/526.html.

10. Hannah Arendt. *Eichmann in Jerusalem: A Report on the Banality of Evil.* Viking, 1963.

11. Kim Stanley Robinson. *The Wild Shore.* Robinson, 1984.

12. Associated Press. "Pat Robertson calls for assassination of Hugo Chavez." *USA Today,* August 23, 2005. [cited January 11, 2008]. usatoday.com/news/nation/2005-08-22-robertson-_x.htm.

13. Jimmy Carter. "This isn't the real America." *Los Angeles Times,* November 14, 2005, p. B-11.

14. Jimmy Carter. *Our Endangered Values: America's Moral Crisis.* Simon and Schuster, 2005, pp. 3, 13, 75, 79, 179, 184, 187, 195.

15. C.J. Campbell. *The Coming Oil Crisis.* Multi-Science, 1997, p. 115.

Chapter 5

1. James Howard Kunstler. *The Geography of Nowhere: The Rise and Decline of America's Man-Made Landscape,* Simon and Schuster, 1993.

2. Jeremy Rifkin. *The Hydrogen Economy.* Tarcher, 2002, p. 184.

3. Joseph J. Romm. *The Hype About Hydrogen: Fact and Fiction in the Race to Save the Climate.* Island, 2004.

4. US DOE Hydrogen Program. *Background.* [cited November 22, 2007]. hydrogen.energy.gov/background.html.

5. Donald L. Barlett and James B. Steele. "Why America is running out of gas." *Alexander's Oil & Gas Connections News & Trends: North America,* Vol 8, #15 (August 8, 2003). [cited November 22, 2007]. gasandoil.com/goc/news/ntn33212.htm.

6. US Department of Energy and US Council for Automotive Research. *FreedomCar: Energy Security for America's Transportation.* February 2, 2002. [cited January 11, 2008]. hydrogen.energy.gov/pdfs/freedomcar_agreement_2002.pdf.

7. US DOE Hydrogen, Fuel Cells and Infrastructure Technologies Program. *President's Hydrogen Fuel Initiative.* [cited January 11, 2008]. www1.eere.energy.gov/hydrogenandfuelcells/presidents_initiative.html.

8. Spark M. Matsunaga Hydrogen Act of 2005, 805(a).

9. George W. Bush. *Advanced Energy Initiative.* February 20, 2006. [cited January 11,2008]. whitehouse.gov/stateoftheunion/2006/energy/index.html.

10. Romm, *The Hype About Hydrogen,* p. 23.

11. Paul Hawken, Amory Lovins, L. Hunter Lovins. *Natural Capitalism: Creating the Next Industrial Revolution.,* Little, Brown , 1999, p. 26.

12. Jeremy Rifkin. *The Hydrogen Economy: The Creation of the Worldwide Energy Web and the Redistribution of Power on Earth.*, Tarcher/Putman, 2002, p. 207.

13. Yahoo Finance. Basic Chart for Ballard Power Systems. [cited November 22, 2007]. finance.yahoo.com/q/bc?s=BLDP&t=my&l=off&z=m&q=l&c=.

14. J-Cast Business News. *New Fuel-Cell Vehicles Need 20 Years To Prevail?* May 6, 2006. [cited November 22, 2007]. en.j-cast.com/2006/05/06001199.html.

15. James Woolsey."The War on Terror: The Energy Front." *FrontPageMagazine.com*, May 2, 2006. [cited November 22, 2007]. frontpagemag.com/Articles/ReadArticle.asp?ID =22286.

16. Amory B. Lovins. *Twenty Hydrogen Myths.* White paper #E03-05 updated February 17, 2005, pp. 4-5. [cited February 19, 2008]. rmi.org/images/other/Energy/E03-05_20HydrogenMyths.pdf.

17. CRC Handbook of Chemistry and Physics, 77th Edition. *The 10 Most Abundant Elements in the Earth's Crust.* [cited January 11, 2008]. education.jlab.org/glossary/abund_ele.html.

18. Ulf Bossel. "The Hydrogen Illusion: Why electrons are a better energy carrier." *Cogeneration and On-Site Power Production*, March-April 2004, pp. 55-59. [cited November 21, 2007]. efcf.com/reports/E11.pdf.

19. Plug-In America. *Plug-In Vehicle History and Status.* September 27, 2006, chart 1. [cited February 19, 2008]. arb.ca.gov/msprog/zevprog/symposium/presentations/ scott_sexton.pdf.

20. California Air Resources Board. *ZEV Program History Tutorial*, p. 8 of 41-50. [cited February 19, 2008]. arb.ca.gov/msprog/zevprog/factsheets/tutorial/ 2history41thru50.pdf.

21. *Who Killed the Electric Car?* Chris Paine Director, 93 min. Sony Pictures Classics, 2006. [DVD].

22. HybridCars.com website. *History.* [cited November 23, 2007]. hybridcars.com/ history.html and *The Great Hybrid Car Cover-up of '74.* [cited November 23, 2007]. hybridcars.com/history/the-great-hybrid-car-cover-up-of-74.html.

23. Green Car Congress. *Cumulative Reported US Sales of Hybrids Edge Past the One Million Mark in 2007.* January 9, 2008. [cited February 19, 2008]. greencarcongress.com/2008/01/cumulative-repo.html#more.

24. Daniel J. Weiss and Nat Gryll. *Flex-Fuel Bait and Switch.* Center for American Progress, June 18, 2007. [cited February 19, 2008]. americanprogress.org/ issues/2007/06/flexfuel.html; US Transportation Energy Data Book. *Table 2.12 — Passenger Travel and Energy Use, 2004.* Edition 26. [cited February 19, 2008]. cta.ornl.gov/data/tedb26/Edition26_Chapter02.pdf.

25. Daniel J. Weiss and Nat Gryll. *Flex-Fuel Bait and Switch.* Center for American Progress, June 18, 2007. [cited February 19, 2008]. americanprogress.org/issues/2007/06/flexfuel.html.

26. Union of Concerned Scientists. *Dual-Fuel Loophole.* [cited February 19, 2008]. ucsusa.org/clean_vehicles/cars_pickups_suvs/dual-fuel-loophole.html.

27. Joe Lieberman. "What We Can and Must Do Now to Break America's Dependence on Foreign Oil and Bring Down Energy Prices" Loewy Lecture, Georgetown University, October 7, 2005. [cited November 23, 2007]. lieberman.senate.gov/newsroom/release.cfm?id=247129.

28. US DOE Fuel Economy website. *How can a gallon of gasoline create 20 pounds of carbon dioxide?* [cited January 11, 2008]. fueleconomy.gov/feg/co2.shtml.

29. US Department of Energy and US Environmental Protection Agency. *Carbon Dioxide Emissions from the Generation of Electric Power in the United States.* July 2000, p. 3. [cited January 11, 2008]. tonto.eia.doe.gov/ftproot/environment/co2emiss00.pdf.

30. Ibid, p. 5.

31. *Energy Technology Perspectives 2006: Scenarios and Strategies to 2050.* OECD/IEA 2006, p. 179.

32. Sherry Boschert. *Plug-in Hybrids: The cars that will recharge America.* New Society, 2006, pp. 125 and 156.

33. James Kliesch and Therese Langer. *Plug In Hybrids: An Environmental and Economic Performance Outlook;* American Council for an Energy-Efficient Economy, Report Number T061,September 2006. [cited January 11, 2008]. aceee.org/pubs/t061.pdf?CFID=212783&CFTOKEN-93630913.

34. Charles F. Kutscher, Editor. *Tackling Climate Change in the U.S.: Potential Carbon Emissions Reductions from Energy Efficiency and Renewable Energy by 2030.* American Solar Energy Society, January 2007, p. 73. [cited January 11, 2008]. ases.org/climatechange/climate_change.pdf.

35. Neela Banerjee. "Pushing Energy Conservation Into the Back Seat of the S.U.V." *New York Times,* November 22, 2003.

Chapter 6

1. Yinon Bentor. *Chemical Elements.com — an Online, interactive Periodic Table of the Elements.* [cited November 21, 2007]. chemicalelements.com.

2. *Energy Technology Perspectives: Scenarios and Strategies to 2050.* International Energy Agency, 2006, p. 179.

3. *Energy Independence and Security Act of 2007* (Enrolled as Agreed to or Passed by Both House and Senate). [cited January 16, 2008]

govtrack.us/congress/billtext.xpd?bill=h110-6.

4. *Energy Policy Act of 2005* (Enrolled as Agreed to or Passed by Both House and Senate). [cited January 16, 2008]. frwebgate.access.gpo.gov/cgibin/ getdoc.cgi?dbname=109_cong_public_laws&docid=f:publ058.109

5. Hosein Shapouri, James A. Duffield and Michael Wang. *The Energy Balance of Corn Ethanol: an Update.* United States Department of Agriculture, 2002. [cited May 21, 2007]. transportation.anl.gov/pdfs/AF/265.pdf

6. David Pimentel D and Tad W. Patzek. "Ethanol Production Using Corn, Switchgrass, and Wood; Biodiesel Production Using Soybean and Sunflower". *Natural Resources Research* Vol 14 #1 (March 2005), pp. 65-76. [cited January 16, 2008]. springerlink.com/content/r1552355771656v0/.

7. Gerrit Buntrock." Food Prices Cheap No More." *Economist,* December 6, 2007. [cited January 16, 2008]. economist.com/displaystory.cfm?story_id=10250420.

8. W. W. Wilhelm et al. "Corn Stover to Sustain Soil Organic Carbon Further Constrains Biomass Supply." *Agronomy Journal* Vol 99 (2007), pp.1665-1667. [cited January 16, 2007]. agron.scijournals.org/cgi/content/abstract/99/6/1665.

9. US Department of Energy Press Release. *DOE Selects 6 Cellulosic Ethanol Plants for Up to $385 Million in Federal Funding.* [cited January 16, 2008]. iogen.ca/news_events/press_releases/2007_02_28_biorefineries_press_release.pdf.

10. See W. W. Wilhelm et al., note 8.

11. See note 3.

12. Reference 13 - Denis Lenardic. "A Walk Through Time." *A History of Photovoltaics.* [cited November 21, 2007]. pvresources.com/en/history.php.

13. Travis Bradford and Paul Maycock."PV market update: Demand grows quickly and supply races to catch up." *Renewable Energy World,* July 2007. [cited January 17, 2008]. renewable-energy-world.com/articles/print_screen.cfm?ARTICLE_ID=305266.

14. These details of wind history were taken from the "Illustrated History of Wind Power Development" on Telosnet, a Colorado web site which includes a focus on alternative energy (telosnet.com/wind/20th.html) and a Danish wind history site (vindhistorie.dk/English.htm).

15. Sylvia Westall."World wind energy market growth seen in 2008." *Reuters,* January 22, 2008. [cited February 20, 2008]. enn.com/energy/article/29745.

16. Kurt Cobb. *Charlie Hall's Balloon Graph.* Scitizen website, December 19, 2007. [cited January 17,2008]. scitizen.com/screens/blogPage/viewBlog/ sw_viewBlog.php?idTheme=14&idContribution=1305.

17. Ryan Wiser and Mark Bolinger. "Report Summary." *Annual Report on U.S. Wind Power Installation, Cost, and Performance Trends: 2006.* US Department of Energy,

May 30, 2007, p. 19. [cited January 17, 2008]. www1.eere.energy.gov/windandhydro/pdfs/wiser_data_report_summary_2006.pdf.

18. Ted Trainer. *Renewable Energy; What are the Limits?* (April 2004). [cited November 21, 2007]. ssis.arts.unsw.edu.au/tsw/D74.RENEWABLE-ENERGY.html.

19. E.ON Netz. *Data and Facts Relating to Wind Power in Germany*, Supplement 2006. [cited January 17, 2008]. eon-netz.com/frameset_reloader_homepage.phtml?top=Ressources/frame_head_eng.jsp&bottom=frameset_english/law_eng/law_windenergy_eng/ene_win_windreport_eng/ene_win_windreport_eng.jsp; E.ON Netz. *Wind Report 2005*. [cited January 17, 2008]. eon-netz.com/Ressources/downloads/EON_Netz_Windreport2005_eng.pdf.

20. Ted Trainer. *Renewable Energy Cannot Sustain a Consumer Society*. Springer, 2007, p. 39.

21. Howard C. Hayden. *The Solar Fraud — Why Solar Energy Won't Run the World*, 2nd ed. Vales Lake Publishing, 2004, pp. vi, 38.

22. Ulf Bossel. "The Hydrogen Illusion: Why electrons are a better energy carrier." *Cogeneration and On-Site Power Production*, March-April 2004, pp. 55-59. [cited November 21, 2007]. efcf.com/reports/E11.pdf.

23. Pete V. Domenici. "Opening Statement — Energy Forecast Hearing." US Senate Committee on Energy and Natural Resources, February 2006. [cited November 26, 2007]. energy.senate.gov/public/index.cfm?FuseAction= Hearings.Statement& Statement_ID=14. Alternate or supplement to this could be Buildings Energy Data Book.

24. Alexis Madrigal. "FutureGen 'Cleanish Coal' Plant Cancelled." *Wired Science*, February 1, 2008. [cited February 20, 2008]. blog.wired.com/wiredscience/2008/02/futuregen-clean.html.

25. Calculated from coal, oil and natural gas consumed in: Nelson Fugate. *Every American Born Will Need* ... Mineral Information Institute, March 2007. [cited February 20, 2008]. mii.org/pdfs/2007_mii_Baby_Info.pdf.

26. Makoto Akai. "Some Introductory Remarks on Geological Storage: Workshop on CDM Methodological Issues in regard to Carbon Dioxide Capture and Storage (CSS)." April 20-21, 2006. [cited January 18, 2008]. meti.go.jp/policy/global_environment/kyomecha/060602CCS_WS(20-21,April)/presentations/420/14.15%20-%20Makoto%20Akai%20-%20060420_Akai_Dist.pdf.

27. Michael Graham Richard. *Important! Why Carbon Sequestration Won't Save Us.* Treehugger.com website, July 31, 2006. [cited January 18, 2008]. treehugger.com/files/2006/07/carbon_sequestration.php quoting Tim Flannery. *The Weather Makers*. Harper Collins, 2005, p. 253.

28. Jan Lee Martin. "Stealing from the future (or how to destroy the planet in seven easy steps)." *The Futures Foundation website*, January 30, 2006. [cited November 23, 2007]. futuresfoundation.org.au/Future-News/Features-%28General%29/Stealing-from-the-future-%28or-how-to-destroy-the-planet-in-seven-easy-steps%29-20060129246/.

Chapter 7

1. M. King Hubbert. *Nuclear Energy and the Fossil Fuels.* Publication 95, Shell Development Company, June 1956. [cited November 6, 2007]. hubbertpeak.com/hubbert/1956/1956.pdf. This paper was presented at the spring meeting of the Southern District Division of Production, American Petroleum Institute, March 7-9, 1956.
2. Rachel Carson. *Silent Spring.* Houghton Mifflin, 1962.
3. Senator Gaylord Nelson. *How the First Earth Day Came About.* Envirolink website [cited January 28, 2008]. earthday.envirolink.org/history.html.
4. Donella H. Meadows et al. *The Limits to Growth: A report for the Club of Rome's Project on the Predicament of Mankind.* Universe, 1972.
5. Morris Berman. *Dark Ages America: The Final Phase of Empire.* Norton, 2006, pp. 55-56.
6. Jason Hamilton. *Sustainability Introduction: "The Earth: Mission Status Briefing."* Cornell University course BioNB 321 (The State of the Planet), Powerpoint slide #32. [cited January 24, 2008]. nbb.cornell.edu/neurobio/BioNB321/schedule.html.
7. "Is Torture on Hit Fox TV Show "24" Encouraging US Soldiers to Abuse Detainees?" *Democracy Now*, Thursday, February 22nd, 2007. [cited January 29, 2008]. democracynow.org/article.pl?sid=07/02/22/1448252.
8. From the Editors. "The Times and Iraq." *New York Times*, May 26, 2004. [cited January 29, 2008]. nytimes.com/2004/05/26/international/middleeast/26FTE_NOTE.html?ex=1400990400&en=94c17fcffad92ca9&ei=5007&partner=USERLAND.
9. Maxwell Boykoff and Jules Boykoff. "Balance as bias: global warming and the US prestige press." *Global Environmental Change* 14 (2004), pp. 125-136. [cited January 29, 2009]. calvin.linfield.edu/~rgardne/ET/FTN/WK%208%20-%20boykoff.pdf.
10. Donella H. Meadows et al. *The Limits to Growth: A report for the Club of Rome's Project on the Predicament of Mankind.* Universe, 1972.
11. Jack Rasmus. *The Trillion Dollar Income Shift, PART 1.* [cited January 29, 2008]. kyklosproductions.com/posts/index.php?p=57.

12. Barbara Ehrenreich. *Nickel and Dimed: On (Not) Getting By in America*. Metropolitan, 2001.

13. Rick Crawford. *What Lincoln Foresaw: Corporations Being "Enthroned" After the Civil War and Re-Writing the Laws Defining Their Existence*. [cited January 28, 2008]. ratical.org/corporations/Lincoln.html.

14. Ted Nace. *Gangs of America: The Rise of Corporate Power and the Disabling of Democracy*. Berrett-Koehler, 2003, p. 15.

15. This definition is taken from the Merriam-Webster Online Dictionary. [cited January 28, 2008]. m-w.com/.

16. Ted Nace. *Gangs of America: The Rise of Corporate Power and the Disabling of Democracy*. Berrett-Koehler, 2003, pp. 15-17.

17. Bob David, John Lyons and Andrew Batson. "Globalization's Gains Come with a Price." *Wall Street Journal*, May 24, 2007.

18. Ibid. The higher the Gini index number, the greater the inequality in income.

19. Alex Carey. *Taking the Risk Out of Democracy: Corporate Propaganda versus Freedom and Liberty*. University of Illinois Press, 1995.

20. Ibid, p. ix.

21. Ibid.

22. Alex Carey. *Taking the Risk Out of Democracy: Corporate Propaganda versus Freedom and Liberty*. University of Illinois Press, 1995, p. 83.

23. The definitions are taken from the Merriam-Webster Online Dictionary. [cited January 28, 2008]. m-w.com/.

24. Al Gore. *The Assault on Reason*. Penguin, 2007, p. 1.

25. A summary of points in *The Assault on Reason*.

26. Al Gore. "Book Excerpt — The Assault on Reason." *Time*, May 16, 2007. [cited February 20, 2008]. time.com/time/nation/article/0,8599,1622015,00.html.

27. Al Gore. *The Assault on Reason*. Penguin, 2007, p. 20.

28. Avner Offer. *The Challenge of Affluence: Self-Control and Well-Being in the United States and Britain since 1950*. Oxford, 2006, p. 185.

29. Jerry Mander. *Four arguments for the elimination of television*. Morrow, 1978.

30. Carnegie Mellon University, *The HomeNet Project*. [cited March 11, 2008]. homenet.hcii.cs.cmu.edu/.

31. Victoria Rideout, Donald F. Roberts and Ulla G. Foehr. *Executive Summary - Generation M: Media in the lives of 8- to 18-Year-olds*. A Kaiser Family Foundation Study, March, 2005, p. 6. [cited January 30, 2008]. kff.org/entmedia/upload/Executive-Summary-Generation-M-Media-in-the-Lives-of-8-18-Year-olds.pdf. Note: The data on homework and chores were collected among 7th- to 12th graders only. All figures are averages across seven days of the week.

32. Worldwatch Institute. *Vital Signs 2006-2007*. Norton, 2007, p. 55.

33. Avner Offer. *The Challenge of Affluence: Self-Control and Well-Being in the United States and Britain since 1950*. Oxford, 2006, p. 186.

34. Plato trans. Benjamin Jowett. "The Allegory of the Cave" from *The Republic*. [cited January 31, 2008]. wsu.edu:8080/~wldciv/world_civ_reader/world_civ_reader_1/plato.html.

Chapter 8

1. *An Inconvenient Truth*. Davis Guggenheim, Director, 96 min. Paramount, 2006. [DVD].

2. Jimmy Carter. *Our Endangered Values: America's Moral Crisis*. Simon & Schuster, 2005, p. 170.

3. This designation is not based on the book by Lester Brown nor do the comments made here about Plan B necessarily apply to him (Lester Brown. *Plan B 2.0*. Norton, 2006).

4. See Chapter 6.

5. See John M. Polimeni et al. *Jeavons' Paradox and the Myth of Resource Efficiency Improvements*. Earthscan, 2008.

6. Bill McKibben. "Remember This: 350 Parts Per Million." Washington Post, December 28, 2007, p. A21. [cited February 22, 2008]. washingtonpost.com/wpdyn/content/article/2007/12/27/AR2007122701942.html.

7. Bill McKibben. *The Enigma of Kerala*. Utne Reader Web Specials Archives. [cited December 22, 2007]. utne.com/archives/TheEnigmaofKerala.aspx; For Cuba, see The Community Solution. *Cuba: Life After Oil*. New Solutions #2 (May 2004). [cited October 16, 2007] communitysolution.org/pdfs/NS2.pdf.

8. Barry Jaruzelski and Kevin Dehoff. "The Customer Connection: The Global Innovation 1000." *Strategy + Business Resilience Report*, December 10, 2007. [cited January 21, 2008]. strategy-business.com/resiliencereport/resilience/rr00053?pg=7.

9. John German. *Testimony before US House of Representatives Subcommittee on Energy of the Committee on Science*. May 17, 2006. [cited January 21, 2008]. science.house.gov/commdocs/hearings/energy06/May%2017/German.pdf.

10. Worldwatch Institute. *Vital Signs 2007-2008: The Trends that Are Shaping Our Future*. W.W. Norton and Company, 2007, p. 52.

11. Andres Duany and Elizabeth Plater-Zyberk. "The Second Coming of the American Small Town." *WQ* (Winter 1992). [cited October 29, 2007]. ite.org/traffic/documents/Tcir0058e.pdf.

12. Ibid, pp. 21-22.

13. See chapters 9 and 10 for derivation of boe/c.

14. A formula to be derived from data noted.

15. Mario Giampietro and David Pimentel. *The Tightening Conflict: Population, Energy Use, And the Ecology of Agriculture.*1994. [cited January 21, 2008]. dieoff.org/page69.htm.

16. Leo Horrigan, Robert S. Lawrence and Polly Walker. *How Sustainable Agriculture Can Address the Environmental and Human Health Harms of Industrial Agriculture.* Environmental Health Perspectives (Vol 110, #5, May 2002). [cited October 17, 2007]. ehponline.org/members/2002/110p445-456horrigan/ horrigan-full.html.

17. David Pimentel and Marcia Pimentel. "Sustainability of meat-based and plant-based diets and the environment." *American Journal of Clinical Nutrition,* V78, # 3 (September 2003), pp. 660S-663S. [cited February 25, 2008]. ajcn.org/cgi/content/full/7813/6605.

18. Danielle Nierenberg. *Happier Meals: Rethinking the Global Meat Industry.* Worldwatch Paper 171, September 2005, pp. 9-10.

19. Gidon Eshel and Pamela Martin. *Diet, Energy and Global Warming.* May 2005. [cited October 17, 2007]. geosci.uchicago.edu/~gidon/papers/nutri/nutri3.pdf; Jolinda Hackett. *What does eating meat have to do with fossil fuels?* [cited October 17, 2007]. vegetarian.about.com/od/vegetarianvegan101/f/fossilfuels.htm; VegSource Vegaism Discussion Board. *How to Win an Argument With a Meat Eater.* [cited October 17, 2007]. vegsource.com/how_to_win.htm; Michael Bluejay. *Bicycling Wastes Gas?* [cited October 17, 2007]. bicycleuniverse.info/transpo/beef.html.

20. Worldwatch Institute. *Vital Signs 2006-2007: The Trends that Are Shaping Our Future.* Norton, 2006, p. 65.

21. *Energy Independence and Security Act of 2007* (Enrolled as Agreed to or Passed by Both House and Senate), Sect 102(b)(2)(A). [cited January 16, 2008]. govtrack.us/congress/billtext.xpd?bill=h110-6.

22. US Department of Energy. *Figure 8.1 — Average Vehicle Occupancy by Vehicle Type.* Transportation Energy Data Book, Edition 26 page 8-11. cta.ornl.gov/data/tedb26/Edition26_Chapter08.pdf.

23. See Chapter 10.

Chapter 9

1. In particular see Figure 4 in Chapter 2 (repeated as Figure 2 in Chapter 8) and Figure 9 Chapter 1.

2. Lester W. Milbrath. *Envisioning A Sustainable Society — Learning Our Way Out.* State University of New York, 1990, p. 20.

3. Edward R. Schreyer. "The Politics of Energy and the Environment." *Ecclectica,* December 2005. [cited October 23, 2007]. ecclectica.ca/issues/2005/3/index.asp?Article=13.

4. International Energy Agency. *Total Final Consumption by Region: OECD.* Key World Energy Statistics 2007, pp. 51, 53. [cited December 23, 2007]. iea.org/textbase/nppdf/free/2007/key_stats_2007.pdf

5. Nelson Fugate. *Every American Born Will Need* ... Mineral Information Institute, March 2007. [cited December 23, 2007]. mii.org/pdfs/2007_mii_Baby_Info.pdf.

6. International Energy Agency. *Total Final Consumption by Region: OECD.* Key World Energy Statistics 2007, pp. 48, 49, 57. [cited December 23, 2007]. iea.org/textbase/nppdf/free/2007/key_stats_2007.pdf

7. Walter Youngquist. *GeoDestinies: The Inevitable Control of Earth Resources over Nations and Individuals.* National Book Company, 1997, p. 369.

8. US Energy Information Administration. *Environmental Indicators.* Energy in the United States: 1635-2000. [cited October 24, 2007]. eia.doe.gov/emeu/aer/eh/frame.html (click on "Environmental").

9. International Energy Agency. *Total Final Consumption by Region: OECD.* Key World Energy Statistics 2007, pp. 49, 57. [cited December 23, 2007]. iea.org/textbase/nppdf/free/2007/key_stats_2007.pdf. Calculated by dividing world CO_2 output by world fossil fuel consumption.

10. Elizabeth Royte. *Garbage Land: On the Secret Trail of Trash.* Little Brown, 2005, p. 275.

11. Ibid, p.11.

12. Paul Winistorfer et al. "Energy Consumption and Greenhouse Gas Emissions Related to the Use, Maintenance and Disposal of a Residential Structure." COR-RIM Phase I Final Report, June 1, 2005, p. 19. [cited November 29, 2007]. corrim.org/reports/2005/SWST/128.pdf.

13. In this scenario, coal is used as the source for electricity since most of US electricity is provided by burning coal.

14. International Energy Agency. *Total Final Consumption by Region: OECD.* Key World Energy Statistics 2007, pp. 48, 49, 57. [cited December 23, 2007]. iea.org/textbase/nppdf/free/2007/key_stats_2007.pdf.

15. Leon Glicksman. *Strategic Challenges in the Energy Sector — Ecoefficiency and Sustainability.* MIT Building Technology Program, February 11, 2008, p. 7. [cited February 22, 2008]. lsc.mit.edu/schedule/2008.2q/bpp-slides/glicksman.pdf

16. David Pimentel and Mario Giampietro. *Food, Land, Population and the U.S. Economy.* Carrying Capacity Network, 1994, [cited January 22, 2008]. dieoff.org/page55.htm.

17. This is a calculation from previous data.

18. Calculated using: US Energy Information Administration. *Energy Basics — Converting Energy Units 101.* [cited February 22, 2008]. eia.doe.gov/basics/conversion_basics.html.

19. Dale Allen Pfeiffer. *Eating Fossil Fuels: Oil, Food, and the Coming Crisis in Agriculture.* New Society, 2006, page 8.

20. Folke Günther. *Sustainability through local self-sufficiency.* Before the Wells Run Dry: Ireland's Transition to Renewable Energy. [cited October 30, 2007]. feasta.org/documents/wells/.

21. US Department of Energy. *Tables 3.1 and 3.2.* Transportation Energy Data Book, 26th edition, 2007. [cited January 22, 2008]. cta.ornl.gov/data/download26.shtml.

22. Ibid., *Table 2.12.*

23. Carnegie Mellon University. "Automobiles: Manufacture vs. Use." Institute for Lifecycle Environmental Assessment *Leaf*, Summer 2002. [cited November 28, 2007]. ilea.org/lcas/macleanlave1998.html.

24. US Department of Energy. *Transportation Energy Data Book*, 26th edition, 2007, p. 8-11. [cited January 22, 2008]. cta.ornl.gov/data/download26.shtml.

25. Ibid, p. 8-12.

26. US Department of Energy Vehicle Technologies Program. *Fact of the Week #473 (June 11, 2007): Vehicle-Miles per Licensed Driver.* [cited January 22, 2008]. eere.energy.gov/vehiclesandfuels/facts/2007_fcvt_fotw473.html.

27. US Department of Energy. *Table 4.14.* Transportation Energy Data Book, 26th edition, 2007. [cited January 22, 2008]. cta.ornl.gov/data/download26.shtml.

28. US Department of Energy. *Tables 2.6 and 2.12.* Transportation Energy Data Book, 26th edition, 2007. [cited January 22, 2008]. cta.ornl.gov/data/download26.shtml.

29. Matthew A. Kromer and John B. Heywood. *Electric Powertrains: Opportunities and Challenges in the U.S. Light-Duty Vehicle Fleet.* Sloan Automotive Laboratory, Publication No. LFEE 2007-03 RP, May 2007, p. 29.

30. Green Car Congress. *Reported US Hybrid Sales Up 36% In December, 38% for 2007.* January 4, 2008. [cited January 22, 2008]. greencarcongress.com/2008/01/reported-us-hyb.html#more.

31. Electric Drive Transportation Association. *Hybrid Sales Figures/Tax Credits for Hybrids.* [cited February 22, 2008]. electricdrive.org/index.php?tg=articles&topics= 7; Alan Durning. *Hybrids hammer Hummers, II.* Sightline Institute. The Daily Score, February 15, 2005. [cited February 22, 2008]. sightline.org/daily_score/ archive/2005/02/15/hybrids_hammer_.

32. US Department of Energy. *Table 2.1.7.* 2007 Buildings Energy Data Book. [cited January 22, 2008]. buildingsdatabook.eren.doe.gov/default.asp?id=view_book&c=2.

33. Ibid., Table 3.4.2.
34. Ibid., Table 3.4.1.

Chapter 10

1. As annual energy consumption in the US is about 100 quads, the numbers for energy used measured in quads and percentage of total consumption are almost identical. US Department of Energy. Table 1.1.1, "U.S. Residential and Commercial Buildings Total Primary Energy Consumption." *2007 Buildings Energy Data Book.* [cited December 3, 2007]. buildingsdatabook.eren.doe.gov/docs/1.1.1.pdf. The 40 quads for buildings is divided into 18 quads for commercial buildings and 22 quads for residential buildings (Table 1.1.3).

2. US Department of Energy. Table 3.1.1, " Carbon Dioxide Emissions for U.S. Buildings, by Year." *2007 Buildings Energy Data Book.* page 2.[online]. [cited December 3, 2007]. buildingsdatabook.eren.doe.gov/docs/3.1.1.pdf.

3. Gil Friend. *The 2030 Climate Challenge and West Coast Green.* WorldChanging.com website, October 2, 2006. [cited December 3, 2007]. worldchanging.com/archives/005005.html.

4. J. Randolph and G. M. Masters. "Chapter 6: Energy Efficiency for Buildings" in *Energy for Sustainability: Technology, Policy, Planning.* Island Press, 2008.

5. See Figure 3, Chapter 9. Canadian Architect. *Measures of Sustainability — Operating Energy.* [cited February 1, 2008]. canadianarchitect.com/asf/perspectives_ sustainaibility/measures_of_sustainablity/measures_of_sustainablity_ operating.htm.

6. US Department of Energy. Table 1, "Building Data Summary Sheets", p. 1. *2007 Buildings Energy Data Book.* [cited February 4, 2008]. buildingsdatabook.eren.doe.gov/.

7. US Department of Energy. Table 12, "Building Data Summary Sheets", p. 2. *2007 Buildings Energy Data Book.* [cited February 4, 2008]. buildingsdatabook.eren.doe.gov/.

8. US Department of Energy. Table 2.2.1, "Total Commercial Floorspace and Number of Buildings, by Year." *2007 Buildings Energy Data Book.*[online]. [cited December 3, 2007]. buildingsdatabook.eren.doe.gov/docs/2.2.1.pdf.

9. US Department of Energy. Table 2.1.1, "Total Number of Households and Buildings, Floorspace, and Household Size, by Year." *2007 Buildings Energy Data Book.*[online]. [cited December 3, 2007]. buildingsdatabook.eren.doe.gov/docs/ 2.1.1.pdf.

10. Ibid.

11. US Department of Energy. Table 2.1.2, " Share of Households, by Housing Type and Type of Ownership, as of 2001." *2007 Buildings Energy Data Book.* [cited December 3, 2007]. buildingsdatabook.eren.doe.gov/docs/2.1.2.pdf.

12. Alex Wilson and Jessica Boehland. "Small is Beautiful: U.S. House Size, Resource Use, and the Environment." *Journal of Industrial Ecology*, Vol. 9, Issues 1-2 (Winter-Spring 2005), p. 278. [cited February 1, 2008]. mitpress.mit.edu/journals/JIEC/v9n1_2/jiec_9_1-2_277_0.pdf .

13. Paul Winistorfer et al. "Energy Consumption and Greenhouse Gas Emissions related to the Use, Maintenance, and Disposal of a Residential Structure." *Wood and Fibre Science*, 37 Corrim Special Issue, 2005, p. 131. [cited December 3, 2007]. corrim.org/reports/2005/swst/128.pdf.

14. PBS. "Empire State Building." Building Big, Wonders of the World databank. [cited December 3, 2007]. pbs.org/wgbh/buildingbig/wonder/structure/empire_state.html.

15. US Department of Energy. Table 2.1.1, " Total Number of Households and Buildings, Floorspace, and Household Size, by Year." (note 9 above) and Table 2.1.6, " Construction Statistics of New Homes Completed/Placed." *2007 Buildings Energy Data Book*.[online]. [cited December 3, 2007]. buildingsdatabook.eren.doe.gov/docs/2.1.6.pdf.

16. Lehman's. *Calculating fuel costs of wood stoves, coal stoves, etc.* [cited February 1, 2008]. mostwoodstoves.com/lehcalc.html.

17. US National Association of Home Builders. "Green Building to Skyrocket by 2010 to Half of New Homes." *Nation's Building News*, April 2, 2007. [cited February 4, 2008]. nahb.org/news_details.aspx?newsID=4380.

18. US Environmental Protection Agency. "About ENERGY STAR New Homes." [cited December 4, 2007]. energystar.gov/index.cfm?c=new_homes.hm_earn_star.

19. "Energy Star Overview of 2005 Achievements ." [cited December 4, 2007]. energystar.gov/ia/news/downloads/2005_achievements.pdf.

20. Alex Frangos. "Is It Too Easy Being Green?" *Wall Street Journal*, October 19, 2005, p. B1.

21. US Green Building Council. LEED for New Construction Rating System v. 2.2. October 2005. [cited February 25, 2008]. usgbc.org/ShowFile.aspx?DocumentID=1095.

22. Alex Frangos. "Timber Business Backs A New 'Green' Standard." *Wall Street Journal*, March 29, 2006. [cited December 4, 2007]. realestatejournal.com/propertyreport/newsandtrends/ 20060331-frangos.html.

23. US Department of Energy. Table 2.2.9, " U.S. LEED Certified Projects, by Certification Type and Selected State." *2007 Buildings Energy Data Book*.[online]. [cited December 3, 2007]. buildingsdatabook.eren.doe.gov/docs/2.2.9.pdf.

24. "LEED Delivers on Predicted Energy Savings." *Environmental Building News*, December 2007, p. 18. [cited February 25, 2008]. buildinggreen.com/auth/article.cfm/2007/12/4/LEED-Delivers-on-Predicted-Energy-Savings/.

25. Bill Prindle et al. *The Twin Pillars of Sustainable Energy: Synergies between Energy Efficiency and Renewable Energy Technology and Policy.* American Council on Renewable Energy, May 2007, ACEEE Report Number E074, Page 15. [cited February 4, 2008]. aceee.org/pubs/e074.pdf?CFID=212222&CFTOKEN= 13176081.

26. US Department of Energy Building Technologies Program. *Building America: Research Project Locations.* [cited February 25, 2008].
eere.energy.gov/buildings/building_america/cfm/project_locations.cfm.

27. US Department of Energy. "Building America Puts Residential Research to Work," Building America website. [cited December 5, 2007].
eere.energy.gov/buildings/building_america/pdfs/35851_ba_puts_research.pdf.

28. US Department of Energy. "BIRA Brings Energy Efficiency to Family in Need." Building America website, March 2005. [cited December 5, 2007].
eere.energy.gov/buildings/building_america/rh_0305_extreme_makeover.html.

29. J. Douglas Balcomb. "Passive Solar Comeback Ahead." *Solar Today*, September/October 2006. [cited December 5, 2007].
solartoday.org/2006/sept_oct06/passive_comeback.htm.

30. Jeff Christian. "Near Zero Energy for Affordable Housing." Oak Ridge National Laboratory, Sustainable Communities Workshop, June 8, 2006. [cited December 6, 2007]. sustainablecommunities.scgov.net/ssDocuments/1270/pdfs/near_zero.pdf.

31. Jeff Christian. "Zero Energy Housing — A Habitat for Humanity Project." Beyond Energy Alternatives: Third US Conference on Peak Oil and Community Solutions, September 22-24, 2006, Yellow Springs, Ohio. [cited December 6, 2007]. communitysolution.org/06conf.html.

32. Joint UK-Sweden Initiative on Sustainable Construction. *Case Studies — Lindås, Göteborg.* [cited December 7, 2007]. ukswedensustainability.org/projects/lindas.jsp.

33. Henk F. Kaan and Bart J. de Boer. *Passive Houses: Achievable Concepts for Low CO_2 Housing.* [cited December 7, 2007].
ases.org/chapter_newsletter/2005/JA05/SWC_Passive_Solar_Design.pdf.

34. Passive House Institute. *Examples of Residential Passive Houses.* [cited December 7, 2007]. passivhaustagung.de/Passive_House_E/Examples_passive_houses.html.

35. Jacqueline LaMuth. *Indoor Air Quality: Molds and Dust.* Ohio State University Extension Fact Sheet. [cited February 4, 2008].
ohioline.osu.edu/cd-fact/0191.html.

36. Worldwatch Institute. *Good Stuff?* Housing. [cited December 7, 2007]. worldwatch.org/node/1493.

37. Cindy Skrzycki. "Agency Cools Off on Insulation Rule.", *Washington Post*, October 25, 2005, p. D01. [cited February 4, 2008]. washingtonpost.com/wpdyn/content/ article/2005/10/24/AR2005102401786.html.

38. Harvey Sachs et al. *Emerging Energy Saving Technologies and Practices for the Buildings Sector as of 2004.* ACEEE Report Number A0242, October 2004.

39. Efficient Window Collaborative. Design Variations-Orientation. [cited February 4, 2008]. efficientwindows.org/var_orient.cfm.

40. Calculated using data from US Department of Energy. Table 5.10.19, "Major Residential and Small Commercial Appliance Lifetimes, Ages, and Replacement Picture." *2007 Buildings Energy Data Book.* [cited February 25, 2008]. buildingsdatabook.eren.doe.gov/docs/5.10.19.pdf

41. Calculated by author from data in Figure 10.9.

42. US Department of Energy. *A Consumer's Guide to Energy Efficiency and Renewable Energy — Caulking.* [cited February 4, 2008]. eere.energy.gov/consumer/your_ home/insulation_airsealing/index.cfm/mytopic=11270.

43. See notes 30 and 31.

Chapter 11

1. Entrepreneur.com website. *Toyota is bullish on U.S. market, due to rapid population growth.* Manufacturing & Technology News, August 17, 2006. [cited February 26, 2008]. entrepreneur.com/tradejournals/article/150676280.html.

2. John German, Manager of Environmental and Energy Analysis, American Honda Motor Company. Statement before the US Senate Committee on Energy and Natural Resources. January 30, 2007. [cited January 10, 2008]. energy.senate.gov/public/index. cfm? FuseAction=Hearings.Testimony&Hearing_ID=1604&Witness_ID=4548.

3. Automotoportal website. *New Survey: Driving Safety is Parents' Greatest Concern for Teens on Prom Night.* May 3, 2007. [cited February 26, 2008]. automotoportal.com/article/ new-survey-driving-safety-is-parents-greatest-concern-for-teens-on-prom-night.

4. Britannica Concise Encyclopedia "Mass Transit". *US History Companion: Public Transportation — The Twentieth Century.* [cited February 26, 2008]. answers.com/topic/ public-transport?cat=biz-fin; US Government Accountability Office. Highway and Transit Investments: Options for Improving Imformation on Projects' Benefits and Increasing Accountability for Results. Report GAO-05-172, January 2005, p. 1. [cited February 26, 2008]. gao.gov/new.items/d05172.pdf; US Department of Transportation. Highway Indicators Table in *Our Nation's Highways – 2000.* Office

of Highway Policy Information. [cited February 26, 2008].
fhwa.dot.gov/ohim/onh00/onh2p1.htm.

5. US Department of Energy. Table 2-12 – "Passenger Travel and Energy Use, 2004."
Transportation Energy Data Book, 26th Edition. [cited December 11, 2007].
cta.ornl.gov/data/chapter2.shtml.

6. US Department of Transportation, National Highway Traffic Safety Administration.
"Event Data Recorders — Notice of proposed rulemaking." Federal Register Vol
69, # 113 (June 14, 2004), Document # FR Doc 04-13241, pp. 32932-32954. [cited
February 5, 2008]. a257.g.akamaitech.net/7/257/2422/06jun20041800/
edocket.access.gpo.gov/2004/04-13241.htm.

7. See Figure 4.5, Chapter 4.

8. See note 8, Chapter 8.

9. US Department of Energy. Figure 4.2 — "Fuel Economy by Speed, 1973, 1984,
and 1997 Studies." *Transportation Energy Data Book*, 26th Edition, p. 4-23. [cited
February 5, 2008].cta.ornl.gov/data/tedb26/Edition26_Chapter04.pdf.

10. Robert Mullins. *HP case wraps up but pretexting problem remains.* PC World website,
March 17, 2007. [cited February 5, 2008].pcworld.about.com/od/privacy/
HP-case-wraps-up-but-pretextin.htm.

11. For Liftshare see liftshare.org/uk/comstart.asp; for Mitfahrzentrale, see
carpool.co.uk/mediadaten.php?partner=&.

12. Kevin Spurgaitis. "Castro's Cuba: is Fidel's socialist paradiso really lost and in
peril?" *Catholic New Times*, March 20, 2005. [cited February 26, 2008].
findarticles.com/p/articles/mi_m0MKY/is_5_29/ai_n13592314.

13. See The Community Solution. *Cuba: Life after Oil.* New Solutions #2, May 2004.
[cited November 8, 2007]. communitysolution.org/pdfs/NS2.pdf; *The Power of
Community: How Cuba Survived Peak Oil.* Faith Morgan, 53 min. The Community
Solution, 2006 [DVD].

Chapter 12

1. Norman Wirzba, ed. *The Art of the Commonplace: The Agrarian Essays of Wendell
Berry.* Counterpoint, 2002, p. 238.

2. Ajit Jain."'Father of India's Green Revolution' given Padma Vibhushan." *Rediff India*,
August 24, 2006. [cited February 6, 2008].
ia.rediff.com/news/2006/aug/24borlaug.htm?q=np&file=.htm.

3. US National Corn Growers Association. *More Corn on Fewer Acres.* [cited February
6, 2008]. ncga.com/news/OurView/pdf/2006/FoodFuelCharts.pdf#search=
%22U.S.%20Corn%20Yield%20.and.%202005%22

4. Jack Kittredgem. "Community-supported agriculture" in *Rooted in the Land: Essays on Community and Place* ed. William Vitek & Wes Jackson. Yale University Press, 1996, p. 260.

5. Wendell Berry. "Nation's destructive farm policy is everyone's concern." *Herald-Leader*, July 11, 1999. [cited December 14, 2007]. agrenv.mcgill.ca/agrecon/ecoagr/doc/berry.htm.

6. Marion Nestle. *What to Eat*. North Point, 2006, p. 4.

7. Eric Schlosser. "Why McDonald's Fries Taste So Good." *Atlantic Monthly*, January 17, 2001. rense.com/general7/whyy.htm.

8. David Pimentel and Marcia Pimentel. "World Population, Food, Natural Resources, and Survival." *World Futures* 59 (2003), pp. 145-167.

9. *Agriculture Statistics 2006*. United States Government Printing Office, 2006.

10. Grocery Manufacturers Association — Food Products Association website. [cited December 14, 2007]. gmabrands.com/index.cfm.

11. *Agriculture Statistics 2006*. United States Government Printing Office, 2006, p. I – 28, Table 1-40.

12. *Agriculture Statistics 2006*. United States Government Printing Office, 2006, p. I – 25, Table 1-37.

13. David Pimentel and Marcia Pimentel. "Sustainability of meat-based and plant-based diets and the environment." *American Journal of Clinical Nutrition*. Vol 78 Supplement (2003), pp. 660S-661S. [cited December 20, 2007]. ajcn.org/cgi/content/full/78/3/660S.

14. Data for individual per capita servings in this chapter are calculated using the US Department of Agriculture's Economic Research Service (ers.usda.gov/data/foodconsumption/).

15. *Agriculture Statistics 2006*. United States Government Printing Office, 2006, p. I – 25, Table 1-37.

16. *Agriculture Statistics 2006*. United States Government Printing Office, 2006, p. I – 5, Table 1-7.

17. US Department of Agriculture, Office of Communications. *Agriculture Fact Book 1999*. p. 1 [cited December 17, 2007]. usda.gov:80/news/pubs/fbook99/contents.htm.

18. *Agriculture Statistics 2006*. United States Government Printing Office, 2006, p. I-40, Table 1-57.

19. American Soybean Association. *U.S. Fats & Oils Edible Consumption 2004*. Soy Stats. [cited February 6,2008]. soystats.com/2005/page_23.htm.

20. See Figure 12.2.

21. Ibid.

22. *Agriculture Statistics 2006*. United States Government Printing Office, 2006, p. XIII-7, Table 13-7.

23. See Figure 12.2.

24. David Pimentel and Marcia Pimentel. "Land, Water and Energy Versus the Ideal U.S. Population." *NPG Forum*, January 2005. [cited December 20, 2007]. npg.org/forum_series/forum0205.html.

25. See Figure 12.2.

26. *Agriculture Statistics 2006*. United States Government Printing Office, 2006, pp. XIII – 6 and 7, Table 13-7.

27. Data for individual per capita servings in this chapter are calculated using the US Department of Agriculture's Economic Research Service (ers.usda.gov/data/foodconsumption/).

28. *Agriculture Statistics 2006*. United States Government Printing Office, 2006, pp. XIII – 6 and 7, Table 13-7.

29. Data for individual per capita servings in this chapter are calculated using the US Department of Agriculture's Economic Research Service (ers.usda.gov/data/foodconsumption/).

30. Ibid, plus acreage data from figure 12.2.

31. David Leonhardt. "What U.S. can learn from Europe on health care." *International Herald Tribune*, October 18, 2006. [cited December 19, 2007]. iht.com/articles/2006/10/17/business/view.php.

32. Kaiser Family Foundation Snapshots: *Health Care Costs. Health Care Spending in the United States and OECD Countries, January 2007*. [cited December 19, 2007]. kff.org/insurance/snapshot/chcm010307oth.cfm.

33. USDA Economic Research Service. Food CPI, *Prices and Expenditures: Food and Alcoholic Beverages: Total Expenditures*. [cited February 27, 2008]. ers.usda.gov/briefing/ cpifoodandexpenditures/data/table1.htm. Calculated by dividing total food expenses of $1,082,495 million for 2006 by population in that year of 300 million.

34. Overweight is defined as a body mass index (BMI) greater than or equal to 25; 66.3% of Americans fall in this category. Obese is defined as a BMI greater than or equal to 30; 32.2% of Americans fall in this category. US National Center for Health Statistics. *Prevalence of Overweight and Obesity Among Adults: United States, 2003-2004*. [cited December 19, 2007]. cdc.gov/nchs/products/pubs/pubd/hestats/overweight/overwght_adult_03.htm#Table%20.

35. Randy Udall, Jeremy Gilbert & Steve Andrews. "Peddling PetroProzac: CERA ignores 10 warning signposts of peak oil." *Energy Bulletin*, November 15, 2006. [cited December 20, 2007]. energybulletin.net/22442.html.

36. Danielle Nierenberg. *Happier Meals: Rethinking the Global Meat Industry.* Worldwatch Paper #171, November 2005, p. 9. [cited December 20, 2007]. worldwatch.org/node/819.

37. Select "Red Meat, Poultry and Fish" using USDA Economic Research Service Data Sets. Food Availability Spreadsheets. [cited February 27, 2008]. ers.usda.gov/Data/FoodConsumption/FoodAvailSpreadsheets.htm#mtpcc.

38. Danielle Nierenberg. "Meat Consumption and Output Up" in *Vital Signs* 2006-2007, Norton, 2006, p. 24.

39. Sustainable Table website. *Fossil Fuel and Energy Use.* [cited February 27, 2008]. www.sustainabletable.org/issues/energy/.

40. David Pimentel and Marcia Pimentel. "Land, Water and Energy Versus the Ideal U.S. Population." *NPG Forum,* January 2005, p. 5. [cited December 20, 2007]. npg.org/forum_series/forum0205.html.

41. See Chapter 8, figure 8.2.

42. David Pimentel and Marcia Pimentel. "Land, Water and Energy Versus the Ideal U.S. Population." *NPG Forum,* January 2005, p. 2 (note: numbers converted from kilograms to pounds). [cited December 20, 2007]. npg.org/forum_series/ forum0205.html.

43. David Pimentel and Marcia Pimentel. "Sustainability of meat-based and plant-based diets and the environment." *American Journal of Clinical Nutrition.* Vol 78 Supplement (2003), pp. 660S-661S. [cited December 20, 2007]. ajcn.org/cgi/content/full/78/3/660S.

44. Henning Steinfeld et al. *Livestock's Long Shadow: Environmental Issues and Options.* Livestock, Environment and Development (LEAD) initiative, 2006, pp. 53 and 97. [cited December 20, 2007]. virtualcentre.org/en/library/key_pub/longshad/A0701E00.pdf.

45. Ibid, p. xxi.

46. Ibid.

47. Nicholas Von Hoffman. "Why Milk Costs More Than Gas." *The Nation,* July 17, 2007. [cited February 27, 2008]. commondreams.org/archive/2007/07/17/2576/.

48. Tim Wiseman. *Midwestern manure gets more blame for the "dead zone" in the Gulf of Mexico.* Institute for Rural Journalism and Community Issues Rural Blog, January 31, 2008. [cited February 27, 2008]. irjci.blogspot.com/2008/01/midwestern-manure-gets-more-blame-for.html.

49. Michael Brower et al. *The Consumer's Guide to Effective Environmental Choices: Practical Advice From The Union of Concerned Scientists.* Three Rivers Press, 1999.

50. Martin C. Heller and Gregory A. Keoleian. *Life Cycle-Based Sustainability Indicators for Assessment of the U.S. Food System.* University of Michigan Center for Sustainable

Studies Report # CSS00-04, December 6, 2000, pp. 34-35. [cited February 7, 2008]. css.snre.umich.edu/css_doc/CSS00-04.pdf.

51. See John Robbins. *Diet for a New America*. Stillpoint, 1987; Gail Eisnitz. *Slaughterhouse*. Prometheus, 1997; Born Free USA United with Animal Protection Institute website. [cited December 20,2007]. api4animals.org/.

52. Martin C. Heller and Gregory A. Keoleian. *Life Cycle-Based Sustainability Indicators for Assessment of the U.S. Food System*. University of Michigan Center for Sustainable Studies Report # CSS00-04, December 6, 2000, p. 20. [cited February 7, 2008]. css.snre.umich.edu/css_doc/CSS00-04.pdf.

53. Ibid.

54. Wendell Berry. "Stupidity in Concentration." in *Citizenship Papers*. Shoemaker and Hoard, 2003, p. 131.

55. John Bowe. "A Shameful Harvest." *The American Prospect*, V14# 7 (July 3, 2003). [cited February 27, 2008]. prospect.org/cs/articles?article=a_shameful_harvest.

56. Moneychump website. *Top 10 dangerous occupations in America*. [cited December 24, 2007]. moneychump.org/2006/12/29/top-10-dangerous-occupations-in-america/.

57. L.E. Fleming et al. "National Health Interview Survey: Mortality among US farmers and pesticide applicators." *American Journal of Industrial Medicine*, V43#2 (February 2003), pp. 227-33. [cited December 24, 2007]. ncbi.nlm.nih.gov/entrez/query.fcgi?cmd=Retrieve&db=pubmed&dopt=Abstract&list_uids=12541279.

Chapter 13

1. The tables in this chapter have been compiled using statistics from Table13.7, *Agriculture Statistics 2006*. United States Government Printing Office, 2006, p. XIII-6; the US Department of Agriculture National Nutrient Database (nal.usda.gov/fnic/foodcomp/search/); the US Department of Agricultural Economic Research Service (ers.usda.gov/Data/FoodConsumption/FoodAvailQueriable.aspx and ers.usda.gov/Data/FoodConsumption/FoodAvailSpreadsheets.htm#vegtot).

2. *From Farm to Table: The Economics of Food Safety; Estimating and Addressing America's Food Losses*. Food Review V22# 3 (December 1999).

3. See Chapter 12, note 34.

4. Jane Brody. *Jane Brody's Good Food Book*. Bantam, 1987, p. 42.

5. Andrew Kimbrell, ed. Fatal Harvest: *The Tragedy of Industrial Agriculture*. Island Press, 2002.

6. Ibid. pp. 71-81.
7. Altria Group Inc. *2003 Annual Report —Our Food Company's Products.* [cited February 11, 2008]. www.altria.com/annualreport2003/ar2003_09_0200.asp.
8. Marion Nestle. *Food Politics: How the Food Industry Influences Nutrition and Health.* University of California Press, 2002.
9. Michael Pollan. "Unhappy Meals." *New York Times,* January 28, 2007. [cited February 11, 2008]. nytimes.com/2007/01/28/magazine/28nutritionism.t.htm.
10. Marion Nestle. *What to Eat.* North Point Press, 2006, p. 4.
11. National Agricultural Law Center. *United States Farm Bills.* [cited February 29, 2008]. nationalaglawcenter.org/farmbills/.
12. Michael Pollan. "The 2007 Farm Bill 'You Are What You Grow'." *Sustainable Food News,* April 19, 2007. [cited February 11, 2008]. organicconsumers.org/articles/article_4908.cfm.
13. David Pimentel and Marcia Pimentel. "Land, Water and Energy Versus the Ideal U.S. Population." *NPG Forum,* January 2005. [cited December 20, 2007]. npg.org/forum_series/forum0205.html.
14. Ibid., Population Table 1, page 2.
15. See Chapter 12, note 34.
16. For details, see The Community Solution. *Cuba: Life after Oil.* New Solutions #2, May 2004. [cited November 8, 2007]. communitysolution.org/pdfs/ NS2.pdf; *The Power of Community: How Cuba Survived Peak Oil.* Faith Morgan, 53 min. The Community Solution, 2006 [DVD].
17. Ibid.
18. Ibid.
19. Eliot Coleman. *Four-Season Harvest: Organic Vegetables from Your Home Garden All Year Long.* Chelsea Green, 1999.
20. Martin C. Heller and Gregory A. Keoleian. *Life Cycle-Based Sustainability Indicators for Assessment of the U.S. Food System.* University of Michigan Center for Sustainable Studies Report # CSS00-04, December 6, 2000, p. 29. [cited February 7, 2008]. css.snre.umich.edu/css_doc/CSS00-04.pdf.

Chapter 14

1. Andrew C. Revkin. "Poor Nations to Bear Brunt as World Warms." *New York Times,* April 1, 2007. [cited December 25, 2007]. nytimes.com/2007/04/01/science/earth/ 01climate.html.
2. Solar Energy International. *Energy Facts.* [cited February 12, 2008]. solarenergy.org/resources/energyfacts.html.

3. "The Global Warming Survival Guide: 51 Things We Can Do To Save the Environment." *Time*, April 9, 2007. [cited December 25, 2007]. time.com/time/specials/2007/environment/.

4. Jim Gunshinan. "Energy Star Changes Approach to Programmable Thermostats." *Home Energy*, March/April 2007. [cited December 25, 2007]. homeenergy.org/article_preview.php?id=372&article_title=Energy_Star_Changes_Approach_ to_ Programmable_Thermostats.

5. Pacific Northwest National Laboratory. *Compact Fluorescent Lighting in America: Lessons Learned on the Way to Market.* US Department of Energy, Office of Energy Efficiency and Renewable Energy, Building Technologies Program, June 2006. [cited December 25, 2007]. eere.energy.gov/buildings/info/documents/pdfs/cfl_lessons_learned_ web.pdf.

6. Amory B. Lovins et al. *Factor Four: Doubling Wealth — Halving Resource Use. The New Report to the Club of Rome.* Allen & Unwin, 1997.

7. OECD. *Gross Domestic Expenditures on R&D 2006.* MSTI 2007-2, Key Figures. [cited February 29, 2008]. oecd.org/dataoecd/49/45/24236156.pdf.

8. US Environmental Protection Agency. *U.S. Greenhouse Gas Inventory.* [cited February 21, 2008]. epa.gov/climatechange/emissions/usgginventory.html.

9. For example see Sunfrost Refrigerators: sunfrost.com/refrigerators_main.html.

10. Mohammed Bah Abba. "Development of a low-cost cooler to preserve perishable foods in countries with arid climates." *ITDG Food Chain* 29 (November, 2001), pp. 3-4. [cited December 27, 2007]. itdg.org/html/agro_processing/docs29/FC29_34.pdf.

11. Fastcooking.ca website. *Energy Efficient High Speed Cooking.* [cited December 27, 2007]. fastcooking.ca/pressure_cookers/energy_savings_pressure_cooker.php.

12 Shell.com. *Environment and Society: The History of Sustainable Development.* [cited February 12, 2008]. shell.com/home/content/envirosoc-en/sustainability_and_our_business_strategy/the_history_of_sd/the_history_of_sd_000407.html.

Chapter 15

1. Steve Lampen. *Up for a Quick Game of Ttlachtli?* March 12, 2003. Radio World Newspaper website. [cited january 31, 2008]. rwonline.com/pages/s.0055/t.5705.html.

2. Miranda Hitti. Soaking *Up the Media: Full-Time Job for Kids.* WebMD Medical News, March 10, 2005. [onlione]. [cited March 2, 2008]. webmd.com/parenting/news/20050310/soaking-up-media-full-time-job-for-kids?page=2.

3. See projectcensored.org/.

4. Fortune 500, 2007. *Industry: Publishing, Printing.* [cited January 31, 2008]. money.cnn.com/magazines/fortune/fortune500/2007/industries/ Publishing_Printing/1.html.
5. See worldwatch.org.
6. See stateofworkingamerica.org.

Chapter 16

1. Colin Hines. *Localization: A Global Manifesto.* Earthscan, 2000.
2. Michael Shuman. *Going Local: Creating Self-Reliant Communities in a Global Age.* Routledge, 2000.
3. CNA Corporation. *National Security and the Threat of Climate Change.* 2007, p. 13. [cited December 28, 2007]. securityandclimate.cna.org/.
4. Donald Holley. *The Second Great Emancipation: The Mechanical Cotton Picker, Black Migration, and How They Shaped the Modern South.* University of Arkansas Press, 2000.
5. Richard C. Duncan. "The Olduvai theory: Energy, population, and Industrial Civilization." *The Social Contract* 16 (2) (Winter 2005-2006), pp. 134-144. [cited February 12, 2008] hubbertpeak.com/duncan/OlduvaiTheorySocialContract.pdf.
6. Folke Günther. "Ruralisation — integrating settlements and agriculture to provide sustainability." [cited February 12, 2008]. holon.se/folke/lectures/ Ruralisation-filer/v3_document.
7. Leila Abboud. "Power Play: How Denmark Paved the Way To Energy Independence." *Wall Street Journal,* April 16, 2007, p. A1. [cited December 28, 2007]. winnipeg.indymedia.org/item.php?5034S.
8. *Honda and Climate Energy Begin Retail Sales of freewatt™ Micro-CHP Home Heating and Power System.* Honda Press Release, April 3, 2007. [cited December 29, 2007]. world.honda.com/news/2007/c070403HomeHeatingPowerSystem/.
9. Carol Pier. "Discounting Rights: Wal-Mart's Violation of US Workers' Right to Freedom of Association." *Human Rights Watch,* V19, #2 (May 2007). [cited December 28, 2007].

Chapter 17

1. These definitions are taken from m-w.com/.
2. Robert N. Bellah et al. *Habits of the Heart: Individualism and Commitment in American Life.* University of California, 1986, p. 333.
3. Rhetoric and Cultures: Contextualizing Discourse Communities. *Definitions of Community.* Northern Arizona University, English 521 (Spring 2002). [cited February 12, 2008]. jan.ucc.nau.edu/~sg7/eng521spring02/communitydefinitions.html.

4. Bryon Munson. *Changing Community Dimensions: The Interrelationships of Social and Economic Variables.* Ohio State University, 1968, p. 1.

5. Wendell Berry. *Sex, Economy, Freedom & Community: Eight Essays.* Pantheon, 1994, p. 119.

6. Mark Givens. "Bring It On Home: An Interview with James Howard Kunstler." *MungBeing* Issue 11. [cited January 1, 2008]. mungbeing.com/issue_ 11.html?page=30#870.

7. Arthur Morgan. "What Is A Community?" *The Community Course,* Chapter 1. [cited January 1, 2008]. smallcommunity.org/course/chapter1.asp.

8. United Nations Department of Economic and Social Affairs, Population Division. *World Urbanization Prospects: The 2005 Revision.* [cited January 1, 2008]. un.org/esa/population/publications/WUP2005/2005wup.htm.

9. See Robert Putnam. *Bowling Alone: The Collapse and Revival of American Community.* Simon & Schuster, 2000.

10. See Arthur E. Morgan. *The Community — The Primary Unit of Society — A Guide for the Study of Small Community in America.* Community Service, Inc., 1942; Ted Trainer. *The Conserver Society: Alternatives for Sustainability.* Zed Books, 1995; Ted Trainer. *The Simpler Way: Working for Transition from Consumer Society to a Simpler, More Cooperative, Just and Ecologically Sustainable Society.* [cited January 1, 2008]. socialwork.arts.unsw.edu.au/tsw/.

11. See Robert Putnam. *Bowling Alone: The Collapse and Revival of American Community.* Simon & Schuster, 2000.

Index

About the Author

Pᴀᴛ Mᴜʀᴘʜʏ ɪs ᴛʜᴇ Exᴇᴄᴜᴛɪᴠᴇ Dɪʀᴇᴄᴛᴏʀ of Community Solutions, a nonprofit organization which focuses on achieving sustainability by reducing energy consumption in the household sectors of food, housing and transportation. The organization also advocates for small, local, low energy communities as the basic societal response to peak oil and climate change. Community Solutions has hosted annual Peak Oil and Solutions Conferences since 2003 in Yellow Springs, Ohio. Pat was the co-writer and co-producer of the documentary film *The Power of Community: How Cuba survived Peak Oil*. He was educated as a computer scientist and worked in the aerospace, energy and construction industries. He is also a licensed building contractor and has had extensive experience in building energy efficient homes. He has been involved in community much of his life and sees community as the context within which sustainability can be attained. Pat lectures widely across the country on energy, peak oil, geopolitics and lifestyle solutions.

If you have enjoyed *Plan C* you might also enjoy other

BOOKS TO BUILD A NEW SOCIETY

Our books provide positive solutions for people
who want to make a difference. We specialize in:

Environment and Justice • Conscientious Commerce • Sustainable Living
Ecological Design and Planning • Natural Building & Appropriate Technology
New Forestry • Educational and Parenting Resources • Nonviolence
Progressive Leadership • Resistance and Community

New Society Publishers

ENVIRONMENTAL BENEFITS STATEMENT

New Society Publishers has chosen to produce this book on Enviro 100, recycled
paper made with **100% post consumer waste**, processed chlorine free, and old
growth free.

For every 5,000 books printed, New Society saves the following resources:[1]

33	Trees
3,020	Pounds of Solid Waste
3,322	Gallons of Water
4,334	Kilowatt Hours of Electricity
5,489	Pounds of Greenhouse Gases
24	Pounds of HAPs, VOCs, and AOX Combined
8	Cubic Yards of Landfill Space

---

[1]Environmental benefits are calculated based on research done by the Environmental Defense Fund and
other members of the Paper Task Force who study the environmental impacts of the paper industry.

For more information on this environmental benefits statement, or to inquire about environmentally
friendly papers, please contact New Leaf Paper – info@newleafpaper.com Tel: 888 • 989 • 5323.

For a full list of NSP's titles, please call **1-800-567-6772** *or check out our website at:*

www.newsociety.com

NEW SOCIETY PUBLISHERS